THE ULTIMATE TIME TEAM COMPANION

THE ULTIMATE TIME TEAM COMPANION

AN ALTERNATIVE HISTORY OF BRITAIN

TIM TAYLOR

Contributors: Nick Ashton, Professor Mick Aston, Phil Harding, Neil Holbrook,
Francis Pryor, Alan Turton and Steve Vizard
Researchers: Jenni Butterworth, Kate Haddock and Teresa Hall

First published in 1999 by Channel 4 Books.
This edition published in 2001 by Channel 4 Books, an imprint of Macmillan Publishers Ltd,
25 Eccleston Place, London SW1W 9NF, Basingstoke and Oxford.

Associated companies throughout the world.

www.macmillan.co.uk

ISBN 0 7522 6170 3

Text © Tim Taylor, 1999

3 5 7 9 8 6 4

A CIP catalogue record for this book is available from the British Library.

Design by Atyeo Cork Linklater

Illustrations by Victor Ambrus

Special photography for the *Time Team* shoots at Basing, Cirencester, Elveden, Flag Fen and
Wierre Effroy © Paul Lewis Isemonger.

All the photographs by Paul Lewis Isemonger were on Kodak E200 film.

Detailed picture credits can be found on page 215.

Colour reproduction by Aylesbury Studios

Printed and bound in Great Britain by Butler & Tanner Ltd, Frome and London

This book accompanies the television series *Time Team* made by Videotext Communications in association with
Picture House Television for Channel 4.

Series producer: Tim Taylor
Executive producer: Philip Clarke

The time line in this book is not meant to be a graphical representation of the passage of time. It is simply to give
you a sense of chronology – a guide to what happened when. Obviously it is impossible to locate the accurate
date of all artefacts found and so these photographs can only be positioned in a likely place on the time line.
Similarly, periods of history and people themselves cannot be attached to a single date. However, we hope that
you will gain from the time line a better sense of the order of the key events in Britain's history.

We have grouped the events into seven categories, each of which is symbolized by an icon as follows:

INNOVATION AND INVENTION   MONUMENTS   HEROES, HEROINES AND VILLAINS   WAR, BATTLE AND DEATH   RELIGION AND THE CHURCH   DOCUMENTS, LITERATURE AND THE ARTS   KINGS AND QUEENS

THE ULTIMATE TIME TEAM COMPANION

CONTENTS

INTRODUCTION

More than fifty Time Team programmes have been broadcast over the past five years and throughout this period I have carried in my mind an approximate structure of Britain's past. As each new programme has come along it has slotted into this mental time line, which is also full of images from the programmes – words of wisdom from Mick and other experts, and memories of some of the amazing discoveries we have made over the years. My time line also includes the faces of all the people in whose fields, houses and back gardens we have excavated. Time Team has always been about the past that can be found on your back doorstep, or even your own back garden.

Time Team is about making archaeology accessible to everyone.

During the course of making *Time Team*, I have become increasingly aware that a time line – a mental map of the past – is something that other people would also find useful as a guide to navigating through the complexities of Britain's shared inheritance. This book provides just that.

This history of 'what happened when' is presented in *Time Team* style – unstuffy, direct and without obfuscation. Experts have been pushed off their academic fences and asked to tell us what we can say about the past. This provides a framework for a journey into British history, a time line that you can use to explore the areas that interest you in more detail. You will be guided along the way by the Team and some of the country's leading archaeological and historical experts who have contributed to the programmes.

As one of television's most popular programmes on archaeology, *Time Team* has a great advantage for which I have always been grateful: experts are always willing to talk to us and, on our viewers' behalf, we have access to some of the best. Their answers and explanations have to be clear and expressed in terms we can all understand – they go through the filter of Tony, myself and the Team's relentless pursuit of the clarity that is necessary to create the kind of programme millions now watch.

As a non-historian, I still have the capacity to be both both surprised and delighted by the nuggets of historical information that appear during the course of each programme. I can still remember, for instance, my shock at realizing just how long ago our ancestors were bashing away at flint; and my surprise at seeing the beautiful objects Bronze Age men and women saw fit to commit to the black swamps of the Fens.

Dealing with objects is another of *Time Team*'s great advantages. I have often said to Mick that I prefer a decent artefact to a host of theories and our pursuit of archaeology has been guided by this. This book therefore shows a lot of finds, not only because they are important and, in many cases, beautiful objects, but also because they are useful *aides-mémoire* to acquiring a time line of the past.

The structure of the book could not be simpler: one hundred key events set out chronologically with fifty *Time Team* excavations, including twenty or so artefacts from *Time Team* digs and detailed descriptions of our work on five important sites all acting as milestones. This is British history delivered in *Time Team* style – I hope you enjoy it!

Mick Aston and I going about the business of trying to
balance archaeology and television.

ELVEDEN
SUFFOLK

TONY'S PIECE TO CAMERA: 'This is what Suffolk looks like now, but 400,000 years ago the Stone Age men and women who lived around here would have been surrounded by lots of lush vegetation. There was plenty of animal life too, including lions, rhino and elephants – but contrary to what the movies tell us, definitely no dinosaurs. Today the exotic animals have all gone and the temperature has dropped a few degrees, so the vegetation has died out. But Time Team have come to Center Parcs in Elveden to try and find out more about the Stone Age people who lived and died here over 400 millennia ago.'

Prehistoric sites always present a challenge. The number of finds is likely to be limited and the information that can be gathered is open to different interpretations. However, I have always felt that because the Palaeolithic period – the Old Stone Age – represents such a long and important part of our past it is important for *Time Team* to work on these sites. It is one of Phil's favourite periods and, thanks to his contacts with Nick Ashton, we had been given access to one of Britain's major palaeolithic sites.

On Day One, as we stood looking across the vast pit dug by Victorian brick-makers in their search for clay, we knew that 450,000 years ago we would have seen rivers created by melting water from glaciers. Some of our earliest ancestors hunted in similar areas, and the only human remains from the palaeolithic period to be found in Britain were unearthed at sites like Elveden: a skull was uncovered at Swanscombe in Kent, and later a tibia and two teeth were discovered at Boxgrove in West Sussex. The skull is important because it gives us an idea of the brain size of Stone Age men and women: approximately 1,300 cubic centimetres. Because human brains have gradually been increasing in size – today their capacity is about 1,400 cubic centimetres – one of the many ways of approximately dating a skull is by its likely brain size. In general the larger the skull's capacity, the later it is. However, Neanderthal man had a slightly larger brain capacity than human beings of today.

Skeletal fragments of human beings are rarely found, but flint tools survive and they were likely to be the main artefacts we would uncover. On Day One Trenches One and Two were located where they would reveal part of the beach that had lined the banks of one of the ancient rivers. Nick Ashton, Mark White and their team had previously discovered evidence that flint tools had been made in the area, and also uncovered the tools themselves. In some cases they had been able to find the waste flint and piece it together to re-create the shape of the original nodule, a process known as refitting.

Another of our aims was to find out whether Elveden was part of the same ancient river system, or palaeochannels. At Barnham, 8 kilometres (5 miles) west, John Gater and Sue Ovenden set off to do a geophysical survey and Stewart Ainsworth studied the topography and started to map features like clay pits to see if there was a link between the two sites. In the lower levels of stratification there is a very good match between them. At Barnham, however, the upper layers contain a veritable zoo of ancient animals: elephant, rhino, lion, bear, bison, aurochs, deer and wild boar. We were hoping that Carenza and Mark White would be able to find more evidence of the flint tools that were used to butcher them. The critical evidence already found at Barnham was of butchery – some of the bones had cut marks on them and had been deliberately smashed to release the marrow.

Tony and Phil trying to make some sense of the palaeolithic artefacts.

Trench One at Elveden – excavating at the prehistoric river beach levels.

Because the Victorian brick-makers had dug deep into the earth Elveden also gave us the opportunity to see the palaeolithic period in section. Understanding it involves getting to grips with stratigraphy – layers of archaeology. As each geological and biological process occurs it leaves a layer of material. The one at the bottom is the oldest and is the start of a time line that becomes more recent as it heads towards the surface. Events like glaciation can mix the layers up but at Elveden we had a chance to see them in a relatively undisturbed state.

As well as excavating the beach site, we also wanted to expose the layers on the other side of the pit and opened Trench Three there. Andy Currant, an expert palaeontologist, was on hand to sample the various layers for bones and see if this would date and identify them. Sampling involved sieving tons of material in search of elusive clues to this distant period of our past.

For much of the Palaeolithic period our ancestors experienced the coming and going of periods of glaciation and these are the key to dating layers. Throughout Europe, until as recently as 11,000 years ago, palaeolithic hunters enacted a strange *pas de deux* with advancing and retreating ice sheets. As the ice melted, relatively warmer and more fertile conditions followed and our ancestors took advantage of these. Ice ages occur at regular intervals and seem to be related to changes in the tilt of the earth. As the ice came and went the cold and warm periods left geological traces.

Proof of this comes from the dark depths of the great oceans where sediment has been forming for millions of years, relatively undisturbed by geological events that make land-based geology more difficult to interpret. In this sediment are the remains of small shells from creatures – foraminifera – which should have a monument erected to them by grateful archaeologists. 'Foram' for short are useful because their skeletons absorb oxygen in the form of isotopes 16 and 18, which are sensitive to changes in sea temperatures. During an ice age the lighter isotope 16, which evaporates more easily from the sea, is locked up in the ice and less of it appears in foraminifera remains. During warmer periods melting ice releases isotope 16 back into the sea and the foraminifera return to a normal balance of 16 and 18. By boring cores deep in the sediments and recording the changes in isotope levels in the foraminifera, a time line of the various cold and warm spells can be created. To show the duration of glacial periods and when they started, these are cross-checked with sediments in ice cores that come from volcanic eruptions for which we have dates.

Two climatic events were relevant to us at Elveden. The Anglian glacial epoch approximately 474,000 to 427,000 years ago and the Hoxnian interglacial or warmer period that followed, 427,000 to 364,000 years ago. It is a sobering thought that we are now in an interglacial epoch and that another ice age may begin with relatively short notice. Some geologists believe the change from warm to cold can take as little as fifty to a hundred years.

We were hoping to find signs of the end of the Anglian glaciation, which is described by Phil as being the 'mother of all glaciations'. He regards its effects as being, and I quote, 'worse than the

Victor begins his reconstruction of the palaeolithic landscape.

eighteen years of the Tory government's roads policy'. The glaciation did something the Tories couldn't do: it moved rivers. The present course of the Thames, for example, is further south than it was before the Anglian ice age.

A glaciation ends virtually all possibility of life in its immediate environment because freezing cold locks up all biology. But when the ice melts the process of life starts – a process which eventually led to Elveden being settled by our ancestors. Micro-organisms begin to colonize the watery bogs at the edge of the retreating glaciers, and organisms living in rock that has been ground up by the ice begin to create the first soil, which is populated by insects and worms – what Andy refers to as the 'black goo' layer. Created about 400,000 years ago this is the earliest evidence of the earth coming to life again. Then come dwarf birches – the first trees to become established on the ice-free land surface.

A few thousand years pass and an increase in small mammals and fish produces a distinct layer – at Elveden the 'fish layer' contained evidence of roaches, rudd, stickleback and pike. At Barnham the remains of terrapin turned up. Small pieces of vole remains were also found and are useful because over time there are minute changes in their skeletons. This means they can be used as a dating tool, referred to by Simon Parfitt as the 'vole clock'. Evidence of larger mammals and of human beings is found on top of this layer.

Phil with his new, bespoke, long-handled shovel.

The foraminifera and animal and plant remains reflect the chronology of the palaeolithic period and, along with the geology, take us to the time of the first hunters. It is at this point that we can begin to see the flint artefacts discovered by archaeologists, however the earliest artefacts show very few changes across time and it is only later that we can begin to see clear differences to measure our place in time. As man developed his tool-making skills there was a progression from simple devices to more complex ones. This created a typology that can be used to date finds and the layer of archaeology in which they are present.

On Day One the archaeologists in our main trenches began to work down through a sandy layer that covered the cobbles that would have originally been a prehistoric river bank. Small fragments of flint began to appear, the first evidence that *Time Team* had located to indicate that flint tools were being made on the site.

Later in the day Phil was joined by John Lord, an expert in flint technology. Between them they would reconstruct some key tools that were used during the Stone Age – the cameo for this programme. One of John's tasks was to reconstruct a paleolithic spear. The famous Clacton spear was found at Clacton-on-Sea in Essex around 1911. Dated to around 450,000 years ago, it is the earliest wooden object discovered in Britain. Complete pine spears have also been found elsewhere in Europe, and it would be a pine spear that John would make for our cameo. Until recently it was accepted that tools associated with the Clacton site – basically cores

Tony looks at the layer at Barnham where we were finding flints. Denis Borrow and Steve Shearn stand by.

with flakes removed to create simple cutting-edges – were the earliest stone ones. They were thought to pre-date hand-axes and this had apparently been confirmed by work at Swanscombe, site of the famous skull, where different types of flint tool appeared in sequential chronological layers. It therefore seemed possible to divide up the palaeolithic period by referring to the Swanscombe sequence.

At Swanscombe there were flaked cores and flakes, but no hand-axes, in the lower gravel and this layer was thought to be Clactonian. Pointed hand-axes that signalled the start of the Acheulean period of technological development around 400,000 years ago came next and above these there were ovate hand-axes. Flaked cores followed by pointed hand-axes followed by ovate hand-axes was therefore considered to be the key sequence. Archaeologists working in the palaeolithic period settled back with what must have been a collective sigh of relief at the fact that the order was nailed down at last. Then in 1970–74 and again in 1998, John Wymer, a flint expert and archaeologist, excavated at Hoxne in Suffolk and began to find pointed hand-axes over ovate ones. Then came Boxgrove, where beautiful flaked, ovate hand-axes often with tranchet edges (an edge created by a transverse blow to the axe which left a sharper edge) came from around 500,000 years ago – a very early period that should have been chronologically Clactonian. Archaeologists who have looked at the wear pattern on these axes suggest that they were used for butchery. Other excavations began to disturb the Swanscombe model:

Prehistoric flint find.

so-called Clactonian cores turned up at much later sites and Clactonian flakes were found alongside Acheulean hand-axes. As Andy Currant put it, things in the palaeolithic period were becoming 'excitingly fluid'.

Faced with the inevitable, Nick Ashton, working with John McNabb, decided to ignore the Swanscombe sequence and assume that the Lower Palaeolithic technologies – Clactonian and Acheulean – were part of a continuum. He excavated at Barnham between 1989 and 1994. It was a site that had always been regarded as typically Clactonian site and he soon found Clactonian chopper-type cores in the same layer as hand-axes. Clactonian tools now appear to have been used in particular circumstances – when flint was in short supply or where a simple cutting-edge would do the job. Worldwide, Oldowan flakes from the Olduvai Gorge in Tanzania are still considered to be the earliest tools.

Archaeologists are always looking for ways to bring some sense of order to events that occurred during the nearly half a million years, that make up the palaeolithic period in Britain. At the start of Day Two we asked Phil to demonstrate just how far away it is from the twentieth century with Tony. With each stride representing a year, and beginning in the present, he headed off down a road in Center Parcs, our base for the shoot. His first hundred steps took him to the beginning of the century. To get back to the end of the Palaeolithic period he would have had to walk to Cornwall!

Camera crews and assistants prepare to follow Phil back in time.

For a small handful of specimens we had to sieve a lot of stuff. The buckets contained earth mixed with mild acids to separate out the clay, which also had the effect of bleaching the diggers' feet.

By the end of Day Two John had made his Clactonian spear. This involved wedging a long straight branch into a 'V'-shaped log embedded in the ground and then using a flint spokeshave to straighten the branch. It was a useful reminder that our ancient ancestors may have used other organic tools – wooden digging sticks and slings, for example – that have been lost.

In Trenches One and Two we found flakes and coincidentally our first flint tool: a spokeshave – a type of plane – that may have been used to produce wooden implements similar to the spear being made by John.

As Day Three began Andy and his team were finding the going tough in Trench Three. Mud and clay were being sieved by the bucketload and combined to create an adhesive material that made sorting out fragments of plant and animal remains difficult. Mild acids like vinegar and hydrogen peroxide were added to the buckets and they were soon bubbling away nicely. These acids break down the clay particles allowing any other material to float free in the water.

Back at our Stone Age encampment John had produced flint flakes and was using these to butcher the carcass of a small deer. Flint can be used to create an incredibly sharp cutting-edge and the ease with which a skilled knapper can make a complete range of tools, from arrow-heads and axes to scrapers and borers, brings home what an efficient technology it was.

Meanwhile Phil laid out a simplified chronology of flint tools along one of the terraces cut into the Elveden sections. The earliest stone tools in Britain, the handaxe and flake, were made by the island's first inhabitants around 500,000 years ago. The Neanderthals, around 200,000 years ago, still used

Ella Galinski, the assistant producer, works out the scene with cameraman Andrew Ridoutt. Phil prepares his timeline of tools.

John Lord, looking very much the nineteenth-century explorer, contemplates the reconstruction ahead.

John Lord and Phil set up their palaeolithic campsite.

hand-axes and flakes, but also had a new type of stone tool called the Levallois flake, named after the Parisian suburb where they were first recognized. However, with the arrival of modern humans around 40,000 years ago, stone tools changed a great deal. They began to make blades – thin, parallel-edged flakes. This was very economical as lots of blades could be struck off a core and also meant that a huge range of different tools could be made, including the first arrowheads. The last glaciation which finished in 9,000 BC saw the arrival of the Mesolithic hunter-gatherers who made very small flints, called microliths, and the first woodworking axes. The first farmers in Britain, the people of the Neolithic period around 4,000 BC, were the last people of the Stone Age. They polished stone axes, making them very beautiful and very long-lasting. Subsequently, metals were the predominant material for tools. However, in the Bronze Age, some very fine flint daggers that copied bronze examples were made, probably for ceremonial purposes.

Using a cleft tree as a vice, John begins works on the spear.

Day Three also saw our first evidence of black goo, and the small bones we had been looking for gradually emerged out of Andy's buckets. Disappointingly, they were from relatively small mammals – and there were no bones from voles to allow us to check out the vole-clock theory.

John, Chris and Stewart had found enough evidence to persuade Nick that there was a connecting system of palaeochannels between Elveden and Barnham and, in the final hours of the shoot, we found more flakes handled by our hunting ancestors more than 400,000 years ago. In Trench One and Trench Two at Elveden we found over 200 flakes as well as flint chips and cores. The three key artefacts we had found were the spokeshave, a notched flint that may have been used as a spokeshave, and a scraper.

Eight kilometres (5 miles) away at Barnham work continued at the other *Time Team* site. Previously a team from the British Museum led by Nick Ashton and Mark White had uncovered large numbers of mammal bones and evidence of butchery. These included one large bovine bone, possibly from a bison, which showed cut marks and there was evidence that another had been deliberately smashed by a rock. The deposits at Barnham had avoided decalcification – when ground water seeping through a deposit over thousands of years removes all the calcium from shells, bones, etc. and

Butchering meat with a hand axe.

destroys the evidence. We also found worked flint, although we weren't near the main areas of bone deposits.

From the evidence we were able to create a picture of a prehistoric valley between Elveden and Barnham, populated by lions, rhinos and other animals. Some of our earliest ancestors produced a wide range of flint tools to butcher their prey and to create wooden spears that would have been used to despatch them. These ancestors would have looked very different from ourselves, with sloping shoulders and protruding eyebrow ridges. Although *Time Team* achieved a great deal in three days of scraping around in the Palaeolithic, my strongest memory will be the gradual uncovering of the surface at the beach area, and our first vew of flints that had been used by people who were at a much earlier stage of evolution than ourselves.

PREHISTORIC BRITAIN

STANTON HARCOURT
OXFORDSHIRE

SERIES 3
Broadcast
14 January 1996

Somewhere under this lot there are mammoths!

Numerous archaeological sites in Britain have been discovered as a result of commercial gravel extraction. At Stanton Harcourt in Oxfordshire workmen uncovered muds and silts dating back 200,000 years to the Lower Palaeolithic period – the earliest era of human occupation in Britain. These very rare deposits included the remains of thousands of mammoths, elephants and other animals as well as stone tools. Archaeologists from Oxford University moved in to excavate the site and asked *Time Team* to help them find evidence of human occupation as they rushed to complete their task before the quarry was filled in again.

In the Stone Age, or Lower Palaeolithic period, Stanton Harcourt was a good location for humans and animals because it was on the banks of a river. Our first target was to pinpoint the route of this ancient waterway as we hoped it would provide us with rich environmental information. Stewart Ainsworth began surveying on the ground while Carenza examined air photographs of the site. Meanwhile, Phil joined palaeolithic expert Kate Scott from Oxford in a trench near what had been the edge of the river. Day One ended with their discovery of a huge mammoth tusk, a bison skull and a collection of other animal bones.

By Day Two overnight analysis of the muds and silts from the trench had revealed evidence that, as well as these large animals, much smaller creatures – beetles – had lived by the river. Because they have hard shells, their remains survive in the ground and provide a picture of what conditions were like when they were alive. Beetle expert Russell Coope was able to tell us that the species we found at Stanton Harcourt suggested that the climate 200,000 years ago was much warmer than it is now – and, because they would have needed food, the finds indicated that there had been rotting material and dung (probably from mammoths) on the river banks. Kate showed Mick earlier excavations at the edge of the river that had yielded evidence of trees and plants, as well as tiny shellfish, preserved in the mud. The geophysics survey suggested that there were more water channels – our targets for the final day.

At the start of Day Three Phil resorted to a mechanical digger to try to expose more of the palaeolithic land surface. Several trenches were dug and soon dark areas indicated the water channels identified

First humans in Britain

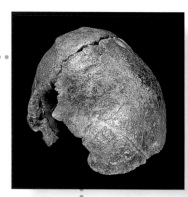

The earliest evidence of human habitation in Britain comes from sites like Boxgrove in West Sussex and Swanscombe in Kent and and gives us a date of about 500,000 years ago. This compares with an approximate date of one million years for human expansion into the rest of Europe from Africa. The key bits of evidence from Boxgrove – tooth remains and a broken tibia or shinbone – allow us to learn quite a lot about early human beings. The closest comparison is with *Homo heidelbergensis*, who would have looked different to modern man with huge brow ridges, a sloping forehead and a heavy jaw.

The first human remains were uncovered at Boxgrove in 1993, along with hand-axes and the remains of bones from animals including giant deer, lion, brown bear, wild horse and rhino. The thickness of the tibia – comparable to that of a top-class athlete today – is evidence that our ancestors were highly active physically. The animal bones show flint-tool cut marks, indicating that they had been butchered. Killing large animals would have required a considerable amount of hunting skill and organization, which may have involved exchanging vocalizations. However, it is believed that speech had not yet developed. It is likely that these hunters used wooden thrusting spears although, because the weapons are organic, only one example – found at Clacton-on-Sea in Essex – survives. It is Britain's oldest wooden tool.

Phil doing a little careful dentistry around a mammoth tooth.

by geophysics. More analysis of the soils from the trenches built up a picture of palaeolithic life at the site. The river banks then were covered with oak and willow trees and, in addition to beetles, there was evidence of other small animals such as snails and tree frogs. Horses and elephants, as well as bison and mammoths, roamed the region. In the river itself, eels and pike abounded.

Although *Time Team* didn't find any direct evidence of human occupation, tiny soil samples allowed us to piece together a detailed picture of one ancient river valley, and the plants and animals that Stone Age men and women would have seen there.

Mammoth tooth found at Stanton Harcourt

COOPER'S HOLE
SOMERSET

SERIES 6
Broadcast
24 January 1999

Cheddar Gorge in Somerset is famous for its spectacular caves and the discovery of Cheddar Man – the oldest intact human skeleton in Europe, dating to 7,000 BC – in Gough's Cave. Further up the gorge, the lesser-known Cooper's Hole was our target for three days. Cavers in the 1960s had found fragmentary remains of Iron Age pottery and animal bones, but nothing else was known about the site. Could we find evidence of earlier, palaeolithic, occupation in the cave, so that it could be scheduled as a site of archaeological interest and protected from intrusions by casual visitors?

After a briefing by members of the Mendip Cavers Group about health and safety, we set off to Cooper's Hole. The entrance was next to a car park and the cave shelved away into the darkness. Our first job was to remove the large quantity of debris and mud that had flooded into it since the 1960s. This proved to be a much more difficult job than we had expected, with teams of diggers emptying sloppy mud into trugs and hauling them to the surface by hand.

Meanwhile, John Gater and Chris Gaffney used ground-penetrating radar (GPR), which provides detailed information about the depth and form of deposits, to reconstruct the original entrance to the cave. It would have been further out than it is now, in the area covered by the car park. As they reported a much wider opening than we had anticipated, it was decided to open Trench One in the car park to investigate the stratigraphy – the order and positioning of the rock strata – there. Badger teeth and Iron Age pottery were soon being uncovered. Trench Two was opened in a tunnel deep in the cave, on the right-hand side. Day One ended on an exhausting note with diggers still bringing up modern debris.

Day Two opened to wet weather, which made working conditions in the cave even more difficult. While the diggers continued to bring up more mud, the surveying team turned to new equipment to create a three-dimensional model of the interior of Cooper's Hole.

After three gruelling days our piece of prehistoric bone emerged. Later examination revealed flint butchery marks.

Our first target was to locate the 'stal' floor, the layer of calcified material that would seal palaeolithic deposits beneath it, so John used seismic refraction to measure how far down it was beneath the modern floor of the cave. To the rest of the Team the technique looked like hitting the ground with large hammers, but the results were good: the blows generated energy waves that changed speed as they passed through the surface and different layers and bounced back again, allowing John to record the layers in a vertical section through the earth. Mick watched from the entrance, frustrated at the slow progress inside the cave. Meanwhile Trench One, in the car park, was worrying Phil because its unstable sides looked near to collapse. Finally, at the end of the day, the diggers inside the cave reached the stal floor, to great relief and excitement.

Although Trench One had not yielded any animal bones or pottery dating to before the Iron Age, the arrival of a snail expert on Day Three produced new results. His analysis suggested that Phil had uncovered a complete ecological sequence dating from the Upper Palaeolithic to the early Mesolithic period. Halfway through the day, solid rock – the collapsed roof of the cave – was reached in the trench and, after being recorded, the unstable hole was filled in.

In Trench Two, the diggers were battling high water-levels and floods of mud and finding little in recompense. None of the animal bones that were coming up were dated any earlier than the Iron Age by *Time Team*'s expert, palaeontologist Andy Currant. At the end of the day, however, Carenza located one small bone with cut marks on it in the deposits below the stal floor in Trench Three, in the left-hand corner of the cave. At the end of the dig we all had high hopes that this would be palaeolithic, but analysis showed that it dated from the Iron Age too.

Cheddar was a difficult site to excavate because of the physical conditions and restricted working space. However, although *Time Team* didn't find the evidence of palaeolithic occupation inside the cave that we had hoped for, the trench in the car park proved the existence of important prehistoric deposits in Cooper's Hole.

As much civil engineering as archaeology, Cooper's Hole presented one of our toughest challenges.

The Upper Palaeolithic Period

There were revolutionary changes in human development during the Upper Palaeolithic period and these are reflected in the flint tools that were made then, and the appearance in Europe of what might be called the first examples of representational art: beautifully carved ivory figures and wall paintings. There is no evidence of these in Britain, which only has the odd bit of engraving on bone from Robin Hood's Cave in Derbyshire.

Evidence of our Upper Palaeolithic ancestors has been uncovered in sites like Gough's Cave in the Cheddar Gorge in Somerset, where archaeologists have found human and animal bones and flint tools. The tools are based on blade technology – blades of flint are struck from a core and are worked to produce a wide range of implements including scrapers, borers, backed blades, spokeshaves and a variety of arrowheads. In addition, sets of blade pieces were mounted in a wooden handle to produce a composite tool with a long cutting edge. There are also new bone tools, including the mysterious *baton de commandement* which, as *Time Team* convincingly demonstrated in the Cheddar Gorge programme, is best used as an extra lever for pulling in a length of rope. Palaeontologist Andy Currant found cut marks on human bones uncovered in Gough's Cave, which might suggest ritual cannibalism, and other evidence implying that soft body tissues were ritually removed after death and stored within the cave.

The Neanderthal line of our ancestry was probably dying out in Europe and it is likely that *Homo sapiens* – the first human beings who looked like us – appeared in Britain during the Upper Palaeolithic. The period also seems to coincide with more elaborate burial practices, when flowers and bone objects were deposited with the dead; evidence of this, dated to around 24,000 BC, was found at Paviland Cave in South Wales.

FINLAGGAN
ISLAY

SERIES 2
Broadcast
8 January 1995

The island of Islay, off the west coast of Scotland and within sight of Ireland on a clear day, was at the centre of the kingdom of the Lords of the Isles for 500 years. In 1156 the King of Argyllshire drove out the Norse settlers and made Islay his headquarters. His descendants settled at Finlaggan in the middle of the island and from the fourteenth century they called themselves the Lord of the Isles. The National Museums of Scotland invited *Time Team* to Islay to help in the final phase of an excavation there. The museum's archaeologists were digging on the main island in Loch Finlaggan and our mission was to find out whether the area around the loch had been inhabited in the fourteenth century and how it related to the island's history.

The weather on the morning of Day One was appalling – driving rain and low mist over the hills. This proved no deterrent to our intrepid team and the geophysics team were sent out to survey Cnoc Seandda, a large mound at the side of the loch which, it was thought, might have been used as a ceremonial site by the Lords of the Isles. Phil opened Trench One in another area beside the loch, known as Rudna Chrocain, where seventeenth-century documents record that turf-built guard huts had been located next to a jetty. Despite the heavy rain and having to continually bail out the trench, he managed to find turf walls, but there was very little datable evidence.

Geophysics were unaffected by the weather and managed to locate what appeared to be walls on top of Cnoc Seandda, and Mick Aston and Phil got on with deturfing the mound so that we could investigate further. As work progressed it became clear that we were finding evidence from a very much earlier period than that relating to the Lords of the Isles: Mesolithic flint cores, blades and a small flint tool from between 10,000 and 3,500 BC. Bernard Thomason and Stewart Ainsworth also started to survey other earthworks around the loch using a global positioning by satellite (GPS) system. This very fast and accurate technique enabled us to record the whole area in just three days, and produce a three-dimensional map on the computer.

This central mound revealed Mesolithic flints, sending the whole dig in a totally different direction.

On Day Two Tony was off to assist the Scottish Trust for Underwater Archaeology with their excavations between the islets in the loch. They had found what appeared to be the top layer of a medieval rubbish tip or midden. A feature like this can be invaluable in unravelling medieval sites – Tony found a large piece of bone with butchery marks on it. The bone assemblage would be analysed to show the kind of meat people ate. In addition, the lack of oxygen under water had prevented valuable organic material, that does not survive on dry land, from deteriorating.

Back at Cnoc Seandda, Phil and Carenza were uncovering a stone structure that they thought might be a souterrain – an underground stone chamber or tunnel – that had possibly been used for storage or been associated with burials. Would we be able to identify its purpose on Day Three?

*Indian 'spear' head fou
at St Mary's City*

10,000BC 8,500BC 7,000BC

Our final day was ushered in by a howling gale. Phil continued to excavate the structure on Cnoc Seandda while Carenza set off to look at Finlaggan's only standing stone. Robin Bush's preliminary research had indicated that there may have been two stones in the seventeenth century and when Carenza reached the site she was immediately struck by the variation in the height of the grasses around the stone. With the help of a sharp steel rod she confirmed that there were features of some kind, possibly stones, below the areas of short grass and that these were impeding the growth of the grass. Geophysics were called in to search the

A flint scraper.

field with the magnetometer, which, with good results, would enable us to see the shapes of the features as though we were looking at them from above.

Back at Cnoc Seandda, Phil had cleared out the soil from the base of the structure and uncovered bones. A closer examination revealed that they were the bones of animals that may have been deliberately buried, probably for ritualistic purposes, as the animals had not been butchered but buried whole. As the structure was obviously very important and the weather was deteriorating again, it was decided to call a halt to Phil's excavation in order to continue the work at a later date in better conditions. The geophysics team had located what appeared to be a series of pits or features – possibly a row or circle – surrounding the single standing stone.

This was an exciting end to our visit to Finlaggan. We had arrived looking for evidence of medieval occupation of the area around the loch and had uncovered evidence to show that it had been in use since the middle of the Stone Age. Was this why the Lords of the Isles were attracted to the site in the first place? The prehistoric remains may well have helped to legitimize their title to the land.

First farmers

The Neolithic period gradually heralded the arrival of what might be called farming. Our ancestors no longer depended solely on the hunting and gathering that had characterized the previous Mesolithic period. Animals were domesticated, woodland was increasingly cleared in order to plant crops and cultivated versions of plants like wheat and barley were used. Domestication and cultivation produced detectable changes in animals and plants and carbonized grain fragments have provided important evidence of a change from wild to cultivated wheat.

There was also a transition from enclosures, reached by causeways, to monuments like henges and, increasingly, tools like polished stone axes became the key to clearing woodland. An axe of similar construction was used to fell a tree when I first met Phil nearly ten years ago. It was on this memorable occasion that the head departed company with the handle at the first blow.

It took hours of work to polish these axe-heads until they were smooth – a process that strengthened them – and they must have had both a practical and symbolic importance as they were often deliberately deposited under Neolithic structures like the trackways discovered in the Somerset Levels.

The dead were often buried in long barrows like the example at West Kennet in Wiltshire, where there were multiple burials. Towards the end of the Neolithic period sarsen stones were erected at Stonehenge and its blue ones were imported from Wales. It must have required a great deal of organization and co-operation to build structures like these, which suggests the existence of a specialist group with the time to devote themselves to activities other than hunting and farming.

6,000BC   4,500BC   3,000BC

SANDAY
⊙RKNEYS

SERIES 5
Broadcast
18 January 1998

Each mound might turn out to be a Viking grave.

The Orkney islands lie just off the far north of the Scottish mainland, a position that made them especially vulnerable to the first raids of pagan Vikings from Norway in the early ninth century. Sanday is within the north-east quarter of the group and *Time Team* was invited there by Shona Grieves, a pupil at the local school, who wanted us to investigate four mounds on the Ness of Brough, a headland on the island. An antiquarian investigated the area in the second half of the nineteenth century, but his notes were poor. He had, though, found a Viking sword, axe and shield boss associated with a skull, all of which probably came from the same mound. Could we find the Viking grave?

Day One began with Carenza and Sue Francis examining aerial photographs showing the four mounds. Two had been surveyed by John Gater and Chris Gaffney with a magnetometer which indicated magnetic activity – maybe from a midden or rubbish tip – just to the side of one them. John Gater thought that the other 'quiet' mound was a grave and Phil dug Trench One across it. Before long, however, we found a prehistoric pot lid, amid growing evidence that the mound was a Bronze Age cairn. We decided simply to clean up the trench and record what we had excavated in order to concentrate on our search for the Viking grave. Another mound, which was being eroded by the sea, lay on the seaward side of the Ness and by the end of the day it was clear that this, too, was a Bronze Age cairn.

Stewart's fieldwork survey of all four mounds revealed that a series of field boundaries ran down from the most southerly mound to the sea, covering what might be a broch – a fortified tower similar to a castle. Extending from this was a boat-shaped feature, possibly a Viking hall or house. A broch would be too complicated to dig in the time we had, so we opened a small trench on the edge of the mound, close to the boat-shaped enclosure, to look for dating evidence. The geophysics results from a third mound showed two 'ferrous spikes', possibly from metalwork, that might be Viking grave goods.

A rune stone found before our arrival.

Day Two saw us examining this possible grave mound, which had stones that looked remarkably like a cist, or slab grave, sticking out of its surface. Another trench was positioned at the edge of the mound, in order to limit damage to the monument, over what appeared to be a kelp-burning pit, edged with stone. Phil and the diggers worked hard on the excavation throughout the day and, by the time the sun began to set, they still hadn't encountered any signs of the burning that would be associated with a kelp pit. This must be a burial site, after all. The ferrous spikes appeared to have been produced by a few pieces of burned stone, not metal, and, as there was no evidence of burning in situ, they must have been carried to the site and added to the burial cairn. The trench near the mound that had indicated magnetic activity was producing a lot of Iron Age pottery and flints.

On the morning of Day Three this trench was extended to allow us to take a look at a boat-shaped feature. A piece of bone was discovered in the area that we had thought was the kelp pit, and Caroline Barker, our expert in osteology, pronounced that it could well be human. The curve of stones that we had thought was part of a kelp-burning pit had turned out to be part of a boat-shaped stone grave. Was this the Viking burial place we were looking for?

Carenza pointing out the layers in a Norse or Viking midden.

When we uncovered the curved wall of the boat-shaped enclosure in the trench we found a series of deposits containing Iron Age pottery on either side of it. However, there were none in the central feature, which appeared to be an earlier building that had collapsed and seemed to be contemporary with the Iron Age broch.

Time Team had uncovered the probable sequence of events on the headland through geophysics and excavation: the Vikings arrived on Sanday in the ninth century and found a headland covered with Bronze Age cairns and the remains of an Iron Age broch. They then reserved the area as a special place in which to bury their dead.

Skara Brae

Skara Brae is one of my favourite sites, a snapshot of mid-Neolithic life in the Orkneys. The survival of this 5,000-year-old cluster of stone houses is staggering, especially as 3 metres (10 feet) of wall still stands. There are remains of other similar Neolithic settlements on the islands, but none are as complete as Skara Brae.

The settlement is made up of six huts, each of which consists of a single rectangular room about 4.5 metres (15 feet) across inside. They were cut into a rubbish dump left by previous settlers, and are deep in the ancient midden material that has gradually built up round the site. The huts are joined by long, narrow passages and are entered through a single small doorway. One or more round cells with drains in the floor lead off each room.

Amazingly, the rooms contain furniture. Built of flagstones, it has survived almost perfectly, allowing us to see first-hand what a Neolithic interior looked like. Nearly all the rooms follow the same plan with a two-shelf dresser, big enough to make it the dominating feature, opposite the entrance. There are stone-lined hearths which probably burnt peat, sunken tanks, perhaps for keeping fish, and even little box-beds which may have been filled with bracken or heather. All around the walls there are more nooks and crannies for storage. It seems that Skara Brae was a self-contained settlement and that the buildings possibly included a workshop – there is no furniture in one of the rooms and evidence of flint-working has been found.

To look down into these Neolithic huts once occupied by our ancestors is a rare and touching experience, and symbolizes how family values were as important in the distant past as they are today.

GREYLAKE
SOMERSET

SERIES 5
Broadcast
11 January 1998

Greylake lies to the south of the Polden Hills, on the Somerset Levels – peat moors which were flooded every winter until the seventeenth century. These wetlands provided a rich hunting ground for our prehistoric ancestors, whose settlements were mostly on small areas of slightly higher ground ingeniously connected by wooden trackways. An antiquarian had suggested in 1926 that one of these might be in a peat field near Greylake, and *Time Team* went to Somerset to test the theory.

The geophysics team went to work on Day One, but although they reported a linear anomaly it appeared to be running at the wrong angle for the trackway. However, this result and the antiquarian's reported find-spot were used to locate the site of Trench One while geophysics moved on to the slightly higher ground. Very soon the first timber was uncovered in the trench, and it looked as if it had been deliberately placed and shaped. Stewart Ainsworth examined the edge of the drainage ditch on one side of the field and found some timbers that were possibly aligned with the one in the trench, so it was decided to investigate these further and Trench Two was opened next to the ditch. The geophysics team, meanwhile, had encountered earthworks associated with a post-medieval farmstead, but nothing relating to the possible trackway.

More timbers appeared in Trench One, including a piece in which a mortise hole had been cut. The planks were at different angles and fairly spread out, leading Mick to suggest that the structure might have been a platform at the end of a trackway, rather than just a walkway. Peat samples were taken from the trench to examine the environmental evidence and help build up a picture of what the landscape would have looked like when the platform was constructed. Then, towards the end of Day One, Phil excavated two pieces of handmade pottery – possibly Bronze or Iron Age – from the level of the timbers. It was an amazing end to a successful day.

On Day Two the Team extended Trench One. It was becoming difficult to work in it because of the high water-table and had to be bailed out. Our dendrochronologist, Robert Howard, arrived and took a

searching for Bronze Age deposits in yet another trench.

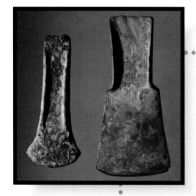

The Bronze Age

The use and exploitation of natural sources of metal occurred later in Britain – about 2,300 BC – than elsewhere in Europe, where copper was smelted as early as 4,000–6,000 BC. There is no evidence of a 'copper age' or 'charcoalithic period'. Copper and bronze artefacts appear at the same time – some of the earliest objects are flat copper axes, known in some places as 'Celts', which were produced by pouring the metal into a flat mould. Britain is rich in deposits of tin and in time it was added to copper to produce the harder material, bronze. It is likely that this alloy was discovered when elements of arsenical tin were accidentally added to copper during the smelting process.

The earliest metalwork is associated with the Beaker people. Despite the efforts of archaeologists to prove otherwise, they seem to be one of the few groups who brought new ideas and technology to Britain. Archaeologists have rightly reacted against the theory that all new ideas arrived as the result of invasion, but, as evidence in burials shows, the Beakers do appear to have brought with them a different cultural package ≃ which included beautiful copper or bronze daggers.

The Bronze Age also saw exploitation of gold deposits which led to the creation of gold *lunalae* – crescent-shaped collars found mainly in Ireland and sometimes in Cornwall. Flint-working continued with the production of distinctive thumbnail scrapers and beautiful barbed and forged arrowheads. *Time Team* found a leaf-shaped one from the early Bronze Age during the excavation at Flag Fen.

number of samples for dating. The timbers in Trench Two, beside the drainage ditch, turned out to be 'natural' wood, with no tool marks, and it was closed down. Geophysics had picked up two curving ditches, possibly forming part of an enclosure, on the higher ground and Trench Three was opened to see if they were significant.

But the first trench was still the centre of the excitement. A human upper-arm bone had turned up – something quite rare on the Somerset Levels as the peat is very acidic and bone is not usually preserved. This was soon followed by a piece of rib and a collar-bone. Were they from human bones that had been ritually deposited there, possibly to define the edge of a territory along a boundary?

Back in the incident room, the timber in Trench One had been identified as hazel and oak, both from dry environments, and the pollen specialists had found grains from a similar environment. Trench Three, on the higher land, was disappointing as there was no evidence of any settlement. Nevertheless, we were excited at the possibility of having uncovered a burial platform of some sort.

At the start of Day Three, Robert Howard contacted us to say that one of the samples he had taken from Trench One indicated that an upright timber had a groove down one side. The excavators decided to remove it and discovered that one side had definitely been cut at an angle. The environmental specialists painted a picture of an area at the edge of water with adjacent dry land, perhaps with a few open pools surrounded by willows.

Meanwhile, the 'dendro-date' had arrived. All three samples came from wood cut down in about 900 BC – the timbers were 3,000 years old! As the day progressed the excavation in Trench One showed a line of upright timbers rather than a platform. It was likely that the bones might have formed part of a ritual deposit along a boundary, like the one previously found at Flag Fen, near Peterborough.

Our visit to the Somerset Levels did not turn up the evidence we had thought we would find. Instead we uncovered something completely new, in that area, for the archaeological record: a ritual burial site along a boundary line – the planks we had initially thought were a walkway. Greylake will give archaeologists food for thought for many years to come.

Pottery finds which had been preserved by the damp conditions.

Stonehenge

One of the greatest monuments of the prehistoric world, Stonehenge is unique and represents at least three different phases of work that started in about 3,000 BC and continued for over 600 years until about 2,400 BC, when its massive trilithons – two upright stones with a third across the top – were erected and the blue stones put in place.

It is part of a huge complex of earthworks, barrows and other monuments, and would have been preceded by earlier wooden structures. The stone joints that hold the trilithons together can be seen as a sophisticated development in stoneworking technology. Work by a number of archaeologists has shown that Stonehenge is aligned to astronomical movements associated with events like midwinter sunrise and midsummer sunset, and also marks the phases of the moon. This is accepted by many archaeologists, as it is highly improbable that the alignments were achieved by chance.

We know for certain that Stonehenge had nothing to do with the Druids, who only came to Britain in about the third century BC. Connections with the Myceneans have also been abandoned in favour of the view that it is a purely indigenous structure in a direct line of descent from earlier wooden circles and other monuments.

Recent arguments over access and rerouting of roads tends to obscure the fact that the entire landscape surrounding Stonehenge is an invaluable and unique area, and that the monument needs to be seen in this context.

2,400BC

DEYA
MALLORCA

SERIES 5
Broadcast
1 February 1998

Deya, on the small island of Mallorca in the western Mediterranean, was the location for *Time Team*'s second venture abroad. American archaeologist Bill Waldren has found twenty-eight Copper and Bronze Age sites there, dating from 2,500–1,300 BC, and invited us to investigate three of them and help him to build up a picture of the landscape that prehistoric Mallorcans lived in.

Mallorca is dry and rocky compared to Britain and presented new problems for the Team. Many of the sites were covered with boulders that had been piled up by farmers clearing fields and these had to be removed from the sites we wanted to investigate – no easy task in the island's hot weather. In addition, the dry, rocky conditions made geophysics almost impossible as these either rely on moisture – of which there wasn't enough – or magnetic fields, and the presence of volcanic rocks distorts these results.

On Day One Phil began digging Trench One at Son Oleza, a complete walled settlement, to try and find evidence of Beaker people – a Copper Age community characterized by the distinctive earthenware beakers found in their graves. Meanwhile Carenza, also in search of Beaker pottery, started clearing stones at a nearby group of prehistoric houses called the Maze.

By the start of Day Two, there had been little progress with the archaeology. Phil had uncovered some fragments of pottery, but Carenza was still clearing stones. Mick suggested digging small test pits, while Carenza wanted to do some fieldwalking and look for pottery on the surface. Because local labour

On Mallorca we found pieces of Beaker-period pottery by the handful. In Britain we are lucky to find the odd fragment.

was very short, we decided to stop working on the Son Oleza site and concentrate on fieldwalking and test-pitting at the Maze. Soon Carenza had collected large quantities of Copper Age pottery.

Meanwhile Mick visited the Sanctuary, an important ritual site nearby. The surviving foundations were Iron Age – later than Copper Age – but he was keen to find out if there was a Beaker sanctuary underneath them. He arranged for radiocarbon dating and astronomical analysis of the site.

Excavations at the Maze had yielded no further evidence of Beaker inhabitants by Day Three except Carenza's pottery, and Phil concluded that the surviving walls were Iron Age rather than Copper Age, although there must have been an earlier settlement somewhere nearby. However, exciting results came from the Sanctuary. The astronomical alignments of the stones there, combined with the radiocarbon dates, suggested that parts of it were Beaker. The position of the stars had shifted over the millennia and, as a result, the site had been unused for 400 years until the surviving Iron Age structures were built.

Mallorca's environment made working on the island a difficult venture for *Time Team*. However, we felt that the results we had achieved in three days had made a small but significant contribution to an important research project.

The spectacular stonework of prehistoric people in Mallorca, including irrigation systems to channel water.

KEMERTON
WORCESTERSHIRE

SERIES 6
Broadcast
7 March 1999

In 1990 a photographer took a series of aerial photographs of fields at Kemerton in Worcestershire, which clearly revealed crop marks showing ditches, structures and boundaries. Local archaeologists knew there was an area of Bronze Age and Iron Age settlement nearby, so were keen to investigate further. They invited *Time Team* to join them and find out what lay beneath the fields.

The most distinct feature on the photographs was a long trackway across the fields, so on the first day two trenches were opened to investigate this. Meanwhile Stewart Ainsworth got to work looking at old maps of Kemerton, identifying features that might be contemporary with the trackway. Back in the fields, Phil soon found fragments of pottery and located the drip trench from the roof of a round thatched house. However, the pottery was Saxon, not Bronze Age. Although Phil was surprised at this, the local archaeologists were happy because Saxon pottery is rare in Worcestershire.

The archaeology was quite different to what everyone was expecting and on Day Two, after much discussion overnight, two long strips of topsoil were cleared from one of the fields to try and make sense of it. Carenza soon unearthed a hearth and a series of post holes and ditches. Meanwhile a soil scientist, David Jordan, took samples across the field to look for signs of burial, burning, food debris and other evidence of occupation. By the end of the day, pottery finds in the strips suggested we were looking at a large Iron Age enclosure, with a later Saxon farmstead nearby.

On Day Three, with an increasingly complicated landscape emerging, two more trenches were opened in the enclosure and Phil found evidence of Iron Age occupation in round houses: pottery,

Part of an Iron Age quern.

potboilers and quern stones from hand-mills for grinding corn. It appeared that the enclosure had also been occupied in the Bronze Age – pottery and even a piece of bronze from a shield or scabbard was found there. Finally, Stewart's study of old maps revealed a whole area of Bronze Age and Iron Age fields and boundaries that would have surrounded the settlement.

The evidence *Time Team* found at Kemerton showed a small settlement of round houses inside an enclosure that had been occupied from at least as early as the Bronze Age. The people living there created fields and boundaries in the surrounding countryside, and these had been in use right through to the Saxon period. Yet again, our excavations had shown that good sites have often been lived in, and farmed, for many thousands of years, and not during just one period.

Sometimes you can only see archaeology from above, and even then it is not very clear! Iron Age ditches and embankments at Kemerton can just be made out in the late-afternoon sun.

FLAG FEN
CAMBRIDGESHIRE

PHOTO STORY
FROM SERIES 7

TONY'S PIECE TO CAMERA: 'This is Flag Fen near Peterborough in the Cambridgeshire Fenlands, probably the most important Bronze Age Site in Britain. The archaeology here has been pickled under a deep layer of waterlogged peat, and even wooden and delicate objects have been perfectly preserved so that we get a detailed 'snapshot' of how people lived 3,000 years ago. The problem is that a cycle-track is being constructed to celebrate the millennium and it's going to cross one of the most important areas of the site. Time Team's been asked to rescue the archaeology before it is destroyed.'

The start of the Bronze Age metal working.

The Bronze Age (2,300–700 BC) is one of my favourite archaeological periods. It was a time of change and innovation when metal objects initially associated with the Beaker people, who came to Britain during the second millennium BC, first appeared. Single burials with bodies placed in a crouched position to some extent replaced the multiple ones of the Neolithic period and there seems to have been a growth in ritual activity: objects were thrown into water and large-scale monuments were created – chiefly the stone circles that culminated in the wonders of Stonehenge.

A new group of craftsmen skilled in metalsmithing came into being. They had the advanced technological skills to produce alloys – tin is added to copper to make bronze – and design innovative objects like laminated bows and wheels; and combined these skills with an aesthetic sensibility that created objects which still hold a fascination for us today. One of my favourite archaeological artefacts, a *lunalae* – a gold collar with incised Beaker-style decoration – comes from this period.

Phil and Margaret Cox study the remains of a Bronze Age cremation.

The material wealth of certain individuals suggests the existence of an élite group of ruling chiefs who were capable of organizing their followers to carry out grand schemes. The Wessex culture of around 1,700 BC is associated with high-status grave goods and these people produced beautiful objects which some archaeologists believe suggest contacts with Mediterranean peoples. The late Bronze Age certainly seems to have been a time when trade increased – and woodworking skills were undoubtedly up to constructing boats capable of undertaking long-distance journeys. One of the main factors that contributed to this development may have been the need to find sources for the tin used in the production of bronze.

Flag Fen is one of Britain's most fascinating Bronze Age sites. The life's work of two remarkable archaeologists, Francis Pryor and Maisie Taylor, it is renowned both for its bronze finds and its wood: Bronze Age wood. Large numbers of objects have been discovered there in circumstances that suggest that they were thrown into the Fenland waters on purpose. Some seem to be imperfect or made in a way that suggests their primary use was not entirely practical. Some are perfect and would have been of great value. Others were deliberately broken and thrown into the water – a ritual 'killing' and sacrifice.

The desire of our Bronze Age ancestors to spend time and precious resources creating masterpieces of the metalsmith's art, only to throw them in a swamp, takes a bit of adjusting to. It's one of those rare events in archaeology when artefacts and their location give us a glimpse into the mind of our predecessors. Interestingly, the concept has a resonance in Britain's more recent mythological past – when Arthur died Sir Bedivere is supposed to have returned the king's sword, Excalibur, to the Lady of

A handful of diggers covered in Bronze Age mud. Behind, Joe Ellison, our Communications supervisor, searches for metal.

the Lake, perhaps an echo of our Bronze Age past. However, we were faced with an archaeological dig and had to get to grips with more mundane realities.

Venturing on to the site of a previous excavation is always a challenge for *Time Team* and when the site is as famous as Flag Fen this is even more the case. The presence alone of Francis and Maisie made it attractive, but what could we add to their exhaustive work?

A millennial cycle-track that would be cutting through the archaeology and the lure of the organic provided the impetus. We rarely see organic finds – bone, wood and cloth. The figure varies, but most archaeologists agree that 70 per cent to 80 per cent of remains are lost because of decomposition. Organic material rots on most sites and we will never know just how much we are missing unless we look more closely at 'wet sites' like Flag Fen. Here remains are immersed in water, and so are protected against the deadly, decaying effect of oxygen. These are a rarity in Britain – unlike in Denmark, which has many boggy expanses. A quick glance through books about these areas – I particularly enjoyed finding *The Bog People* by the wonderfully named P.V. Glob – brings home how little organic material survives on the average 'dry site'. Most 'wet site' archaeologists have an undeniably superior air – as if their 'dry site' peers are missing the point! Excavating in the Fenland bogs would give *Time Team* an opportunity to get to grips with organic remains and the special techniques needed to excavate them.

When I arrived on the site the evening before the dig commenced, there was an air of general confusion which seemed to centre on the fact that Francis had already dug up an area we thought we were supposed to be digging. A combination of over-enthusiasm and a slightly inexact research brief had helped to create the situation. This meant an anxious few hours doing a complete rewrite on Tony's opening piece to camera. Entering into the mire of the Fenland bogs was providing an unusual range of challenges from the start.

The business of excavating in bogland certainly presented new challenges to our diggers. The dark peaty soil had to be carefully eased away from the wooden logs and planks that 3,000 to 4,000 years ago formed walkways and fences across the Fens. Their survival is amazing in itself. Some of the timbers in the huge Preservation Hall at Flag Fen are still hard, preserved by the anaerobic (oxygen-free) conditions of the peatbog and carefully conserved. As soon as wooden artefacts are exposed to the air they become dry and desiccated and rapidly turn to dust if they are not conserved. Maisie and her team of excavators were on hand to help us with our excavation and demonstrate their conservation techniques.

The Flag Fen team had excavated at various points on a trackway in previous years and we hoped to find where it went to, in particular whether it continued to an area of high ground where a number of barrows – likely Bronze Age burial sites – were located. Francis was keen to establish that they were contemporary with the trackway and find out how long the high ground had been an 'island of the dead'. Aerial photographs showed crop marks and these suggested a lot of activity that included farming, but was not necessarily from one period.

On the first day, one of Stewart Ainsworth's jobs was to sort out the tangle of field boundaries and other features revealed by the crop marks, and see how they related to the trackway. Trenches were opened alongside the trackway and soon revealed upright timbers surrounded by a spaghetti-like cluster of smaller horizontal ones. The diggers used wooden spatulas – later reinforced by a supply of used lolly sticks because of the hot weather – to gently tease black mud from Bronze Age wood.

Crop marks and an initial survey of the barrow site by the geophysics team: Chris Gaffney, Louis Harvey and David Weston, suggested the location of Trench Two – over one of the barrows. We hoped it would enable us to find out when the site had been used for burials. Barrows with an initial single burial then later 'satellite' ones are a distinctive feature of the Bronze Age.

We enrolled the services of Paul Middleton, an environmental archaeologist, who set up a miniature laboratory by the side of the road to analyse the phosphate content of the soil. Burials can leave a high trace of the mineral and this can be detected by mixing soil samples with a reactive chemical that changes colour depending on the level of phosphate. Garden centres sell similar, but less sensitive, kits for testing garden soil.

Despite the clear crop marks, Phil's early excavations in Trench Two were not hopeful. The large areas of gravel that were emerging looked alarmingly natural. Had the barrow been ploughed out? Francis remained confident, but by the end of the day there was still no trace of burials, cremations or the distinctive ditch that often surrounds a barrow.

A Bronze Age pike jaw – clearly a formidable creature.

Digging in barrows such as these was considered a fine day out for some of our more recent ancestors. The Victorians in particular liked to pack their picnic hampers and shovels and see what they could discover, taking along the necessary workmen to do the digging. Often they went straight to the middle in their search for valuable artefacts and skulls. Pieces of pottery and other such finds were cast to one side and the material at the periphery of the barrow was often ignored.

Day Two saw more timbers appearing in Trench One and dry weather meant they had to be sprayed to prevent them drying out. The geophysics team had moved to the part of the high ground where the trackway – or 'post alignment' as Francis insisted on calling it – should end. We opened Trench Three here to see if the timbers continued into the area.

By now our metalsmith, Dave Chapman, had arrived to start on the cameo – the technology re-enactment featured in every programme. He would combine copper with tin, and use the bronze produced to copy an axe found at Flag Fen.

One of our earliest and most successful cameos was smelting tin. I can still remember the sense of magic when the tinsmith at the fogou site in Boleigh in Cornwall (see page 50) produced globules of bright metal from the dark coals of the furnace – tin, extracted from shiny black pebbles lodged in Cornish streams. When it is added to copper it has a hardening effect – this is the reason why bronze will take and keep a sharp cutting-edge.

Dave takes his trade seriously and has researched his techniques to make sure they are as authentic as possible. It is likely that bronze was discovered when early smiths smelted copper that contained elements of arsenical tin. They would have realized that the new metal produced a harder edge – that something magical had happened in the heat of the furnace. We know that in many cultures smiths were thought to have magical powers.

Encamped in a circular tent on a wooden framwork Dave set to work building a bowl furnace – the kind that was used throughout the Bronze Age and Iron Age. With Mick's help it soon took shape. It turned out to be smaller than we had expected and was placed in a hole dug in the soil at the centre

Interior of the replica Bronze Age hut at Flag Fen.

Dave Chapman and Mick check the molten bronze in the bowl furnace.

of the tent. Two goatskin bellows supplied draughts of air through bone or clay pipes – *tuyéres* – which prevent the bellows catching fire. Copper melts at around 1,000°C (1,800°F), bronze at 1,150–1,200°C (2,100–2,190°F) and iron at 1,500–1,600°C (2,700–2,900°F), so the temperature in the furnace had to reach well above 950°C (2,010°F) to get the bronze in a good pouring state. It was also important to balance the ratio of tin to copper in order to achieve the right combination of sharpness and strength. Bronze for making weapons normally contains about 12 per cent tin. A proportion of 15 per cent produces a sharper edge – for a razor, for example – but a weapon like the axe Dave was making would easily shatter if the bronze was made with this amount of tin.

Francis and Carenza examining Bronze Age objects.

The way bronze axes developed has enabled archaeologists to create a typology. The early copper and bronze ones were flat, almost two-dimensional, designs. The bronze was poured into open moulds and the axe was often etched with decorations similar to those found in Beaker burials. The basic design gradually increased in complexity, with a hammered edge to hold the haft – the wooden handle – in place. Over time what are known as palstave axes were developed, with edges large enough for the flanges to take a haft with a V-shaped section cut out of it. Later still, axe-heads became hollow, sometimes with rings for cord so that the head could be tied to the haft. These socketed axes require a fairly sophisticated mould but create a secure place for the haft. Moulds to creat these have been found on archaeological sites.

When an axe strikes a tree – or an enemy – it carries a great deal of force and bronze was too valuable to risk repeatedly losing the axe-head because of poor design. A way had to be found to secure the head to the haft and the gradual development of the necessary technology provides a relatively secure bronze-axe typology: a system that enables archaeologists to suggest a date for a site based on axe finds that can be placed on a typological time line. One where a simple flat axe with increased decoration is found is likely to be earlier than one that produces an axe with socket loops and other sophisticated additions. Later axes tend to show the addition of lead to the alloy, which makes the bronze pour more smoothly. It is interesting, though, that Dave did not find this to be the case. Lead does not produce a true alloy and he dislikes the bronze it makes.

Most axes found at Flag Fen were from the Wilburton group – socketed axes from the late Bronze Age – and the one we were copying had been made in a reusable stone or bronze mould with a ceramic core. Dave pointed out that the seams along the centre were evidence of this. Victor Ambrus created a wax copy of the axe which was wrapped in a mixture of clay and horse manure – the latter to reduce clay's tendency to crack – then left to dry and form a mould for the axe-head. The horse's digestive system reduces vegetable fibres until they are fine enough to mix in easily with the clay.

Assembled diggers waiting for the appearance of prehistoric woodwork.

With preparations to cast the bronze axe well under way, Phil was dispatched to the woods with Maisie to look for suitable wood for a haft. Hafts have been found at Flag Fen, rare evidence of the organic element in Bronze Age axes. Maisie has great respect for the woodworkers of the period and believes that, aside from their expertise in constructing axes, one of their greatest skills was their ability to choose the right piece of wood, from a particular tree, for the haft. For example, the angle where the branch and trunk meet should be the same as the angle between the haft and axe-head.

Jenni Butterworth keeping the Bronze Age wood moist. One of the uprights of the trackway can be seen on the right.

Back in the trenches, pottery, a critical artefact for dating Bronze Age sites, had begun to appear. The shards we found are known as Post-Deverel-Rimbury ware and, like the socketed axes, are later Bronze Age and typical of this area of the Fens. They seemed to show encrusted deposits that may have been associated with metalworking. The Bronze Age produced a variety of pottery from the beautiful drinking cups of the Beaker burials to the more complicated collared urns of the later Bronze Age. Interestingly the earlier Beaker-ware is often finer than the later pottery. At Waddon (see page 59) we were lucky to find a small piece of Beaker-ware which enabled us to date a possible henge monument.

Trench Two, the barrow excavation, at last produced the required ditch and Francis was happy – Paul's phosphate analysis of the layers of soil below the surface had indicated two possible locations for a burial. With Phil back on the job the surface of these areas was gently picked away and we began to see white: flecks of material that Margaret Cox, *Time Team*'s osteoarchaeologist, recognized as tooth enamel. In addition, small fragments of bone and the edge of a Bronze Age urn gradually appeared. As it turned out, there were no further deposits. Aggressive soil conditions – high acidity – had probably rotted the bone. However, we did find a triangular flint arrowhead adjacent to the main trench. Arrows were among the main objects that were buried with the dead in the early Bronze Age and Phil was ecstatic about the workmanship this one revealed. It was a timely reminder that flint production did not cease with the start of the Bronze Age.

On Day Three Trench Four was opened on the 'post alignment' and produced a number of objects that, like those from the barrow excavation, suggested ritual activity – they had been deliberately buried there. Large fragments of a Bronze Age pottery bowl appeared and both Carenza and Francis felt that they had been broken in one place on purpose. We also found the remains of a horse's skull, another object associated with Bronze Age ritual deposits.

Carenza with a part-finished Bronze Age arrowhead.

The centre of the furnace. Bronze alloy at a temperature of over 950°C.

Molten bronze ready to pour.

Phil had carved a haft and it was time to pour the bronze into the mould. The results were impressive. When the metal had cooled the mould was broken open to reveal a perfect copy of a Flag Fen axe-head. This was reheated until it was hot enough to burn the wood and the haft was forced into the socket. Tony used the axe to chop wood and produced shallow scoops like the ones we had begun to find on the wood in Trench One, which had produced a dendro-date of 1,071 BC.

For Francis, Time Team's most important achievement was uncovering evidence that the barrow had been in continuous use. We found material from the early to late Bronze Age; and when we reached its base, ditches that might indicate an earlier Neolithic structure on the site were revealed. We also showed that the 'post alignment' continued on to the higher ground and the evidence in Trench Four suggested that this too may have been a site of ritual deposits. Further excavation over a wider area would almost certainly have produced bronze objects.

There was one final act to perform. Dave, our metalsmith, suggested that it would be appropriate to return a bronze object to Flag Fen – an offering of thanks for all the objects archaeologists had found there. He gave a beautiful bronze sword – appropriately marked to avoid any future confusion – to Francis, who volunteered to carry it into the lake at the edge of the site. This moving moment was rather undermined by Phil's laughter at the sight of our colleague wading into the water still wearing shoes and trousers, but we felt we had made an offering, and an appropriate one at that, to our Bronze Age ancestors.

Director, cameramen and crew stand by to film as Francis quietly sinks deeper.

Roman Britain

BOLEIGH
CORNWALL

SERIES 3
Broadcast
7 January 1996

The discovery of Iron Age pottery at last confirme we were in the right spot.

Fogous – underground tunnels or passages – are enigmatic features of Britain's Iron Age landscape. They are found in the south-west and although they are generally associated with settlements, their function is unknown. There are many theories: that they were refuges from attack or underground storage areas, or that they enabled early men and women to get spiritually close to the earth. Western Cornwall is rich in prehistoric sites and Joe Kay invited *Time Team* to investigate a fogou in his garden in Boleigh. We hoped that by locating the settlement that accompanied it we might be able to understand more about why these mysterious structures are built.

On Day One Stewart Ainsworth began by surveying the complexes of small walls and ditches around the fogou. He identified the outlines of houses and buildings. Meanwhile, the geophysics team led by John Gater identified a strong anomaly on the nearby lawn and Phil opened Trench One to investigate it. Trench Two was away from the fogou where the outside wall of the Iron Age settlement might be located. By the end of the day Phil's chief find, in Trench One, was an iron water pipe – the earlier anomaly.

On Day Two, after consulting nineteenth-century plans of the fogou, Stewart decided to look for the settlement outside the garden and set off into the undergrowth. Phil began to uncover large quantities of Iron Age pottery in Trench Two, along with the remains of a substantial building. Carenza decided to open Trench Three nearby, and was soon inundated with pottery, as well as a stone for grinding corn.

Excavations around the fogou continued on Day Three and confirmed that the Team had located the settlement where its Iron Age builders would have lived. Meanwhile, Stewart turned his attention to

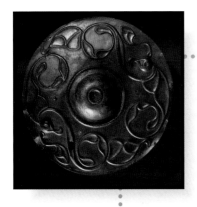

The Iron Age

The Iron Age was characterized by a deterioration in climate which led to changes in society and politics during the first millennium BC. As temperatures dropped, less land was available to farm or live on, and competition for any that was usable increased. Tribes began to protect their territories with boundaries and fortified sites – hillforts – to fend off aggressive neighbours. There are more than 3,000 hillforts in Britain, dating from about the fourth century BC, and excavations and geophysics have shown that they were used for a variety of purposes, including settlement, storage and as places of trading.

Iron was more accessible than bronze and the technology for processing it had been developed and was widely known by the third to fourth centuries BC. Evidence for this comes from blacksmiths' tools like hammers and tongs, and smelting furnaces that have been found on Dartmoor and other areas.

The first coins come from about the first century BC, with the development of early *oppida* – 'urban' centres that attracted crafts and industry – where indications of coin production have been uncovered. The introduction of coins into Iron Age society confirms that a trading network that required a standardization of values was in place at this time. Indeed, the range of this network is shown by the Mediterranean artefacts that have been found in Britain.

Celtic art is another classic feature of the Iron Age. Exquisite decoration on weapons, pottery and brooches, with interlocking spirals and knots and rich inlays, shows a wide range of styles and designs. Despite the apparent predominance of conflict in this period, Iron Age craftsmen were capable of producing objects of great beauty.

Wooden stake from the trackway at Greylake

the fogou itself and produced an accurate survey of its tunnels. Finally, at the end of the day, the geophysics team returned triumphantly from a nearby site called Treveneague. They had managed to find a fogou, the location of which had been discovered in the nineteenth century but subsequently lost.

Time Team had located the settlement that accompanied the fogou at Boleigh and so made a good contribution to the study of these enigmatic structures. It is always important to study the landscape in order to understand single features like fogous. By investigating the villages of the Iron Age people who built and used fogous, and examining the landscape around them, archaeologists can get closer to understanding why they were built and what they were used for.

Phil prepares to explore the depths of an underground chamber.

Rim of an Iron Age bowl found at Boleigh

Bowl awl found at Waddon

Navan
County Armagh

SERIES 3
Broadcast
4 February 1996

Navan in County Armagh, Northern Ireland, was the ancient Emain Macha, the seat of the kings of Ulster. Legend has it that one of them, Conchobhar, had three palaces there and Dr Chris Lynn, Principal Inspector of Monuments for Northern Ireland invited *Time Team* to see if they could locate these legendary Bronze Age sites in the surrounding area.

Day One found us examining a set of ditches at Creeveroe, an area of settlement and a possible palace site, close to Navan. Phil opened Trench One across one of the ditches and, most unexpectedly, found a Neolithic stone axe-head from a quarry in County Antrim. This didn't shed any light on Bronze Age Creeveroe, but the Team were soon finding iron slag, possibly medieval, and then pieces of Bronze Age domestic pottery – the first evidence that could be dated to the period associated with Conchobhar. It seemed that the ditch was an early one that had been reused at a later date.

Our next target was a set of crop marks that seemed to connect Haughey's Fort, an adjacent hillfort, with the King's Stables, a natural pool that was known to have been used for ritual purposes and which had produced numerous prestigious objects in an earlier excavation by Dr Chris Lynn, in 1976. A survey by the geophysics team pointed to a useful location for Trench Two that might show up a link between the fort and pool. A survey by Stewart Ainsworth and Carenza produced another candidate for a possible palace site – a nearby hill called Bally Doo, which is approximately the same distance from Haughey's Fort as the fort is from Navan. Stewart had spotted a carved stone on the side of the hill when he was examining the hill top. Did this point to an earlier settlement?

One of Phil's
favourite finds –
a prehistoric polished
stone axe.

At the beginning of Day Two the results of the survey of Bally Doo were discussed and we decided to open Trench Three and to excavate what looked like a defensive ditch. Back at Creeveroe, in Trench One, the layer of later soil containing iron slag could clearly be seen above the layer in the bottom of the ditch that contained the Bronze Age pottery. The day ended with the discovery in Trench Three at Bally Doo, of the edge of what might be a pathway surface that lined up with Haughey's Fort and with the King's Stables.

On Day Three new material, including a fragile piece of metal that turned out to be a medieval stirrup, appeared in Trench Three. Geophysics did a concentrated survey of the hill top which suggested there were structures there so Trench Four was opened. Stonework and large amounts of souterrain-ware were soon located suggesting the site dated to the early Christian period. Towards the end of the day the discovery of a glass bead confirmed this view: only two kinds of sites – early ecclesiastical and royal – ever produce this kind of find.

Time Team did not unearth a palace, but a number of the secrets of this ancient landscape were unlocked over three days. It had been thought that the Iron Age landscape around Navan might be quite extensive and *Time Team* had shown that this was the case, with cropmarks and geophysical surveys revealing the routeways that linked the different elements of the landscape. In addition, we had discovered that this ritual landscape had its roots in the Bronze Age period, and that it had still been considered important enough as a site for later generations to locate their Christian sites in the same area.

A rare prehistoric
carving at
Navan. Victor
later managed to
create a drawing
of a deer from
this unpromising
start.

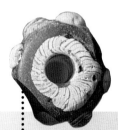

Glass bead found
at York

200BC

ΠETHERAVOΠ
WILTSHIRE

SERIES 4
Broadcast
9 February 1997

In 1907 an army officer, Lieutenant Colonel William Hawley, located the mosaic pavement of a Roman villa near the sergeants' mess of the cavalry barracks at Netheravon in Wiltshire. His description of where he found it was vague and for this reason, and because the barracks buildings that might have helped to identify its location were demolished, the site of the villa had been lost. The Ministry of Defence was planning to redevelop the old barracks area and invited *Time Team* to try and locate the villa before the builders moved in.

A Roman tile. Objects like this suggested the existence of a building, but it proved frustratingly hard to locate.

At the start of Day One the site looked less than promising. It was littered with rubble and building foundations and was partly covered with tarmac and concrete. We knew that these were difficult conditions for the geophysics team, but John and Chris started surveying anyway. Because the location of the villa was so vague, Mick decided to open a number of 1 x 1 metre (3 x 3 foot) test pits across the site – a common method of assessing below-ground archaeology over a wide area. In addition, Carenza opened Trench One and Trench Two where we hoped the villa would be. By the end of the day, neither the trenches nor the test pits had produced anything except one Roman brick.

On Day Two geophysics attempted deeper readings and, after a tip-off from a local resident who could remember the location of the sergeants' mess, more test pits were dug, in new areas. Roman pottery was soon being unearthed from these new pits. Meanwhile, Trench Two, one of Carenza's trenches, had started to uncover hard evidence of the villa itself. Building materials from the house – stones and roof tiles – provided a vivid picture of what it would have looked like. The diamond-shaped tiles were made of three types of stone – red, white and green – so the villa would

Julius Caesar

Although he is one of the best-known Roman leaders in British history, Julius Caesar never conquered, or ruled, any part of Britain. However, gaining territory does not appear to have been his objective: his invasions of 55 BC and 54 BC were probably intended to prevent the Britons assisting his enemies in Gaul and gain him personal glory in Rome.

Despite Caesar's brilliance as a military strategist and commander, his first invasion started badly when he failed to lead his fleet successfully and quickly into a safe British harbour. The Britons had time to organize themselves and waded into the shallows to meet the Roman army when it eventually arrived in what is now Kent. Once Caesar's men had slowly and painfully gained a foothold on dry land their military training came into its own, and they were able to win skirmishes with the British forces. However, a violent storm prevented the arrival of their cavalry and damaged their ships. Lacking horse-power, the Romans lost a further skirmish to the Britons and Caesar was forced to cut his losses and return to Gaul.

He returned to Britain the following year with a larger fleet of about 800 vessels. His men were unchallenged when they came ashore and stormed northwards to what is now Hertfordshire. Here – possibly near Wheathampstead – Caesar defeated a coalition of British tribes led by Cassivellaunus, king of the Catuvellauni, who was forced to pay tribute.

Caesar made treaties with his opponents and returned to Gaul where a rebellion was brewing. Establishing a Roman presence in Britain had not been his aim: he had achieved the victory he desired and was hailed as a hero in Rome.

have had a striking patterned roof. The day ended on an optimistic note when Carenza found the first tesserae from the mosaic pavement in Trench Two.

Lindsay Allason-Jones, *Time Team*'s Roman expert, was convinced that the tesserae came from a corridor in the villa, but Day Three yielded little evidence to confirm or deny this. Carenza's trenches produced more building materials, but no foundations or floors to confirm the location of the villa. Finally, Phil and Mick opened a third trench and located the edge of the terrace on which it would have been built. This provided a boundary for the site, and suggested where the villa might have been.

Netheravon was a frustrating but useful site for *Time Team* to excavate. It demonstrated that an archaeological investigation can be like solving a jigsaw puzzle: many small pieces combine to provide a lot of information. Although we didn't find the location of the villa itself, the evidence we did find revealed a great deal about what it would have looked like and how it was built.

Phil refused to be beaten and worked his way deeper into the potential Roman terraces.

Claudius Invades

In August 43 the emperor Claudius launched the second successful Roman invasion of Britain when four legions and auxiliary troops, in total over 40,000 men, landed unchallenged on the Kentish coast. The army was led by Aulus Plautius, who became Britain's first Roman governor, and marched unopposed to the River Medway. Here they met the Britons under the command of Caratacus, chief of the Catuvellauni, and gained a spectacular victory after a two-day battle. The Britons fled to the Thames and into Essex and, with final victory close at hand, Claudius travelled to Britain from Rome and led his army into battle on 23 September.

The emperor brought with him elephants and twelve camels, which may seem surprising today, but the animals proved their worth. The elephants could penetrate dense hawthorn thickets while the unfamiliar smell of camels drove the native horses mad and upset the British charioteers. I have always been tempted to look for a burial ground full of elephant bones and camel skulls!

After his victory, Claudius led a triumphal entry into what the Romans called Camulodunon (modern Colchester), the Catuvellaunian capital. Some 4,700 Britons were dead and 8,000 were taken prisoner, while the Romans lost 380 men, with 600 wounded. The emperor spent only sixteen days in his newly conquered province, then returned to Rome leaving Plautius to lay the foundations of Roman Britain.

Maiden Castle

Maiden Castle, perhaps the most impressive hillfort in Britain, was the last refuge of a fierce British tribe, the Durotriges, and the scene of what appears to have been the fiercest battle fought during the Roman conquest. Hillforts represent and reflect increased competition for the slowly diminishing areas of fertile land during the Iron Age, and the degree to which they were fortified reflects the attempts of individual chiefs to secure power. However, even a great fortification like Maiden Castle was not safe from the advancing Roman army who attacked it in 44, probably led by the brilliant general, and future emperor, Vespasian.

The hillfort was well defended. Its huge defences enclosed 20 hectares (50 acres), with enormous banks more than 38 metres (125 feet) high towering over the surrounding fields. However, the Durotriges fought with slingshots – a cache of over 22,000 slingstones has been found on the site – which were ineffective against the shields that protected the legionaries, while the Romans fired metal arrows from a kind of catapult – *ballista*.

The Romans were victorious, once again displaying their superb military skill. Their brutal efficiency can be seen in the shallow pits where the twisted and damaged bodies of men and women were buried. The dead showed signs of mutilation and gaping head wounds – one man had been hit at least nine times, while a *ballista* arrow was in another's spine, leaving no doubt as to his slayers.

Memories of this brutal and bloody battle may well have lingered in the area, leaving a tradition of ghosts and death on the hill. Whether or not this is the case, no one built on Maiden Castle for the next 300 years.

Boudica

The rebellion of Boudica is one of the best-known events in Romano-British history. The widow of Prasutagus, King of the Iceni, she opposed the Roman governor, Suetonius Paulinus, who seized power over the tribe after her husband's death in about 60. Her lands and those of her nobles were annexed, the Romans destroyed her palace and legionaries assaulted her and her two daughters. Anger at this, and resentment over taxes and the loss of their own lands, prompted many of the former British tribes to make a stand: the stage was set for a dramatic attack on Roman authority.

As luck would have it, the rebellion was perfectly timed as Paulinus was in north Wales extending the Roman conquest. Colchester fell in two days and Verulamium (St Albans) and London were practically burnt to the ground by Boudica's marauding army. She gave the Romans the kind of respect they had given her and took no prisoners. The Roman historian Tacitus estimated that 70,000 people died in the wake of her wrath.

However, Boudica had overstretched herself with the result that her supply routes broke down and she lost control over her ill-disciplined army. In the final battle, with Paulinus at the helm, the military discipline of the Romans won outright, despite the fact that Boudica's followers outnumbered them three to one. Tacitus recorded that 80,000 Britons died compared to 400 Romans. Governors who succeeded Paulinus adopted a more conciliatory approach to the British tribes, but Boudicca did not live to see this. She died soon after her defeat, reputedly by taking poison.

Roman Bath

During the Roman occupation of Britain, Bath was a healing centre known as Aquae Sulis – the waters of Sulis – from the hot springs around which the city was built and the Celtic goddess Sulis. The site was dedicated to Sulis and this fact, linked with the discovery of prehistoric flints and late Iron Age coins, is evidence that it may have held a sacred significance for the native British population. The Roman settlement started in about 60 and was centred on the main spring which serves the Great Bath – now known as the King's Bath – and produces 1.1 million litres (250,000 gallons) of water a day.

The temple and bath precinct, the grandest and earliest public buildings in Roman Britain, developed gradually and consisted of a classical temple with a bathing complex to the east and west. The complex consisted of a large lead-lined bath, subsidiary baths and a reservoir that caught the water from the spring that fed the Great Bath. The date, plan, size, style and architecture of the complex made it exceptional in Rome's western empire.

Aquae Sulis was clearly a popular destination for Romans, who made offerings to the goddess Sulis Minerva, an amalgamation of the Celtic and Roman deities. More than 12,000 Roman coins and 130 inscribed lead tablets that have been found in the springs pay testament to this. The tablets were often inscribed with curses, possibly imploring the goddess to turn an enemy's toes black or other such pleas.

The baths fell into disuse in the late fourth century, but became popular again in the eighteenth century when they attracted the fashionable society of Georgian England.

Waddon
Dorset

SERIES 7
to be broadcast in
early 2000

Time Team went to Waddon, a tiny village near Portesham in Dorset, to investigate an archaeological mystery. Two next-door neighbours had found Iron Age and medieval pottery while digging a hole for a septic tank in one of their back gardens. They had put their finds in a bag and sent them to us. Has Waddon been inhabited since the Iron Age? The bag of pottery was our only clue.

Day One started in the garden that had produced the pottery, and while the geophysics team led by John started surveying, Phil worked out where he could put trenches without disturbing the septic tank. He finally opened Trench One upslope from it and Trench Two below it. Meanwhile, in the field next to the garden, Carenza opened Trench Three and Trench Four to investigate some interesting earthworks. She soon found post-medieval pottery and the foundations of a small farmhouse with paved floors. Phil ended the day with a great deal of rubble in his trenches, but little sign of Iron Age activity.

On Day Two Phil began to remove the rubble from Trench One and started finding Iron Age pottery. He also found what he thought was the drip gulley around an Iron Age round house – a shallow ditch formed when water dripped off the thatched roof. Trench Two, downslope from the septic tank, had produced little sign of round houses – just a confusing collection of strangely shaped ditches and gulleys. Mick was sure they were trenches in a market garden that had been used to grow asparagus and other vegetables. By the end of the day, a series of curving walls were starting to emerge upslope from the tank. It appeared that successive houses had been built there throughout the Iron Age.

Stewart Ainsworth produced a surprise on Day Three when he discovered a previously unknown Neolithic henge – a large circular ditch and bank between 4,500 and 6,000 years old – in fields beyond the village. It was a rare find and suggested Stone Age habitation. In one of Carenza's trenches a cobbled floor was found next to the farmhouse, showing that an earlier medieval building once stood on the same spot. In the garden, the walls and floor of the round house Phil had found on Day Two were clearly visible both above and below the septic tank. It had been placed in the middle of an Iron Age building. At the very last moment, one of the diggers presented Phil with a bone awl – a small pointed tool – that had been lying on the floor of the house.

The three days in Waddon exceeded *Time Team*'s expectations. Starting with a bag of pottery, we uncovered settlement there from the Iron Age and throughout the post-medieval period to the present day – and also found new evidence of Stone Age activity.

A beautiful bone awl perhaps used for piercing leather by our Iron Age ancestors.

These medieval house remains were just part of the historical continuity that existed at Waddon.

silvered bronze mirror found at Papcastle

LAVENHAM
SUFFOLK

SERIES 3
Broadcast
11 February 1996

Suffolk was one of the main agricultural regions of Roman Britain, but intensive farming since then has led to much of the evidence of past settlement being obliterated. Adrian Thorpe of Priory Farm, near Lavenham, invited *Time Team* to investigate one of his fields which had been producing vast numbers of Roman pottery shards and coins.

On Day One the geophysics team led by John moved into the field to survey an area where Adrian Thorpe had seen crop marks. However, the results of their survey did not tie in with the marks, and it seemed that different periods of occupation had left differing patterns on the landscape. Trench One was opened to test the results and was also sited near the most intensive area of crop marks. We located some ditches, but nothing that could be considered a building. Mick pointed out that Iron Age archaeology in Suffolk is often a question of analysing stains in the soil – all that is left of the wooden buildings. We also found a scatter of Roman pottery – but not enough to suggest that this had been an area of occupation.

The first hopeful signs of occupation appear.

The field had previously produced two pre-Roman coins, a find that added significantly to information about the early history of the farm, and the Team included two metal-detectors who helped us to scan the spoil heaps from the excavations. Over the three days of the shoot they found brooches and some silver coins.

As Day Two progressed, geophysics covered more areas of the field and located three or four areas of intense activity. We placed Trench Two over a small area of strong magnetic anomalies which could indicate a hearth or area of burning, possibly associated with a building. As soon as the topsoil was removed there were clear signs of red rubble and pottery shards, implying that we had uncovered the source of some sort of industrial activity – possibly a small kiln. Geophysics located what looked like a building next to Trench One so the trench was widened.

Day Three began with the discovery of what seemed to be an area of floor in the newly extended part of Trench One. Dark patches appeared as it was cleaned. Back in Trench Two, the red rubble was pronounced to be a possible kiln. It had produced large pieces of a pottery drinking-cup or flagon dating

Roman roads

The Romans were experts at building roads and constructed the first major ones in Britain. While the British used an informal system of trackways across the country, the Romans built metalled roads that were generally straight and used their skills to go through and over obstacles, rather than round them.

The roads can be divided into three types: those built by the state; those built by local government; and those – probably very similar to the dirt tracks of the pre-Roman period – built by small communities or individuals for private use. Some of the most famous roads are the Fosse Way which eventually stretched from Topsham in Devon to Lincoln, Watling Street from London to Wroxeter in Shropshire and Ermin Street which ran from London to York and by extension to southern Scotland. Their construction reflects the great skill of the surveyors and engineers of Roman Britain.

Main roads were raised on a stone base with a gravel – or sometimes paved – surface and ditches on either side. Although they were expensive to construct, they were fundamental to the movement of military forces and to communication between garrisons. The extensive network of roads spread across Britain and laid the foundations for many routes that are still used today.

A lot of suggestive stains, but no large structures to accompany the wonderful finds at Lavenham.

from the first occupation of the site, possibly around 50 BC. After further work in Trench One we were able to see that the dark patches were post holes and beam slots, and could make out faint traces of a building that had stood in the field in Roman times. Large amounts of pottery, some silver coins and numerous pieces of brooches were associated with it, suggesting that the field had been the site of a small settlement of farms with kilns and some metalworking.

Whilst the results of the *Time Team* dig at Lavenham did not look as spectacular as some of the other Roman sites that the Team have visted, the geophysics and careful fieldwork combined with the precise excavation of the different coloured stains in the soil revealed that we had uncovered a Romano-British settlement where the inhabitants had possibly supplemented their living by making small cheap brooches to sell in the nearby town of Colchester.

Hadrian's Wall

The northern frontier of Roman Britain, Hadrian's Wall stretched for more than 112 kilometres (70 miles), across the narrow neck of Britain from the mouth of the River Tyne in the east to the Solway Firth in the west. After their conquest of northern England in 74 the Romans had endured years of harassment by marauding tribes north of the border and the Brigantes to the south and in 122 the emperor Hadrian decided on a solution to these constant skirmishes: a huge wall, 4.5 metres (15 feet) high, with watchtowers every 500 metres (540 yards) and milecastles – garrisoned gateways with small forts – every mile. This would keep out the northern tribes, while a great ditch or vallum just to the south of the wall would protect the legionaries from the Brigantes. As construction progressed his plan was constantly modified. Great forts like that at Housesteads were built at 8-kilometre (5 mile) intervals, and the lack of suitable local stone meant turf had to be used for the western end of the wall.

Today Hadrian's Wall conjures up images of Roman legionaries standing on top of it and fighting shaggy-haired barbarians against a dark, bleak sky. However, it is clear that in many places the wall was not wide enough to have been used as a platform, but must have been more of a deterrent. Nevertheless, with its impressive proportions it was clearly an effective barrier and played a key role in keeping the peace in Britain for 300 years.

Turkdean
Gloucestershire

LIVE
23–25 August 1997
SERIES 5
Broadcast
25 January 1998
SERIES 6
Broadcast
28 February 1999

Turkdean is a small Cotswold village and in the long, dry summer of 1976 a nearby farmer, Wilf Mustoe, saw parch marks in one of his fields of grass. At about the same time another local, Roger Box, photographed the marks from the air. He contacted the Corinium Museum in Cirencester who confirmed his photographs appeared to show the site of an entire Roman villa. Roger Box invited *Time Team* to investigate and the programme was the first one to be broadcast live.

The Team knew from the photographs that they were dealing with a large, important villa site and Mick had no doubts about where to begin – John Gater, Chris Gaffney and the rest of the geophysics team were set to work early on Day One and by 10 am their initial results were in. They showed, with astonishing clarity, the outline of a villa with ranges of buildings to the north and south, possible gardens in the middle and what appeared to be a gatehouse in the centre of the south side. Phil and Carenza opened two trenches and walls appeared almost immediately in both of them. In Trench Two, Carenza's trench, one of the walls had plaster adhering to it and was associated with finds of fourth-century Severn Valley ware. Mark Corney, *Time Team*'s Roman expert, set about comparing the plan of the villa with plans of villas in other parts of Britain and concluded that the one at Turkdean was among the biggest in the country.

During a brief lull in the rain, Tony and Mick took to the air to survey the site. The situation was ideal for a villa: there was a spring on the hill behind it, a stream downslope and it was only a few miles from the Fosse Way, one of Britain's major Roman roads. Amazingly, the parch marks seen in 1976 were visible again and Mick spotted that they continued well outside the area that had been surveyed on Day One. The geophysics team were sent to the area towards the stream. A geophysics survey earlier in the day had shown a small area of walls on a different alignment to the villa, so Mick decided to investigate the different alignment as it might indicate an earlier phase of building. This third trench contained a mass of stonework that looked very complicated. The results at the end of the day were unexpected. Instead of just two ranges of buildings there appeared to be *another* courtyard and *another* range of buildings to the south.

On Day Two we opened Trench Four over the feature that had originally seemed to be a gatehouse, but which was now in the middle of the complex, and uncovered at least four small rooms just below the surface. The *opus signinum* – a waterproof cement – on the walls of one of them suggested a bath house. It soon became apparent that we had found a plaster-lined plunge pool covered in blue paint – an expensive colour that indicated a high-status site. The well-decorated walls in Trench Two, indicated that this was where the family had

A Roman plunge pool or ornamental bath comes to light.

lived. However, the opulence had been short-lived – the plaster had fallen and been used as flooring, probably in a room used for storage, animals or slaves. As Trench Three had proved so complicated, Mick closed it down so that he could help out on Trench Four.

By mid-afternoon Carenza had persuaded Mick to open up Trenches Five and Six further downslope towards the stream to test the results of the geophysics survey there. Stone structures emerged in Trench Five and finds associated with rubbish – mainly cow bones – were found in Trench Six. Back in Trench Four, the bath-house trench, Neil Holbrook, director of the Cotswold Archaeological Trust, found an amazing roof filial blocking the flue-hole. It was about 30 centimetres (12 inches) tall with four arches and a minute column on top.

During the morning of Day Three the diggers removed all the rubble from the plunge pool. It was about 1 metre (3 feet) deep, with arm rests, and had had a domed, painted ceiling. A coin dating to 367–383 AD was found at the bottom of the pool, indicating the earliest date at which it could have gone out of use. The walls in Trenches Five and Six, downslope from the bath house, were too flimsy to have been in major living quarters and the structures were probably outbuildings. Lots of bones were found in the area, including those of deer and suckling pigs, both of which were high-status foods. The area appeared to be associated with the preparation of food.

These Roman buildings were just below the surface at Turkdean.

The finial from the roof of a Roman bath house.

Trench Seven, over the range of buildings in the east, had produced an escutcheon plate complete with a keyhole, suggesting a major door or a chest, and further digging revealed a bowl furnace containing bits of lead slag, indicating a workshop. Finally, at the very end of the day, further geophysics results showed that there was yet another range of buildings up the hill towards the spring, suggesting that the site might be a palace and temple complex rather than a villa.

Time Team's first live broadcast was amazingly successful. We discovered a massive complex of buildings, and showed that the opulence that had briefly existed on the site during the fourth century came to an abrupt end – probably soon after 410 AD when the Roman legions were recalled to Rome.

Nevertheless, important questions had been left unanswered. Were the buildings running up the hillside towards the spring earlier or later than the villa? Were they part of a shrine or temple? *Time Team* returned to Turkdean the following year to investigate further.

There were rival theories about the buildings from Day One. Mark Corney was convinced that they were the farmsteads and workshops that would have supported the villa, rather than a temple or shrine. Geophysics found evidence of a long aisled building that could be a workshop or livestock shelter, so Phil opened the first trenches to investigate it – and was soon overwhelmed by walls running in different directions. Meanwhile, Carenza found a floor covered in iron slag, suggesting industrial activity. Coins in another trench indicated that the building was fourth century – the same date as the villa.

On Day Two Mick decided that the spring should be investigated to see if it had supplied water to the villa and outbuildings. Two channels that could have carried water to the villa were discovered. Excitingly, the walls in one of Phil's trenches appeared to be standing on even earlier structures, suggesting that there had been buildings on the site for a very long time. There was red-painted plaster on some of the walls and Mark Corney deduced that they might have been in a high-status building – the bailiff's house, or even the main building before the villa was constructed further down the slope.

By Day Three, Phil had found many Roman artefacts, including two first-century brooches and a tiny child's earring, as well as numerous pottery shards. The structures below the walls were looking more and more impressive, with two tower rooms flanking what would have been the front entrance to the building. In addition, pieces of blue plaster were found in the cellar area, prompting speculation that this could have been some kind of underground shrine. Finally, at the end of the shoot, Carenza found a stone bearing the inscription 'FIL' – possibly representing *filius* meaning 'son'; and Mick traced the water supply to the villa and outbuildings – he put dye into the spring and coloured water came out where it emerged at the bottom of the hill.

Time Team's second excavation at Turkdean was as exciting as the first and we answered many of the questions we had set out with after the first excavation. We created a picture of an estate that had been built up across the hillside during centuries of Roman rule, and gained an insight into the life of its inhabitants. However, as with our first visit, we came away feeling that there was more to find out about the villa at Turkdean.

BIRDOSWALD
CUMBRIA

SERIES 7
To be broadcast in
early 2000

The Roman fort of Birdoswald is on Hadrian's Wall just to the south of England's border with Scotland, and Bruce Bennison of Cumbria County Council invited *Time Team* to help evaluate a Roman military cemetery that lies adjacent to the fort — the first-ever Roman cemetery to be excavated near the wall. It had first come to light in 1959/60 when a cremation had been ploughed up in a field. The cemetery was now under threat because of ploughing, rutting caused by farm vehicles, and erosion of the river-cliff at one edge of the field. The fort is a World Heritage Site and in order to dig beside it we had to produce a project design to justify the excavation and to set out the parameters of what we would be doing.

On Day One it was raining hard and John Gater and Chris Gaffney began proceedings by surveying the field. Carenza opened Trench One in its gateway, which was one of the places most under threat. Part of the Team's remit was to establish how well the remains were preserved, and digging here should provide enough information about this to make it unnecessary to risk damaging the better-preserved area by excavation. Before long, Carenza found pieces of burnt bone in the topsoil and Jackie McKinley, *Time Team*'s osteoarchaeologist, identified one of them as part of a tibia. The pieces could be pyre debris — the body would have been burnt on a stack of wood and the bones collected afterwards and put in an urn. The trench also produced a hobnail, showing that one Roman at least had been burnt with his boots on.

Meanwhile, Stewart Ainsworth examined the topography of the area to see if he could discover why the cemetery was 200 metres (180 yards) from the fort, in the direction of the river. Geophysics showed anomalies in the field between the cremations and the fort that might be associated with either burning or occupation and Phil opened Trench Two there. In Trench One the last find of the day was some old wood sealed beneath a small patch of cremated remains. Was the wood Roman?

At the beginning of Day Two Mick decided to open Trench Three in an area nearer to the fort as flagstones and bits of walls in Phil's trench suggested there might have been another *vicus* or settlement on this side of the fort, as well as one that was already known about on the other side. This could account for the situation of the cemetery, which would have been placed outside the *vicus*. Trench One, Carenza's trench, had to be bailed out because of the incessant rain, but the remains seemed to be better preserved than we had hoped. Katy Hirst, one of the diggers, abseiled over the river-cliff at the edge of the field to take a look at the eroding section. Fortunately, she found no signs of cremated material, suggesting that the cemetery did not extend that far. Trenches Two and Three, both over the *vicus*, showed a long linear settlement stretching along the road out of the fort. Meanwhile, the geophysics team had used an extremely sensitive type of magnetometer to survey the cremation field, and revealed what appeared to be a small group of cremations surrounded by a ditch. Trench Four was put in to investigate the feature.

Roman coins were not the only spectacular finds at Hadrian's Wall.

Whatever its date it has to be drawn and recorded! A farmer's attempt to ease his way out of mud gets mixed up with a Roman cemetery.

By now it was apparent that the wood in Trench One covered a large area. It seemed probable that it was only a few decades old and had been laid down by a farmer to improve access into the field. The cremation on top of the wood must have been disturbed and redeposited by ploughing.

At the start of Day Three it was becoming clear that there was nothing in Trench Four, over the geophysics anomaly, and John Gater set off in search of geophysics 'spikes' — high readings that may indicate burnt material. In Phil's Trench Two, over the *vicus* site, Jenni Butterworth found an *intaglio* – a small cut stone from the centre of a ring. This was followed by another interesting find – a small piece of red Samian pottery decorated with an erotic scene.

John's survey produced some very promising spikes and Mick decided to open a small trench — Trench Five — over the top of one to see if it represented a cremation. Almost immediately, Carenza found the top of a cremation urn lying very close to the surface, with a small pot adjacent to it. This showed that the cremations were in good condition. They were buried close to the surface of the field, but should be safe provided no more ploughing takes place there.

Stewart's investigations had revealed that the site had first been a small fort on the river bank, adjacent to the turf wall that preceded the stone-built Hadrian's Wall. It soon faced problems of erosion and when Hadrian's Wall was built in stone further to the north, the fort was also moved northwards, away from the river. The *vicus* developed on either side of the new fort and the cemetery was established beyond it.

In three days *Time Team* established that the cremations were in good condition, and also helped to solve the mystery of why the cemetery wasn't situated immediately outside the fort of Birdoswald.

Inscribed silver brooch found at Turkdean

GREENWICH PARK
LONDON

SERIES 7
To be broadcast in
early 2000

Greenwich Park, on the south side of the River Thames in London, is one of the city's few remaining areas of open land. It was enclosed as a royal park in 1433 and as a result many earthworks survive there. A Roman building has been marked on Ordnance Survey maps since 1903 when it was excavated but, unfortunately, never recorded properly. Three inscriptions from this excavation suggest it may have been a temple. Harvey Sheldon of Birkbeck College, University of London, dug some small exploratory trenches on behalf of the Department of Environment in 1978 and 1979 to ascertain the state of the remains and found two phases of building. However, it was not possible to decipher them without a larger scale excavation and he and Hedley Swain of the Museum of London invited *Time Team* to see if we could identify the structure.

Roman pits and walls appear from beneath a London park.

The 1903 excavation took place in a large mound which now has iron railings at its top, surrounding a very small area of Roman mosaic pavement. On Day One John Gater started to survey the surrounding area but the railings interfered with the magnetometry and had to be removed before he could continue. Mick went up in a crane for a bird's-eye view and could see where Harvey's trenches had been cut. An earthwork enclosure just to the north-east of the mound was also visible. He decided to open two trenches: Trench One, under Phil's supervision, down the north side of the mound away from the railings and Trench Two, looked after by Carenza, in the area of the earthwork enclosure. Geophysics results to the north of the mound showed what looked like a possible building and Gustav Milne, one of *Time Team*'s Roman experts, suggested there might be a settlement in the area – the Thames had started to silt up in about AD 240 and places like Greenwich that were downstream from the port of London became more important than they had been. A small trench (Trench Three) was put over the possible building to check the geophysics results. Meanwhile, Stewart Ainsworth recorded the various earthwork features in the park to see if any of them would tie in with the Roman remains.

Work in Trenches One and Two was very slow because it was difficult to work out whether ground was natural or had been disturbed. By the end of the day it was clear that the feature showing up in Trench Three had no finds associated with it, and so Mick decided to close it down and concentrate on excavating in the other two.

On Day Two the geophysics survey was extended towards Maze Hill Gate, to the north of the mound. Work was still progressing slowly in the first two trenches. Phil was finding it very difficult to see if the mound was natural or artificial and whether the features in his trench were robbed out or were slots for wooden beams that had rotted away. The railings had by now been removed from the top of the mound and Phil moved there to open an area that joined on to Trench One (where Katie Hirst continued the work). This new area – an extension of Trench One – soon produced a large piece of Roman tile. Carenza's Trench Two showed part of a wall and was extended, and Trench Four, manned by diggers from the Museum of London, was opened at the other end of the earthwork enclosure to see if the wall continued into this area.

A Roman coin found at Birdoswald

By the end of Day Two, Trench One had revealed a massive robbed-out construction trench, which must have been part of the temple building. It was difficult to interpret Carenza's trench: Mick and Guy de la Bédoyère, another of *Time Team*'s Roman experts, were uncertain whether the features were genuinely Roman or if they were post-medieval garden remains with bits of Roman walling incorporated.

On Day Three, the Team concentrated on Trenches One and Two to make sense of the features they were finding. An additional small trench, Trench Five, was opened on the west side of the mound. The trench produced a piece of broken limestone on which the letters MIN and LIV could be made out, in two rows, one under the other. Could they refer to the Roman goddess Minerva? Guy de la Bédoyère recently compiled a computer database of inscriptions from Roman Britain, and fed in the letters to identify the words in which they occur most often.

A Roman tile inscribed with the letters PPBR, translating as the Procurator of the Province of Britannia – signifying that it had been commissioned by the highest authority in Roman Britain – was found in Trench Two, which also revealed cobbled surfaces, pits (of Roman date) which might have been tree-planting holes and a boundary wall with a ditch outside it. It appeared that Carenza's trench had uncovered the courtyard enclosure outside the Roman temple.

By lunchtime, another three letters – CVS – had been identified on the stone and Guy had results from his search of the inscription database: the two most likely words for MIN and LIV were NV-*MIN*-E and CAECI-*LIV*-S and CVS probably belonged to PRIS-*CVS*. Caecilius and Priscus were both common Roman names and Mark Hassall, Britain's foremost authority on Roman inscriptions, agreed they were the most likely words for the letters we had found. His explanation that the names were probably from a dedication plaque commemorating two deified Roman emperors confirmed that we had found a temple within an enclosure yard or *teminos*.

One of our most rare finds: an inscribed Roman stone.

In three days, *Time Team* solved the mystery of the Roman building of Greenwich Park. It was definitely a temple and, what is more, it was one of some significance – the letters PPBR inscribed on the tile imply it had been built by the governor of the province. Very few inscriptions have been found in southern Britain and the presence of four on the site of the temple (including the three discovered during the 1903 excavation) further confirms its importance. John's geophysics survey showed a lack of any other features in the area which indicates that the building stood in splendid isolation overlooking the river; and Stewart's earthwork survey indicated that the Roman road from Canterbury to London had been aligned on the temple.

TOCKENHAM
WILTSHIRE

SERIES 2
Broadcast
22 January 1995

About 600 years ago a small Roman sculpture, believed to be a figure of Aesculapius, the Greek god of healing adopted by the Romans, was built into the outside wall of the church of St Giles in Tockenham, a small village in the heart of Wiltshire. There was already evidence of Roman settlement in the area – while ploughing a field to the south of the church, a local landowner, had turned up roof tiles, coins, tesserae from a mosaic and tiles used in Roman central-heating sytems. *Time Team* went to Tockenham to find out where the sculpture had come from: was the church on the site of a Roman temple?

A spring next to the church feeds a pond in an adjacent garden and Day One started with the geophysics team John Gater and Chris Gaffney looking for buried features in this area. There seemed to be little evidence of buildings so Phil and Mike Allen and Julie Gardiner, our environmental experts, took

Diggers on early morning bucket duty. Sometimes we have to bail the trenches out before we can start to dig.

core samples of soil to examine the sediments in the pond. Sediments can contain plant and seed remains and may also show how the strata in soil build up over time. If the spring beside the church had been a ritual site, we could expect to find traces of votive offerings like coins, tablets or offerings of food.

Dr Martin Henig, *Time Team*'s expert on Roman sculpture, examined the statue in the church. In his opinion, the figure was a *genius loci*, a guardian spirit often associated with households, and not Aesculapius. The statue was wearing a Roman toga, whereas Aesculapius was usually depicted in Greek costume. Furthermore, the statue was carrying a horn of plenty, which is not associated with the god of healing. The sculpture might therefore have come from a domestic setting, possibly a Roman villa, rather than a temple. Carenza went off to search the Sites and Monuments Record (SMR) to look for more information about Roman occupation in the area. Was the villa or temple in the field that had already produced Roman artefacts? Geophysics did a preliminary survey.

On Day Two the geophysics results were through and showed an almost complete plan of what looked like a Roman villa, with walls and corridors clearly visible, along with a large building with an apse at one end. The Team and Roy Canham, the county archaeological officer, discussed whether any evaluation trenches should be opened over the villa or whether the site should be scheduled as an ancient monument and left for future generations. The decision was to call in Amanda Chadburn, the local English Heritage inspector, and meanwhile to open two small trenches outside the main area of the villa complex – minimum interference which would help the inspector to see the condition of the remains.

Trench One soon showed evidence of an earthwork and ditch that might have surrounded the villa but there were no structural remains. Phil organized the villagers to walk an adjacent ploughed field and pick up artefacts from the surface. There were soon dozens of new Roman finds, mostly pottery. At the end of Day Two David Barnes, who farmed the field, produced a piece of decorated stone pipe he had found at the bottom of a pond. To everybody's amazement it turned out to be a finely carved Roman water spout, indicating a high-status villa.

Victor's reconstruction of a household god, which led us to the site.

The results of the soil cores were in by the beginning of Day Three and showed cereal grains that had been milled, indicating that they may have been thrown into the pond as ritual offerings. Amanda Chadburn came to see if the villa should be scheduled and decided that more information was needed on how well the site was preserved, and its date. We opened two small trenches, across the walls of the villa and revealed tesserae, building materials and painted wall plaster. Large pieces of a bowl from Samos were also found and their size indicated that little damage had been done by medieval and modern ploughing. However, the walls of the villa had been robbed out and the stones recycled elsewhere. In Trench One on the edge of the complex Mick was surprised to find marks in the sub-soil that had been caused by prehistoric ploughing with an ard, the earliest form of plough.

Our understanding of where the statue had come from had moved from a possible Roman temple sited beside the spring to the major new villa site in the nearby field. In three days *Time Team* located and mapped a major Roman site of national importance.

LAMBETH PALACE
LONDON

SERIES 2
Broadcast
29 January 1995

Lambeth Palace lies on the south bank of the River Thames, in the heart of London. In the 1930s, after undertaking some small excavations, the archaeologist Bernard Davis claimed that gravels he had found there showed that Watling Street, the Roman road from Richborough in Kent to Wroxeter in Shropshire, ran through the palace grounds. The Museum of London Archaeology Service invited *Time Team* to help clarify its route, and survey the local geology to try and locate the underlying gravel levels which would indicate possible early settlements.

Lambeth Palace was founded in 1190, and its buildings were altered over the centuries, with the last phase of restoration in the Gothic style in the nineteenth century. The thirteenth-century crypt of

John Gater gets technical and adds yet another bit of kit to his armoury.

the chapel still remains and the palace is set in about 4 hectares (10 acres) of park and garden, one of the few areas of central London that has been left undeveloped.

The first move on Day One was to send in the geophysics team to find the trenches that Davis had dug in the 1930s. Stewart Ainsworth noticed some faint ridges on the lawn that might be the remains of the excavations, so geophysics concentrated on this area. The positions of the trenches were soon located and the Team decided to reopen one of them. Meanwhile Robin Bush settled into the palace library to search for references to early crossing-points on the Thames. By the end of the day we had located an area of gravel in Trench One which may have been the feature that Davis had thought was the road. Phil had also found our first direct evidence of Roman activity – a piece of a Roman *mortarium* or grinding bowl – in Trench One.

On Day Two a second trench was opened up over the site of Davis's excavations to test whether a possible area of compacted gravel identified by geophysics was a natural feature or part of the Roman road. The Team also started looking for environmental evidence for the crossing-point. It would have been logical for the Romans to have selected a tidal site that would allow them to bring heavily laden boats to the area at low tide. Jane Siddell, *Time Team*'s environmental expert, looked for diatoms, microscopic single-cell algae, that would tell us whether salt water had been present, but none were found. Trench Two produced gravels that Davis had interpreted as being the Roman road, but Phil identified them as being natural Thames gravel. However, there was more early Roman pottery in the trench, and part of a quern stone, for grinding corn, from Germany, where three Roman legions had been based before coming to England. As Davis's theory had been disproved, finding evidence of an early crossing became our focus and Mick suggested exploring the Westminster side of the river.

Day Three saw Mick in a Thames fire-boat carrying out an unscientific survey of the depth of the river around Westminster. There appeared to be a shallower area of water just below Westminster which

Lambeth Palace in all its splendour. Round the back we were busy digging holes in its beautiful gardens!

might indicate a natural ridge of higher land – or just a sandbank – and the captain of the fire boat confirmed that the shallow area did exist as he could feel it against the hull of his vessel at low tide. A crossing here would link nicely with a reference Robin had found to the 'Staingate crossing'.

Time Team's investigations suggested that there may have been an early crossing-point at Lambeth or to the north, associated with a settlement immediately after the Roman conquest in the first century AD. The later route of Watling Street remains a mystery but Time Team had at least established that what Bernard Davis had found was not the Roman road.

RIBCHESTER
LANCASHIRE

SERIES 1
Broadcast
23 January 1994

The village of Ribchester is midway between Preston and Clitheroe, in a tranquil setting beside the River Ribble. In Roman times, however, it must have seemed like the last outpost of the empire to a legionary of the newly conquering army. Jim Ridge, a local resident, asked *Time Team* to investigate the Roman remains in his garden.

Earlier excavations in Ribchester had located a Roman stone fort built in about 150 AD, the wall of which ran through Jim's garden, which also contained the remains of a guard tower set in to the wall. On Day One, Phil's first task was to open Trench One in an attempt to find the floor of the tower, while Carenza collated all the information on Roman Ribchester on a map. A short length of ditch that may have been part of the early Roman defences had previously been found on the edge of Ribchester in an area being developed as a residential home and the geophysics team, John Gater and Chris Gaffney, set to work to trace it. Their first area of survey, in the field adjacent to the residential home, produced the line of the ditch which appeared to run in a south-westerly line across the field before curving round to the south-east, suggesting the typical playing-card shape of a Roman fort. Trenches Two and Three were opened – one on either side of the bend – to test the results.

On Day Two part of the cobbled floor of the guard tower emerged in Trench One and a section dug through this came down on to clay. The clay was part of the earliest wooden fort, the ramparts of which followed the same line as the later stone ones. Trench One had been successful so it was closed down, and the Team concentrated on Trenches Two and Three. In Trench Two, which was on the same line as the area of ditch under the residential home, the clay subsoil of a rampart was emerging. Dr Adrian Olivier, *Time Team*'s local Roman expert, explained that this rampart and ditch

might have been built around an area of civil settlement that had grown up beside the stone fort and need not necessarily be another early fort. If the settlement had been surrounded by a ditch and wall, it would have been of a higher status than had previously been thought. The cobbled foundation of the rampart emerged from underneath the clay, and part of the ditch could be seen dropping down at the end of the trench, which was extended to make the profile of the ditch visible. There was no evidence of a ditch or bank in Trench Three, but some Samian pottery and part of a Roman quern for grinding corn were found.

On Day Three the latest geophysics results threw earlier theories into turmoil: the curving feature running to the south-east was geological and not part of the ditch, which continued on in a straight line. The finds from Trench Three suggested an area of occupation between the fort and ditch, and a post hole from a timber building confirmed this. Meanwhile, Trench Two had revealed that the ditch had been dug in two phases. The first profile belongs to what is known as a Punic ditch, an asymmetrical type often associated with early forts, and was contemporary with the wooden fort in Jim's garden. The later recut was broader and shallower, but still Roman.

In three days *Time Team* rewrote the history of Ribchester's Roman defences. It was already known that a temporary wooden fortress had existed before the stone fort was constructed but *Time Team* had established that this had been surrounded by a large Punic ditch, which had been built for defensive purposes, to protect the settlement immediately outside the fort.

somewhere down there, in a back garden, lies a hidden Roman fort.

BEAUPORT PARK
SUSSEX

SERIES 6
Broadcast
14 February 1999

In the 1960s amateur archaeologist Dr Gerald Brodribb excavated a huge mound of Roman slag – waste from iron production – at Beauport Park in Sussex and found a large Roman bath house. It appeared that this was a major Roman industrial site where officers of the *classis Britannica*, the seaborne wing of the Roman army, were in charge of iron production. But where were their quarters, the administration offices, the commander's house? Gerald invited *Time Team* to investigate.

Mick and Tony began Day One with a guided tour of the bath house. Now close to Beauport Park golf club, it is scheduled as a site of archaeological interest and protected beneath a corrugated iron shelter. The building still stands, up to its window ledges, and has plastered and painted walls; even the clothes lockers and heating system are preserved. Meanwhile the geophysics team began surveying in the surrounding woodland. Gerald and his team had located three platforms that they believed could indicate buildings and the first three trenches were opened on one of them. However, no evidence of Roman occupation was found.

Moulded Roman glass fragments from the 'golf course' dig.

The thirteenth fairway, and we cautiously extend the excavation into the path of oncoming golf balls.

Day Two saw the search for the buildings move further afield and Mick and Stewart Ainsworth went up in a helicopter to get an overview of the area and decide where to look next. Mick was convinced we needed to revise our approach to the site, and that the Team should look at the whole landscape, not just the random trenches Gerald had dug so far. Iron-smelting would have been a smoky, polluting process, and Mick suggested that the bath house was for on-site washing, with other buildings and high-status houses further away from the works. Six more trenches were opened during the day, one of them – Trench Eight – to investigate a geophysical anomaly at the side of the thirteenth fairway, and another – Trench Ten – on the edge of its rough. Stewart found a collapsed wall on the hill at the end of the day – the only 'real' archaeology so far.

On Day Three, Phil and Carenza worked with members of Gerald's group in Trench Eleven, one of the previous excavations, for some time, and two trenches were dug on earthworks. The second of these, Trench Thirteen, produced a furnace base. Geophysics had good results from the golf course and, when Trench Fourteen was opened as a result, a charcoal-working pit was located. Both this and the furnace base indicated that iron-smelting had taken place on the site. Phil also found shards from a pottery flagon and we found a glass bottle that would have been used by workers.

Time Team didn't find any buildings and, although there is a chance that they lie under the slag surrounding the bath house, it is more probable that the men who managed the ironworks lived some distance away. Nevertheless, our three days at Beauport Park showed how applying archaeological methods to an already excavated site could produce new results.

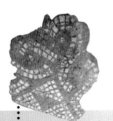

Mosaic found at Cirencester

PAPCASTLE
CUMBRIA

SERIES 6
Broadcast
10 January 1999

In the first century AD Papcastle, now a tiny village outside Cockermouth in Cumbria, was the site of a fort on the northern edge of the Roman empire. It was next to the River Derwent, at the crossing-point of two important roads, and a town or *vicus* grew up around the fort. The Buckingham family, who live in the village, found an enormous number of Roman artefacts in their garden when they were clearing it for a new patio. Their garden is within the area of the *vicus*, and so *Time Team* went to investigate further.

Day One began in the garden, in the area that they had already begun clearing for a new patio. Stones from a building that ran under their house had been uncovered, so this became Trench One and Phil set about cleaning and recording it. Meanwhile *Time Team*'s Roman expert, Lindsay Allason-Jones, examined some of the artefacts that had already been found in the garden. Phil's trench produced large numbers of horses' teeth and it was starting to look as if there might have been a butcher's shop, or possibly a cult centre, under the house.

Ground-penetrating radar has not always been successful for *Time Team*, and on this occasion John Gater and Chris Gaffney were trying out a new system. Very soon, they identified an anomaly 1.5 metres (5 feet) below the surface of the garden and Jenni Butterworth opened Trench Two to test this. The day ended on an exciting note when Stewart Ainsworth and the geophysics team returned from the fields between the village and river with evidence of more structures running down to the water. Could these indicate another fort, or was the *vicus* bigger than anyone had previously guessed?

Figured samian ware: it is always a relief to locate this distinctive high-status potte...

On Day Two Stewart and Bernard Thomason concentrated on mapping the streets of the *vicus*. Meanwhile the garden was yielding exciting results. Phil's Trench One produced, among other finds, a timber building with a hearth of burnt clay, and a large ditch filled with cobbles. In Trench Two, after digging through spoil from a nearby Victorian cellar, the anomaly identified by geophysics turned

Constantine the Great

Constantine made Christianity the favoured religion of the Roman Empire. He also built a new Roman capital in Byzantium on the Bosporus and renamed it Constantinople. He was the son of Constantius I, emperor of Rome, and was in Britain when his father died in York in 306. The troops there acclaimed Constantine as joint emperor and in 307 he left for Gaul to assert his claim.

Constantine defeated his rival, Maxentius, in Italy in 312. Just before the battle he is said to have seen a Christian vision: a flaming cross in the sky inscribed 'In this sign thou shalt conquer'. He adopted the cross and in 313 he issued an edict that Christianity could be tolerated throughout the Roman Empire. Eleven years later he became sole emperor.

A year after his edict three bishops were created in Britain, a mere outpost of the Roman empire, and, although Constantine continued to tolerate paganism, he also encouraged the growth of Christianity throughout the empire. Despite this, there appears to be no archaeological evidence of purpose-built Roman churches in Britain, although there is plenty of evidence for later conversion of Roman buildings for Christian use.

Despite his recognition of Christianity – he presided over the first council at Nicaea in 325 – Constantine was only baptized on his deathbed.

300   315   330

It is amazing what can come out of a small back garden. Another kind family allow us to dig up their lawns.

out to be a row of stones that were aligned with the streets Stewart and Bernard had mapped. The discovery of a polished Roman mirror and cosmetic spoon gave a vivid insight into how the women of the *vicus* lived. Two more trenches had been opened in the fields between the village and the river and during the day they slowly revealed the remains of cobbled surfaces and walls. It was becoming apparent that this was no ordinary *vicus* with a hotchpotch of streets and rambling houses, but a settlement built in regular lines with buildings on well-organized plots.

At the start of Day Three, the discovery that a large piece of stonework (being used as a doorstep) was the cornice from a monumental Roman building coincided with a new interpretation of the features in the garden. Phil was convinced that the cobble-filled ditch in Trench One was the foundation of a huge building that had replaced the timber one with the hearth. Suggestions about its function included one that it was an administrative or civic hall and another that it was a very large pub! However, the end of the shoot hinged on the results from the trenches in the fields, which continued to reveal more walls and surfaces.

In three days *Time Team* uncovered a well-planned settlement on the furthest reaches of the Roman Empire and changed the accepted view of frontier life suggesting that Papcastle was much more orderly and well-planned than anyone had previously thought.

345   360   375

CIRENCESTER
GLOUCESTERSHIRE

TONY'S PIECE TO CAMERA: 'In about AD 300 this was Corinium, the second most important centre in Roman Britain after London(ium). But things have changed quite a bit over the last 1,700 years and today I am on Chester Street in the middle of the Gloucestershire town of Cirencester. Time Team have come here to find out how it fits into the Roman plan for the city, and if Chester Street was connected in any way with the Roman highway or Ermin Street. We also want to see if there is any truth in the rumour that this is the site of a Roman temple.

Cirencester or to give it its Roman name, Corinium Dobunnorum, was an important town in Roman Britain. Neil Holbrook, head of the Cotswold Archaeological Trust and *Time Team*'s expert on the site, estimates that it covered more than 96 hectares (240 acres) making it comparable with a modern European city like Cologne. It was established as a fort and communications centre soon after the Romans conquered Britain in AD 43 and, to a considerable extent, its later development was the result of its position at the crossing of two major Roman roads: the Fosse Way, which ran from Axminster in Devon to Lincoln, and Ermin Street, which linked London with Gloucester.

The town had the advantage of being in a rich and fertile hinterland, the territory of the Dobunni who, unlike some other British tribes, quickly came to terms with their conquerors: there is evidence of amphorae from Bagendon in Gloucestershire, their pre-Roman centre. It was unscathed by the rebellion inspired by Boudica, queen of the Iceni in AD 61 and within thirty years of the Roman conquest it was the capital of the Dobunni *civitas* – the basic unit of local government in the Roman Empire. Early in the fourth century Cirencester became the capital of Britannia Prima, the main province of western Britain, and by the time it reached its high point in the late fourth century it was a typically Roman town with a forum, temples, market-place, amphitheatre and bath house. Although the baths must have been at least as large as those in Bath their site has never been conclusively located: in many parts of Cirencester the archaeology has lain undisturbed ever since. Saxon settlements and the medieval town were located away from the main Roman areas and it is clear that there are large areas of villas, markets and roads still to be discovered. Despite its importance, there are few mentions of Corinium Dobunnorum in surviving records – the only major Roman document to mention it is the *Ravenna Cosmography*.

One of the reasons I was interested in doing a programme in Cirencester was that it might throw some light on the debate about whether Roman Britain ended with a bang or a whimper. Was its decline the gradual result of a failing economy and barbarian threats? The Cotswolds seem to have been blessed with villas that survived and thrived well into the final days of Roman occupation – *Time Team* had touched on this in the Turkdean programmes (see page 62) – but was a town like Cirencester also prospering? It is possible, but not certain, that Cirencester was associated with what might be called the golden age of late Roman Britain, and any new archaeology uncovered there has the potential to provide valuable clues in the hunt for answers to these questions.

Experts also debate the relative importance at this time of Christianity, one of the official religions of Rome since 313, when Constantine declared it to be so at York. In 1891 a late Roman stone was

Time Team at the bottom of the garden. Sieving frame and people washing finds in the foreground. St Michael's Park in the distance.

found in Cirencester. Known as the Septimus stone, it commemorates the restoration of a column that was put up in honour of L. Septimus (we believe the 'L' stands for Lucius), one of the governors of Britannia Prima. The column is dedicated to Jupiter and this seems to be proof that paganism was alive and well and surviving at a high level in towns like Cirencester.

When I expressed an interest in excavating Cirencester, Neil Holbrook suggested we looked at a site in St Michael's Park, a huge open area in the middle of what had been the Roman town, where there was some evidence that fragments of an embrokated – covered with leaf-shaped designs – Jupiter column had been found. These are fairly rare and would have had a figure of Jupiter – probably on a horse – on top of them. The fragments are now in the local museum and more pieces were found when a gardeners' hut was erected in the park . The park has been scheduled as a site of archaeological interest by English Heritage, but a number of houses have back gardens that abut on to it and I was interested in the possibility of working with their owners.

Neil referred us to the work of Thomas Bravender, a Victorian engineer and antiquarian who surveyed Roman finds in Cirencester. He had lived in The Firs, a large Victorian house at the end of Chester Street, near where the embrokated fragments had been located. Tessellated pavements – bits of mosaic flooring – had been revealed in the trenches that were dug when the building was constructed in the 1890s, and Bravender had produced a map containing Xs that indicated where they were and also included all the Roman discoveries he could find. Their location was near where it was thought the remains of the Jupiter column had been discovered and this happy coincidence led us to the back gardens of Chester Street. But would we find enough evidence of Roman occupation to make a *Time Team* programme?

At an early stage I had agreed with Neil that an application to excavate in the main park site was not a good idea. It is a key area in Cirencester's Roman town and a commitment to extensive long-term excavations would be required for any application to

Our adopted Time Team family join in with the pot washing.

The back gardens of Chester Street.

Various members of Time Team joining in the fascinating process of watching a trench being dug. Jenni is crouched in her 'oyster pit' while Katie Hirst is welding her mattock.

be justified. The back-garden approach was one I was keen to retain and our researcher, Pippa Gilbert, assistant producer Ella Galinsky and our contacts at the Cotswold Archaeological Trust had found enthusiastic volunteers among the local residents. However, some small allotments that had originally been part of The Firs garden were within the scheduled area. I felt it was important to have access to this site and our researchers set about obtaining the necessary permission from English Heritage.

The areas to which we would have access were still relatively small and Mel Morpeth, the director, and the researchers were understandably concerned about how this would translate into a three-day *Time Team* excavation. We discussed the problem at a meeting in London two weeks before we were due to begin shooting, and began to refocus the idea of the programme around the notion that Chester Street and its occupants were what mattered. We had access to three or four key gardens and I felt these were where the story had to happen.

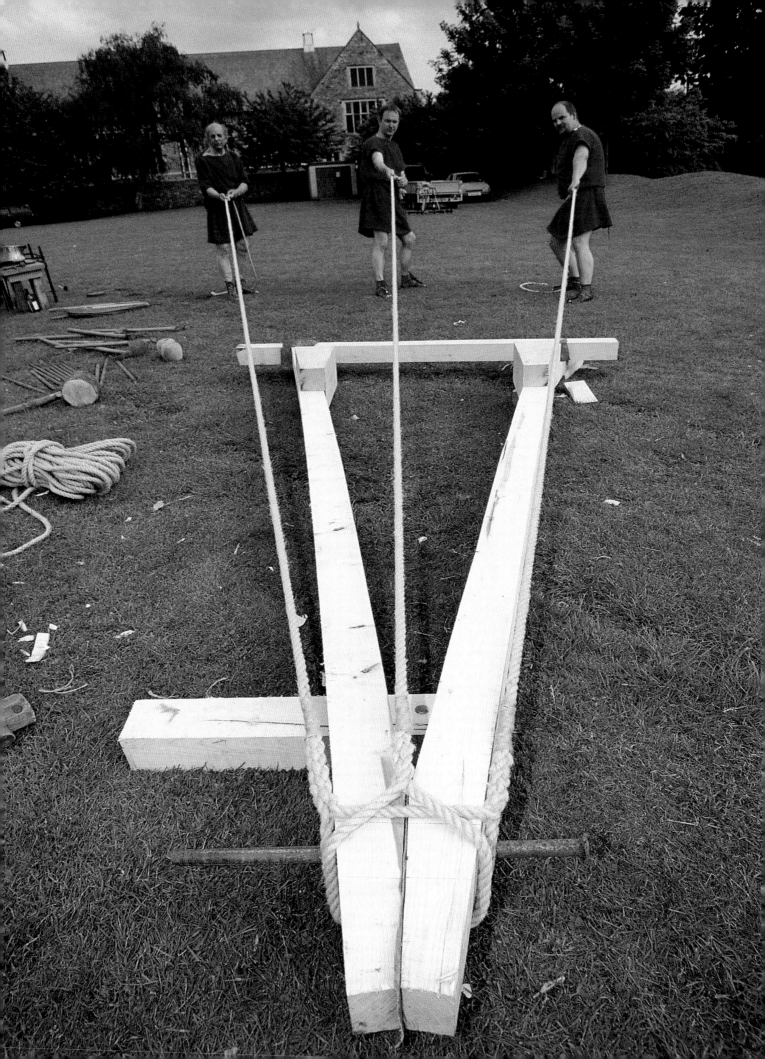

With a bit of geographical licence we were able to include the garden of The Firs at the end of the street. This was important because the fragments of the Jupiter column the site had revealed might indicate a temple and the wider perspective would be useful. In addition, it is larger than other gardens in the street and another trench in a different location, on a bigger scale, would undoubtedly be helpful – three days of staring at small excavations could give us a dose of claustrophobia.

Neil combines enthusiasm and an excellent knowledge of Cirencester – 'Ciren' as he refers to it – with an understanding of how *Time Team* works, and I trusted his judgement implicitly when he said that digging in Cirencester should always produce something. As it had been one of Britain's major Roman towns we ought to find at least the odd bit of pot – but would we uncover a mosaic? We had been down this route before and found only the odd tessera – a depressing outcome when viewers and experts are picturing decorative mosaic floors complete with rampant animals and floral borders.

What we had on 'Ciren' was a nineteenth-century map, Neil's dedication and the enthusiasm of the residents of Chester Street. I kept telling myself that Bravender had been an engineer so there was a chance he might turn out to be an antiquarian who could measure correctly.

On Day One, armed with Bravender's X-marked map, the Team set out on a mosaic hunt. We opened Trench One at the bottom of the back garden of 56 Chester Street, where Bravender had located

the tessellated pavements. The garden was small compared to the amount of earth that came out of the 3 x 3 metre (10 x 10 foot) trench and over the three days of the shoot it was a constant battle to prevent the spoil heap taking over. Because of the size of the garden the earth had to shifted by hand rather than with a machine. In the afternoon, the first Roman walls were revealed. Neil pointed out that because there was no medieval or Saxon occupation in this part of Cirencester it is normal to go from modern remains straight to Roman ones.

By the end of the day the diggers had uncovered a lot of Roman artefacts and, although we had small hand sieves, their richness – in particular the coins that were coming up – called for a large-scale sieving operation. We contacted an old friend of Mick, who agreed to bring a large A-frame sieve to the site as soon as possible.

We had opened Trench Two in the garden of Number 58, located to hit what might be a crossroads connected with Ermin Street. We had obtained permission to do a geophysics survey in St Michael's Park and this showed traces of a road that might pass through one of the gardens of Chester Street. It would be important to find this as Roman houses tended to front on to the street and its route would help Neil to establish another part of the street plan of Roman Cirencester. The trench began to reveal finds, including a coin and substantial stones that might indicate a ditch at the side of the road.

By the end of Day One, although we were still only working the top foot or so of the trenches, Tony was looking at a considerable collection of finds including a bronze pin, discarded glass and a beautiful gaming counter – a rounded glass bead – as well as the coins. We were also uncovering a lot of pottery.

The Ermin Street Guard prepare to erect the A-frame of our Roman crane.

The trench that would eventually reveal the Roman road.

Carenza knocking
out 'embrokations'.

Our very own
Time Team
mosaic – a bit
patched up, but
for us a thing
of beauty!

Day Two saw the start of the cameo. The Ermin Street Guard, a group of Roman re-enactors, arrived to build a typical Roman A-frame crane that would lift a block of sculpted stone on to a base similar to that of the Jupiter column. Giles Macdonald, a sculptor, who had sculpted a Roman altar stone for us at Turkdean, joined us to carve a suitable inscription and to help Carenza cut out the leaf shapes around the stone.

Meanwhile, Trench One was close to reaching the depth at which shoring would be required as the diggers cleared rubble in order to get a look at the layers underneath the demolition debris of the Roman structure. Hoping to hit a floor, they continued to excavate in what they thought was the inside of the building but as they went deeper it became apparent that they were outside it and were digging the outflow point of a drain that exited through a large hole in part of the walls – every trowel of earth brought up quantities of oyster shells, broken pottery and animal bones. Finally, the drainage channel was located on the inside of the drain.

Mark Brett, one of Neil's diggers, had been notably quiet in a corner and suddenly glanced at me with a look that implied something interesting had turned up. I told him to keep going around the area but to go no deeper until I had told Mel Morpeth, the director, and Neil Holbrook to organize the camera crew into position. A dull bit of tessera was visible through the dark soil near the digger's trowel and as he worked around it there was the sound of something solid and cemented in place. There was a wave of excitement as we realized we might be about to see our first *in situ* mosaic.

With the crew in place and Neil on hand in case we had to face any immediate conservation issues we gently eased away the soil. Piece after piece of mosaic started to appear and we began to see geometrical designs and different colours: reds, whites, blacks. What was interesting was that Jenni and the diggers had excavated through undisturbed soil layers, not Victorian backfill, so the mosaic was not from one of the pavements that Bravender had located. This indicated that his map was not as accurate as we had thought.

Ian Powlesland, one of Time Team's diggers, exploring the depths of Trench Three.

Teasing away the earth from our first ever in situ mosaic.

As the mosaic emerged it revealed details of its construction. It had been repaired with square stones in the later Roman period, but there was enough of the original for David Neal and Steve Cosh to describe it as a geometrical corridor mosaic from the latter part of the fourth century.

The coin count was rising in Trenches One and Two and we started to find ones from Theodosius (379–395), the latest to be minted in Roman Britain. We also uncovered shell-tempered pottery made in Bedfordshire and dated to after 360 in Trench One, and Oxfordshire colour-coated ware with white decoration in the same trench. All these finds suggested that Cirencester was still an active and busy town in the fourth century.

Trench Three, which had been opened in The Firs parking area, looked like a building site, with bits of broken tarmac and a huge pile of rubble, but it had revealed a set of walls. Mick was excited by them because they were not in the Roman town alignment but east–west. Could this imply that a later post-Roman church had been built on the site of a Roman temple? This was left unresolved.

At the end of Day Two, with the rest of the mosaic gradually emerging from Trench One, Jenni was sent off to an allotment garden belonging to a Mrs Kelly at the back of The Firs. Our researchers had obtained permission from English Heritage for us to dig here, but as it was a scheduled site it had to be excavated in accordance with the licence we had been given and our research design – a detailed document that specifies the goals and methods of an excavation, and the personnel who will be involved.

The garden was where Bravender had located a tessellated pavement and Trench Four was opened to see whether the mosaic was intact or whether it had been destroyed by nineteenth-century landscaping. Stewart Ainsworth was not convinced the pavement was still there, or that we were digging in the right place, so Jenni decided to start with a 1 x 1 metre (3 x 3 foot) test pit. Just before the end of the day, Trench Four produced one tessera, some Roman wall plaster and an emerging mortar floor.

The trench was extended on Day Three and soon revealed a Roman wall. There was no sign of any Victorian excavation at all, suggesting that the Roman archaeology might be intact. The top of a layer of plaster was just visible, attached to the wall on one side. The diggers excavated on both sides of the wall, to assess what the conditions of the inside and outside of the building were, and as they began to remove the layer of demolition rubble inside the structure an amazing range of finds emerged. Within several minutes they uncovered a bronze brooch, a silver spoon, and several items of worked bone including a dice and a beautiful piece of carved furniture inlay.

It was clear we had uncovered an important high-status building that was well preserved and had not been destroyed by Victorian landscaping, and checked the Scheduled Monument Consent to make

ilt brooch from rench Four.

A piece of Roman bone furniture inlay.

Victor and our family watch the past come to life.

sure we were excavating according to the original brief laid down by English Heritage. It confirmed that we could continue excavating until we reached the upper levels of Roman occupation. We decided that we would continue through the demolition layers in one small section, and through the 'squatter' debris – left by people who had occupied the buildings after they had become ruined – below to assess the condition of the Roman levels. As the end of the dig drew near, Barney Sloane uncovered a sunken but still intact mortar floor. We had not found Bravender's mosaic pavement, but had uncovered a different room with a different floor.

In Trench Two we found evidence of a stone-lined ditch alongside the stone-paved surface, confirming the existence of the Roman road. The mosaic in Trench One was at last revealed in all its glory, complete with patches, and the drain could be seen without the oyster shells and other debris.

This Roman gaming piece, found in the first trench, was still completely intact.

The number and quality of the finds *Time Team* excavated at Cirencester were staggering, not only because there were so many of them and they were so unusual, but because they were such personal items. Artefacts like the dice, spoon and gaming piece provide a vivid insight into the everyday lives of individual people in a way that pottery or coins do not. In addition, we had clearly shown that large areas of undisturbed Roman archaeology are still waiting to be evaluated, and that the area along Chester Street is important to our understanding of the road system and the villas alongside it. From the coins collected in particular we were able to say that 'civilized' life had continued here until the end of the fourth century. If we could make a more general assumption we would say that Roman towns in areas like the Cotswolds were managing to hang on to the comforts of Roman life for a longer period than we had thought, but further work would need to be done in Cirencester to find this out for sure. We were also delighted by the way the residents joined in and clearly enjoyed our invasion of their back gardens. Not every family has a mosaic under their rhubarb patch!

A Roman silver spoon.

Medieval Britain

DOWNPATRICK
COUNTY DOWN

SERIES 5
Broadcast
22 February 1998

Phil attempts to penetrate deeper into the secrets of St Patrick.

Cathedral Hill, a site of Christian worship since the fifth century when a monastery was founded there reputedly by St Patrick himself, dominates Downpatrick in County Down. After the arrival of the Normans in the late twelfth century this early monastery was replaced by a Benedictine one. *Time Team* went to Downpatrick to locate these early buildings beneath later developments on the hill.

A tall circular bell tower that had stood near the church of the early Christian monastery had been demolished in the eighteenth century and, armed with a plan showing the tower, Phil and Mick opened Trench One to try and locate it. Meanwhile Stewart Ainsworth found evidence of a possible bank and ditch encircling the hill, and Carenza opened Trench Two to see if this related to either of the monasteries. By the end of Day One evidence from the trenches was negative – there was no sign of the tower, and tennis courts on top of the hill had destroyed any archaeology that might have been there.

On Day Two the geophysics team, John Gater and Chris Gaffney, identified another two sets of banks and ditches encircling the hill and two new trenches were put in. Early Christian pottery that Phil found in one of the ditches, Trench Three, suggested it was the boundary of the earlier monastery. Meanwhile Mick identified earthworks which he thought could be medieval buildings near the ditches.

On Day Three two more trenches were opened near Trench Three and Carenza found a large kiln and thirteenth- and fourteenth-century green, glazed ridge-tiles from the Benedictine monastery in Trench Four, while Phil discovered the remains of its guesthouse, a building with mortared floors and a slate roof, in Trench Six. The most puzzling area was near the tennis courts on top of the hill.

At last some of the features of t monastic site begin to appear.

St Patrick in Ireland

A great deal is known about St Patrick, Ireland's patron saint, from his *Confessio* (or autobiography). From this and his other writings we know that he was Romano–British and that when he was sixteen he was seized by Irish pirates and taken to Ireland. The six years of slavery that followed allowed him to develop his Christian faith and ideals. He eventually escaped and entered the monastery of Lérins in France before returning to Britain. After experiencing a vision he went back to Ireland to convert what he regarded as a heathen population and established an early form of the Church there, with a cathedral in Armagh. In 1998 *Time Team* searched for a monastery that he reputedly founded at Downpatrick.

It is often thought that Patrick imposed monastic Christianity on the native Irish culture. Mick, however, believes he adapted this tradition to suit the social system that already existed. Elsewhere in the Christian world bishops imposed rules from the top down, but the monasticism Patrick developed was more egalitarian and, as it allowed chieftains to place family members in prominent positions in the Church, was better suited to Ireland's tribal structure. His system was the established form of Christianity before St Augustine's mission in 597.

The remains of a medieval rubbish shute.

Trial pits here revealed more of the Benedictine monastery, but Mick wasn't sure which part. By the end of the day, large quantities of medieval animal bones and refuse suggested we had unearthed the rubbish chutes from its kitchens.

Although *Time Team* didn't find buildings from the early Christian monastery we did find the remains of the Benedictine monastery. Locating the boundary bank and ditch that enclosed the earlier building was important and provides archaeologists with a definite area to work in.

The Saxons Invade

The Saxons did not invade Britain as a single great force that defeated the Britons. After the collapse of Roman authority in Britain in the early fifth century, the state system broke down, leaving local factions and the need to re-establish authority. It is thought that during this period some British chieftains invited Saxon mercenaries, or *federati*, to come from north Germany to fight for their cause.

It was not only military men who came to Britain. There also seems to have been a great migration of settlers – excavations have shown their presence in the south of the country where cemeteries reveal men, women and children – who soon established themselves in southern and eastern areas.

By 600 Britain had been reorganized into new small kingdoms inhabited by Saxons, Jutes or Angles, all of whom had recently arrived from Germany, as well as by native Britons.

GOVAN
GLASGOW

SERIES 4
Broadcast
26 January 1997

The churchyard at Govan, a suburb of Glasgow, contains thirty-one stones that date from the nineth to the eleventh centuries and are sculpted in Celtic, English, Pictish and Norse styles. Local archaeologists have been debating the history of Govan and its stones for years, and legends suggest that what is now a suburban area was an important site in the early medieval period. *Time Team* went to investigate. Our excavations would concentrate on the churchyard and a nearby mound that was thought to be an ancient meeting place, or moot hill. We set off without Mick, who broke his leg shortly before filming, knowing we would miss his knowledge of the period.

We opened Trench One in the churchyard at the start of Day One, but recent burials soon slowed down the digging. Carenza and Phil decided to work out the relationship between the churchyard and the mound and Carenza opened Trench Two in the mound itself. Phil opened Trench Three to try and find the entranceway to the churchyard. It is round, a shape that is often associated with early, important churches, so he was keen to investigate further.

By the start of Day Two, Stewart Ainsworth had formulated a new theory about the mound. He was convinced that it was a previously undiscovered castle site, not a meeting place, because it was in a perfect position to defend what would have been a strategic crossing-point on the River Clyde. In Trench One the archaeology was getting more and more complicated with numerous medieval and later burials cutting through each other. The geophysics team led by John Gater were trying to identify more sculpted stones and a few trenches were opened, but the anomalies they found turned out to be later gravestones. Stewart also had bad news for the Team when his analysis of old maps suggested that the churchyard used to be rectangular, and might not be ancient. At the end of the day, however, in Trench Two, Mick Worthington uncovered the edge of a possible ditch around the mound.

The curved boundary and ancient sculptured stones of Govan led us to this site.

On Day Three, attention focused on this trench, which was filled with different layers of sand and lots of pottery. Mick found nothing earlier than the thirteenth century, supporting Stewart's theory that the mound was a medieval motte-and-bailey castle. Local archaeologists were nevertheless still convinced that the historical evidence showed it was an ancient meeting place. Finally, a structure built of unmortared stones was discovered in Trench One in the churchyard. It was earlier than any other feature we had found on the site, but could not be accurately dated.

This was a fascinating site for *Time Team* because it demonstrated the difficulty of matching history, legend and archaeology in the early medieval period. Stewart's theory that the mound was a castle added yet another facet to the debate about the Govan's origins. In the end, however, we all agreed to disagree about the site and await more evidence in the future.

A trench abandoned by the diggers – it must have been lunch time! Traces of a large defensive ditch wait to be further uncovered.

BAWSEY
NORFOLK

LIVE
29–31 August 1998
SERIES 6
Broadcast
14 March 1999

Today the only indication of past activity at Bawsey in Norfolk is a ruined Norman church that stands alone in rolling arable fields. However, several clues suggested it was once an important settlement, particularly in the Saxon and medieval periods: metal-detectors have found many beautiful objects in the fields over the years, and Saxon sculpture and grave slabs have been found in the church. *Time Team* were going to try to uncover Bawsey's history in three days – our second live programme.

Several different lines of investigation into the site were opened straight away on Day One. Archaeologists in the 1930s had reportedly found an earlier phase of building inside the Norman church but no records survived of the dig, so a trench was opened to re-examine their excavations. An aerial photograph of the fields around the church showed a large ditched enclosure surrounding it, so Carenza put in another trench to look at the ditch. Phil, who was unable to dig because of a back problem, got together with Mick and organized fieldwalking and systematic metal-detecting inside the enclosure. By the end of the day, results were coming in thick and fast. Carenza found thirteenth-century pottery in the ditch and was still going down, while the trenches in the church revealed a fifteenth-century tiled floor and the first human remains. Meanwhile, the fieldwalkers produced the first Saxon finds – a coin and a pair of tweezers – and the geophysics team identified large numbers of ditches, boundaries and other unidentified anomolies.

On Day Two Mick authorized the use of machines to strip off the disturbed and ploughed topsoil from new trenches in the fields and this was sieved and metal-detected for stray finds. Near the church, one of the geophysical anomalies turned out to be an oven base made of burnt clay, with a ring of holes for a wicker-pole frame around the outside. The collection of finds grew at an alarming rate, with items ranging from Bronze Age debris and Roman roof tiles to Saxon silver pennies and, most interestingly, waste from iron-smelting.

On Day Three Carenza produced a crucial find from the bottom of the ditch – a loom weight dating to the eighth century – and one of the trenches located a quarry that probably supplied building materials for the church, with evidence of metal-working nearby. At the very end of the day a trench, near the

Our amazing Bawsey skull, cleaved open by a attacking rider. A rare example of the cause of death being immediately visible.

St Columba

Columba was an Irish monk who converted the Picts, the people of Scotland, to Christianity. In doing so, he was following the great tradition of Irish monks at the time: to spread the Word to the 'unenlightened'.

He was born in County Donegal of royal descent but was exiled from Ireland in 561 and, with twelve companions, sailed to the island of Iona. He built a monastery there in 565 which became the centre of Christianity in northern and western Britain: St Aidan, who converted Northumbria at the invitation of its king, St Oswald, in the seventh century, and founded the monastery at Lindisfarne, was one of its monks. Christian missionaries set out from Iona for much of Europe, and even reached Eygpt.

Columba made missionary journeys to mainland Scotland from his base on Iona, and in his later years he founded abbeys in Ireland. He ranks with St Patrick and St Brigid as one of the three patron saints of the Irish.

Augustine of Canterbury

In 596 Pope Gregory I (the Great), troubled at the pagan practices of the 'Anglei', sent Augustine to England at the head of a Roman mission to convert its inhabitants. Gregory had been impressed by the beauty of English boys for sale in a slave market in Rome, exclaiming that Angles was an appropriate name for, 'they have angelic faces and should become fellow heirs with the angels in heaven'.

Augustine arrived in 597 and went first to the court of King Aethelbert of Kent, whose wife Bertha was a Christian. The king, however, was sceptical about this religion from Rome and insisted on receiving Augustine in the open air to prevent him and his companions performing witchcraft – pagans believed that Christian spells were contained and focused inside buildings but harmless outside them.

The Kentish king nevertheless soon converted to Christianity, together with many of his subjects, and in 601 Augustine became the first Archbishop of Canterbury. He established Christ Church, later a cathedral, there in 603 and founded the monastery of Sts Peter and Paul just outside the city's walls. He later placed bishops in Rochester and London, and helped Aethelbert to draft the earliest written laws to survive in England. However, Augustine never gained the support of the monks of the Celtic Church – the Christian Church in Britain before his mission – who relied on the impact of an ascetic and austere lifestyle to gain converts, and resented his efforts to establish a hierarchical organization.

Mick regards Augustine's efforts as puny – 'He never got further than Essex' – and gives the credit to Theodore of Tarsus, who was appointed Archbishop of Canterbury in 668 and came to England in 669, where he built on the work of Augustine and his successors. Pope Vitalian gave him the authority to reorganize the Church in Britain and he set up a diocesan structure that lasted throughout the Middle Ages. He also established a school for the higher clergy in Canterbury. By the time of his death in 690 Christianity was widely accepted throughout England.

Bawsey's standing medieval remains including a Norman arch.

ooking like mething for aching eggs, our axon hearth eveals its secrets.

church produced the most staggering find of the dig. A complete skeleton dating to the tenth or eleventh century was uncovered, with a nasty sword cut across the front of the skull that would have killed him. Nearby, we found another skeleton with a broken forearm.

The artefacts *Time Team* uncovered at Bawsey showed that the critical phase of occupation at the site started in the eighth century and continued into the Norman period when the stone church was built. However, there were enough Roman finds to suggest a Roman building nearby, and – even earlier – flint, bone and burnt debris from a Bronze Age settlement. The dig demonstrated how complicated sites can be below the ground, even when little survives above the surface, and that important settlement areas were often used continuously for many centuries.

King Arthur

It is disappointing that the great King Arthur may never have existed. The man who inspired the myth was probably a great Romano-Celtic warrior of the sixth century, whose exploits on the battlefield against Saxon invaders were described 300 years later by a chronicler writing under the name of Nennius. Indeed, his fighting prowess must have been great – a Welsh poem, the 'Gododdin', written in c.600 close to the time when he lived, claims that a certain warrior was 'no Arthur'. How a successful war leader came to be seen as the best and greatest of all Britain's monarchs is due to a great British tradition: story-telling.

In the ninth and tenth centuries the Welsh needed a figurehead who would epitomize their national identity, and who would stir their blood and spur them on to victory against the English. Arthur fitted the bill perfectly and his name became a banner around which both Wales and other areas of Celtic culture, such as Cornwall, could rally.

It was Geoffrey of Monmouth who, in the 1130s, gave us the story of Arthur the High King, ruler of all Britain, who presided over the court of Camelot. In his romanticized *History of the Kings of Britain*, he recounts the unsurpassed achievements of a leader who conquered most of Europe and even attacked Rome.

Arthur has long been associated with Glastonbury in Somerset – the Tor is said to be the Isle of Avalon, his final resting-place. This is not totally surprising: in the twelfth century the monks of the nearby abbey 'found' his body and that of his queen, Guinevere – and created a medieval tourist attraction.

The legend of Arthur is so powerful that it has survived through the ages with more and more sites, from Tintagel in Cornwall to South Cadbury in Somerset, associated with this best of British kings. Even today he remains a powerful figure of folk myth, responding to the need for a hero that lies deep within the human pysche.

Sutton Hoo

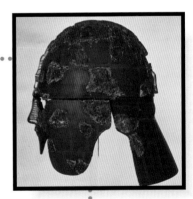

Looking at the grassy mounds in a field at Sutton Hoo in Suffolk, no one could have guessed that one of them hid a wonderfully lavish burial, with some of the finest and richest objects ever seen from Saxon Britain contained in the cabin of a huge wooden ship. There were gold objects made by local craftsmen, artefacts of Mediterranean silver brought from Europe, coins, weapons and dishes.

Getting the ship to the burial site would have been no easy feat. Though Sutton Hoo is close to the Deben estuary, the Saxons had to lift the boat out of the water and lower it into the pit they had dug on the heath, 30.5 metres (100 feet) above the river. The oared ship was 27.5 metres (90 feet) long with places for forty oarsmen and is the largest found in a boat-burial.

Sutton Hoo symbolizes a society that depended on the power and patronage of the chief or king, who gave gifts to his followers to bind them to him. The rich objects found in the burial were the currency of this system.

Although no body was found in the ship, the richness of the artefacts, which include a silver sceptre and elaborate warrior's trappings, leave little doubt that it was a grave fit for a king. Dated coins indicate that the ship was probably buried in the mid 620s and, because of its location, it is possible that the king was Raedwald, who ruled East Anglia between 616 and 627. We can only imagine the pomp and circumstance which went with the burial of this great ship – a fitting tribute to a fallen king.

The Synod of Whitby

The Synod of Whitby in 664 was an important event in the history of Christianity in Britain, because it attempted to impose a set of rules that would reduce the differences between the Celtic Church and the Roman Church. St Augustine had attempted to resolve the matter some sixty years earlier, but was unsuccessful: Celtic monks resented both him and the new hierarchical system he attempted to impose on British Christianity.

Two points at issue at the Synod were variations in the way people were baptised, and monks' tonsures. A Celtic monk shaved the front of his head and left his hair long at the back, while a more Romanized one shaved the hair in the centre of his skull. It is likely, though, that mere differences of appearance were of less importance than the fact that the Roman Church wanted to adapt and assimilate the Celtic Church's hierarchy.

The key point, however, was the date of Easter, which was celebrated at different times according to whether it was calculated by the Celtic or the Roman method. King Oswy of Northumbria, who called and presided over the Synod, was initially in favour of the Celtic date, but was convinced by the arguments of Wilfrid, the Abbot of Ripon, and eventually decided in favour of the Roman one. In doing so, he encouraged the Church in Britain to become more like its continental counterpart.

Beowulf

Beowulf is the oldest epic poem in English – in fact, the oldest in any language of Germanic origin. We do not know exactly when it was written down, but most people agree it was composed in the eighth century.

The story is set in the fifth and sixth centuries, at the court of Hrothgar, King of the Danes, which was plagued by the fiendish exploits of two fen monsters: Grendel and his mother. Beowulf is a young noble who kills these creatures and later becomes a king. He subsequently dies fighting a dragon. The poem is 3,182 lines long, and its rich imagery and vivid pictures of honour, valour, loyalty to one's king and the quest for glory give us a feel for the politics and everyday life of a royal court of the period. It is full of lessons about how young nobles were expected to behave, and how heroes were made – almost like an early medieval *Boy's Own* story.

Beowulf represents an oral tradition of story-telling and, although it is essentially fiction, it gives us an insight into the people to whom it was told – what their lives were like, their attitude to the afterlife and how their society depended on war and gift-giving. In particular, it enables us to understand the relationship between warriors and their king.

WINTERBOURNE GUNNER
WILTSHIRE

SERIES 2
Broadcast
15 January 1995

Over the past thirty years a Saxon cemetery dating to the sixth century has been uncovered in part of Winterbourne Gunner, a small Wiltshire village to the north-east of the cathedral city of Salisbury. A local developer who wanted to build on a plot in the middle of the cemetery area, invited *Time Team* to assess the archaeology – planning conditions dictated that until this was done there would be no decision as to whether or not he could go ahead.

On Day One the first problem confronting the Team was the building rubble and other debris heaped in piles all over the site. There was too much metal for a geophysics survey to be successful so Phil decided to remove a thin layer of topsoil from the front of the developer's plot by machine. The underlying chalk bedrock was revealed and almost immediately Phil saw a possible grave appearing. Sixth-century Saxons were pagans and some were buried with grave goods – objects like jewellery, weapons and knives – that would either help them in the afterlife, or confirm their status: the richer the person, the greater the quantity of grave goods buried with them. While the topsoil was being removed Carenza set about collating previous discoveries: in addition to the Saxon cemetery, there were records of ring ditches in the nearby fields along with an area of what appeared to be medieval earthworks near the village church.

On Day Two the three graves were carefully excavated and began to reveal the skeletons. Dr Margaret Cox, *Time Team*'s bone expert, disclosed that one of them was an elderly woman. The diggers worked very carefully because grave goods are fragile and difficult to spot after lying in the ground for so many years. The second skeleton also proved to be female. The third, smaller, grave contained the body of a child who had been buried in a crouching position, and was near a large patch of brown soil deposits that had been cut into chalk in

An upturned cremation urn awaits lifting. It will later be excavated in the laboratory.

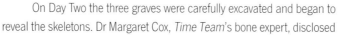

The Venerable Bede

The Venerable Bede began the tradition of documenting history in England when he completed the first-ever English history book, *Ecclesiastical History of the English People*, in 731. Born in Monkwearmouth in Durham he entered the local monastery in 679 when he was seven, and moved to Jarrow, where he spent the rest of his life, about three years later. His history, which provides critical insights into the events and practices of the early medieval period, recorded national events and people of high worth. It is probable that Bede was trying to encourage national unity in an unsettled country – a concept that Alfred the Great later adopted – and to set the moral standards by which its people should live.

Bede also wrote hymns, commentaries on the Bible, and about the state of the Church in Northumbria. He studied chronology and popularized the use of the *anno domini* notation, systematically dating events from the birth of Christ. All his works are well written and researched, and have remained readable and popular through the centuries, with a charm that is unaffected by the fact that he clearly had his prejudices.

His *Ecclesiastical History* was known and appreciated from the eighth century onwards, on the Continent as well as in England, and, together with his other works, had an impact that lasted through the Middle Ages – and beyond.

what was now the centre of the building plot. Mick speculated that brown soil deposits might be the remains of some kind of barrow around which the Saxon cemetery was focused.

A key question was the extent of the cemetery. We had expected to find more than three graves at the front of the plot and on Day Three we decided to examine the area at the back. No sooner had it been stripped of topsoil to open Trench Two than two Bronze Age cremation urns were uncovered, indicating that burials had taken place on the site 2,000 years before the arrival of the Saxons we were investigating. Mick and Carenza went up in a helicopter to view the area and identified three ring ditches in a nearby field and another in the field backing on to the building plot – further evidence of Bronze Age barrows. Phil continued to excavate the Saxon skeletons and found grave goods buried with the elderly woman: a brooch, long pin and large amber bead. X-rays revealed details that would allow the finds to be cleaned with precision, and that were no longer visible to the naked eye because the jewellery had deteriorated in the soil – the pin had a looped head and the brooch, made of gilded copper alloy, was decorated with a simple pattern of rings and dots.

Mick and Carenza went to look at earthworks around the church – Carenza's study of earlier archaeological discoveries had revealed that pottery from an earlier excavation there included pagan Saxon wares, indicating that the Saxons in the cemetery may have lived in this area. Back on site another urn was found in Trench Two, along with part of the ring ditch. The urn was in an area that is unlikely to be disturbed by building works and was left *in situ*. We found a final cremation urn in Trench Two in the middle of the large brown area, confirmation that the Saxon cemetery was centred around a barrow.

Time Team uncovered evidence that two different periods – Bronze Age and Saxon – were linked on the Winterbourne Gunner site. The urn that was found at the end of Day Three was the primary burial in the barrow and attracted other Bronze Age cremations. Over 2,000 years it acted as the marker for the Saxon burials we were originally investigating.

Our Saxon brooch. Later X-rays reveal a dot and a circle design.

The Book of Kells

The *Book of Kells* is a Latin copy of the Gospels, in an unusually large format and elaborately and lavishly decorated. The artistic styles and forms draw on all the conventions of eighth- and ninth-century Irish art, with some European influences. The text was laboriously copied out by monks – possibly in the monastery of Iona – and the many inaccuracies it contains suggest it was used on the altar as a decorative *aide-mémoire* for those familiar with its contents, rather than as a script.

The pages are vellum – prepared calfskin – and their edges are gilded. A variety of brushes was used for the text, which is in ink, and for the illustrations which were created by using compasses and set squares underpinned by complex mathematical formulae – a process that produced the famous intertwined figures of humans, animals and mythical beasts. A relief effect, created by layering the pigments, was used for the original illustrations but was destroyed in the nineteenth century when the pages were dampened and flattened.

The *Book of Kells* was never completed and in the seventeenth century it was given to Trinity College, Dublin. It is still on display there, in the Old Library, where it is seen by more than half a million visitors every year.

750   755   760

YORK
NORTH YORKSHIRE

LIVE
4–6 September 1999

Time Team's third live broadcast was from York, and was our toughest challenge yet. The city's history is long and continuous because of its ideal defensive location on the fork of the Ouse and Foss rivers, and so the Team went to excavate – simultaneously – three different sites from three different periods spanning a thousand years of British history: a Roman cemetery in the Royal York Hotel gardens, a Viking street called Walmgate, and the largest English hospital in the eleventh century.

Geophysics results showed a number of small anomalies in the hotel garden and a large anomaly in the hospital precinct which local people said was an air-raid shelter from the Second World War. Mick and his team opened Trenches One and Two to investigate the shelter as well as medieval traces in the area. At Walmgate, a small trench had revealed Viking archaeology in 1991, and Carenza and her team removed the backfill to get straight to the deposits. Medieval Trenches One and Two were laid out over the anomalies in the hotel garden. Stewart Ainsworth looked at patterns in buildings and streets that might indicate a continuity of house boundaries from the Roman or Viking periods.

By the evening of Day One Walmgate was producing lots of organic finds from the dark, wet soils of the Viking layers – as the soil was removed it was dry- and wet-sieved to catch preserved finds like seeds. In the hotel garden Roman Trenches One and Two had revealed artefacts like an unusual fourth-century coin showing the Empress Helena and high-quality Roman glass, lifting hopes that we would uncover a burial. The air-raid shelter had been uncovered in Medieval Trenches One and Two at the hospital, and the Team were concentrating on the medieval hospital.

At the start of Day Two, Medieval Trench Three was put in on the hospital site to locate the edge of the infirmary hall and a later kitchen. Medieval Trench Four was opened in a garden behind the council offices, to investigate the archaeology in a

A Roman burial from the second or third century.

different area of the precinct. Roman Trench Two in the hotel garden produced the first Roman burial. The grave was lined with stone and there were traces of a wooden coffin. The skeleton was a female over thirty who had never had children. Further excavations revealed a second smaller burial, of a four-year-old girl, to the woman's left. Meanwhile, on the hospital site Medieval Trench Two was extended to try to find more of the pier bases so Mick could determine the layout of the hall. On the other side of the city, at Walmgate, excitement was building as a wattle boundary wall and evidence of a house appeared. Samples were sent off to Sheffield for dendrochronology dating.

By Day Three Medieval Trench Two on the hospital site had revealed two pier bases and the possible location of a third. Whilst Medieval Trenches One, Three and Four had not produced structures, finds indicating cooking and other activities had been discovered. In the hotel garden a third burial – of a man in his early twenties – was found to the right of the other two, and when Roman Trench One was extended a ditch from a huge building, possibly a mausoleum, was found. The Viking site at Walmgate continued to produce wonderful finds and evidence of a wooden house with a clay floor and wattle boundary walls.

In three days *Time Team* uncovered evidence of life – and death – in Roman, Viking and medieval York and confirmed the city's status as one Britain's foremost archaeological sites.

Dressed for action, Phil and Margaret Cox get ready to take DNA samples in our Roman cemetery site.

THETFORD
NORFOLK

SERIES 6
Broadcast
17 January 1999

In the eleventh century Thetford, a small market town in Norfolk, was an important Saxon and early Norman centre, the seat of the bishop of Norfolk and Suffolk and a cathedral city. Today Thetford Grammar School stands on the site not only of the cathedral, which later moved to Norwich, but also of a later Cluniac monastery and Dominican friary. Pupils at the school were intrigued by the remaining walls of the friary. They asked *Time Team* to find out what lay beneath them and Mick, with his love of medieval monasteries, took up the challenge.

The surviving friary walls – which date to the fourteenth century – are the best-known part of the site and on Day One Phil opened Trenches One and Two at their base. This would enable him to relate any below-ground archaeology to the walls and work out the sequence of building on the site – which would, he hoped, go back to the eleventh century or earlier. Meanwhile Carenza and Beric Morley, *Time Team*'s buildings expert, examined the walls and revealed a complex picture of building and rebuilding in the late medieval period. The geophysics team led by John Gater carried out a survey of the school quadrangle but this was complicated by modern services. Carenza decided to open a (very carefully dug) trench, Trench Three, around the gas pipes and water mains to investigate the area. The day ended with Phil's discovery of the first piece of late Saxon pottery.

By Day Two we were wondering what the cathedral had looked like – was it built of timber or stone? The answer would only come from more excavation and survey. Geophysics revealed the ground plan of the friary cloisters under the school playing field, but no evidence of the cathedral. Meanwhile, Carenza was unearthing large quantities of medieval stained glass and window lead from Trench Three in the quad. A further trench, Trench Four, was added in the quadrangle and revealed a substantial wall.

On Day Three final analysis of Trenches One and Two by the friary walls confirmed we had found the friary cloister that linked the walls, but nothing earlier than the fourteenth century. Attention turned

An early Norman column base – enigmatic remains of an early medieval church.

St Alcuin

Alcuin was one of a long line of religious reformers and, like so many of them, he came from the Northumbrian Church of the eighth century. He was born in York, but left there in 780 to go to Rome and then to Charlemagne's court at Aachen, the northern capital of the Frankish empire, where he was an influential adviser to the king. Charlemagne, who became Holy Roman Emperor in 800, led an early medieval renaissance of culture and religion, and Alcuin played an important role in reviving European civilization after the depredations of the barbarians.

His major concern was the relationship between religious and non-religious matters and he was the probable author of a letter Charlemagne wrote to the pope outlining their respective spheres of responsibility. In *The Bishops, Kings and Saints of York*, one of the earliest political essays of the Middle Ages, Alcuin described a unified Northumbria with the Church based at York.

His other works include the standard medieval version of the Bible and the lives of several saints. Alcuin was outspoken in his views and his 300 letters reflect the low standards of the Church in the eighth century and the great need for religious reform in Britain.

Trying to work out which wall went where proved to be a difficult task.

to the wall in the new trench in the quad. Amidst lashing rain, further excavation was carried out and led to the conclusion that it too was part of the friary, although it also incorporated fragments of much earlier buildings.

At the end of three days *Time Team* had not only uncovered the friary cloisters they had also learnt a lot from this site. Ecclesiastical sites such as this are very complicated and the suggestions made by historical sources are not always what you might imagine. It seems likely that the cathedral was a small timber or stone building that had been lost under later structures.

Offa's Dyke

Offa's Dyke survives as a tribute to a great Anglo-Saxon king: Offa, who ruled Mercia from 757 to 796, conquered Essex, Kent, Sussex and Surrey, defeated the Welsh and West Saxons and established the supremacy of his kingdom south of the River Humber.

The dyke marks the boundary with Wales and runs over 112 kilometres (70 miles) of wild mountainous countryside, from the River Dee to the River Severn. Its northern sections have mostly disappeared, but in the southern part there are long stretches of ditch, some disjointed sections of bank and ditch and some places where no traces remain. The distance between the ditch and the top of the bank would have been 8 metres (26 feet). A wall along the top was made from timber or, occasionally, stone. There may have been towers and signal beacons, but no one knows where the gateways were – or, indeed, whether there were any. Offa's achievements are reflected in the fact that he was the first ruler to have his coins inscribed 'King of the English'.

ATHELNEY
SOMERSET

SERIES 1
Broadcast
16 January 1994

Athelney lies in the Somerset Levels, about 16 kilometres (10 miles) from the county town of Taunton, and was the location for the first *Time Team* programme. In the ninth century it was an island deep within marshland and Alfred the Great, King of Wessex from 871 to 899, took refuge there in 878 at the lowest ebb of his reign: the Vikings had conquered Northumbria, East Anglia and Mercia, and killed their kings and Alfred's kingdom had shrunk to a few acres around Athelney. He emerged to defeat the Viking army at the battle of Edington, and the Morgan family, who farm in the area, set the Team the task of locating the site of his fort, and the abbey he built on the island to celebrate his decisive victory. Despite the importance of the site very little archaeological work had been carried out there in the past.

A monument marks the location of Alfred's abbey – and a later one that was built over it during the Middle Ages – and it was assumed that his fort had been at the other end of the island. Because Athelney Abbey is scheduled as an ancient monument we were not allowed to excavate on the site and on Day One the first task for Phil and Carenza was to survey the area of the ninth-century island and create a reference grid across the site for an intensive fieldwalking and geophysics programme. Mick and Tony went up in a helicopter to examine the area from the air. Part of the area was still flooded, as it would have been in Alfred's time, and curving field boundaries picked out the shapes of Athelney and the neighbouring island of Lyng, to which it had been joined by a narrow causeway.

On Day Two the geophysics team revealed that their results showed two linear anomalies; an unusually high magnetic response indicated that they might be ditches filled with industrial metalworking waste. Carenza thought a circular feature on an old aerial photograph might be the fort but Mick was sceptical – it was on the edge of the marsh and he could see no reason why Alfred would build it there. By early afternoon the fieldwalkers had found a large piece of metal slag. Gerry McDonnell, an expert on slag, was contacted in Bradford and asked to come to Athelney to tell us whether or not it came from a Saxon furnace. The geophysics team had been surveying the abbey site. The plan of the

Medieval floor tiles which may have been hiding an earlier church below.

Lindisfarne attacked by Vikings

On 8 June 793 Vikings sacked Lindisfarne, the Holy Island off the coast of Northumbria. They arrived without warning and the horror of their savagery made a lasting impression on the entire Christian world. The raiders ransacked the monastery, and stripped it of most of its treasures. They killed livestock, murdered many of the monks and took others into slavery. The monastery, which had flourished for over 200 years and housed the coffin containing the body of St Cuthbert, never fully recovered from the raid. The attack was all the more offensive because Lindisfarne was a great centre of learning and art, inspiring all the Christian Church. Its monks had established a huge library, which included the beautifully illuminated *Lindisfarne Gospels*.

The English scholar Alcuin of York recorded his outrage: 'Behold, the church of St Cuthbert spattered with the blood of the priests of God, despoiled of all its ornaments; a place more venerable than all in Britain is given as prey to pagan peoples'.

It is a mystery how the *Lindisfarne Gospels* and the relics of St Cuthbert survived the attack – but survive they did. It was only in 875, when a second Viking raid threatened, that the monks fled their island with these two most sacred treasures. They settled at Chester-le-Street near Durham. In 995 the Lindisfarne community made its final move to Durham. With the community went the body of St Cuthbert and the *Lindisfarne Gospels*. The saint's relics reamin at Durham while the *Gospels* are now on permanent display in the British Musuem.

abbey was astoundingly detailed and the outline of the later church could be seen quite clearly. Carenza's feature, however, was looking remarkably prehistoric and was unlikely to be associated with Alfred.

On the morning of Day Three an analysis of the abbey plan revealed that it showed the medieval building as it had been when Henry VIII dissolved the monasteries in the early sixteenth century. After studying the geophysics plan, Chris Gaffney decided that one small rectangular area of walls was aligned differently to the rest of the medieval abbey, which may be evidence of Alfred's abbey.

After his victory over the Vikings, Alfred had established a series of burhs or fortified centres throughout southern England, such as nearby Lyng. These were defended by men of the surrounding countryside. Each hide (a unit of land) big enough to support a family and its dependents had to send a man to defend his local fort. Each pole – 5 metres (5½ yards) – of wall was defended by four men. A large ditch behind the church at Lyng had formed part of the defences of the burh and, as 100 hides had been attached to the fort, Mick worked out that the ditch would have been 125 metres (137½ yards) long. He and Tony measured what survives of it in the churchyard and found that it was about 62.5 metres (69 yards) – half the length Mick had calculated for the ninth-century ditch. The other half would have been on the other side of the road that runs through Lyng today, so that the ditch would have effectively cut off the burh from the adjacent higher land whilst it remained linked to Athelney by a long causeway above the marsh.

At the end of the day we were joined by Gerry McDonnell. A first-hand examination confirmed an Anglo-Saxon date – the furthest west any such waste had been discovered. Because this type of slag occurs mainly in East Anglia it had been thought that it was produced only by the Saxons, when they first came to Britain in the fifth century. However, its presence at Athelney indicated that the process that created it must have been in general use throughout the Anglo-Saxon period.

Time Team's first programme had established the position and layout of the medieval abbey, and possibly of Alfred's church . We had found the first evidence that this was the area where he had prepared for his battle at Edington in the form of metalworking possibly connected with making weapons.

Working around vegetables, or in this case teasels, is an occupational hazard. The monument gave us a clue where to look.

Vikings Attack

The Vikings originally traded with the people of England but, in the eighth century, they crossed the sea bearing axes rather than market goods. They started a series of raids on the English coast, stealing from and destroying coastal settlements. Lindisfarne, tragically sacked in 793, was only the first Northumbrian monastery that they attacked. After 835 the raids intensified – the Vikings were now seeking territory and power in England – and were headed for more ambitious targets like Southampton and London. As the scale of their campaigns increased, they were forced to spend the winter months on English soil, rather than returning to Scandinavia. They seized Dublin in 841 and archaeological excavations show it became their principal military and trading base in Ireland.

Their first real invasion of England took place in East Anglia, which fell to them in 866. When they had established a base there, the Vikings made their way north to York where they built a great city in what became their central kingdom. Battles continued between them and Alfred the Great, who was forced officially to acknowledge their presence in England in 871. In 886 he reached an agreement with Guthrum, King of East Anglia, whereby the Vikings were recognized as rulers of the north-eastern area of England – the Danelaw. Their rule ended in 954, when Erik Bloodaxe, the last Viking king of York, was deposed and killed.

Viking York

After the Vikings seized York in 867 they expanded and developed what had been a large Roman city. During the ninth and tenth centuries it became one of their principal centres in England, and a great industrial town.

The Anglo-Saxon Chronicle records death, disaster and destruction in York during the Viking period, but archaeology has shown quite the opposite. The town was booming with international trade and thriving industry. There were workshops of all shapes and sizes, including one for minting coins. Much of our knowledge has been gained from excavations on a site called Coppergate, a street lined with buildings that were erected between about 930 and 935. It may have been an early example of town planning – the buildings were all of a regular size and plan – and perhaps the street was intended to encourage the development of an industrial estate. It is clear that the workers at Coppergate were industrious, with metalworking, jewellery-making and woodworking included among their activities.

The geology of York produces conditions in which organic material is not decomposed as it is on most archaeological sites. As a result wonderful objects made from leather, wood and cloth can be uncovered, providing a whole new insight into life in the Viking town.

Alfred the Great

Alfred is best known as the warrior who vanquished the Vikings and laid the basis for the unification of England. He became King of Wessex in 871 when his brother, Aethelred I, whom he had assisted in battles against the Vikings, died. In 878 he was forced to retreat to Athelney in Somerset, and emerged from there to win his most famous battle against the Vikings, at Edington in 878. He recaptured London in 886 and in that same year agreed to respect Viking control of the Danelaw – land north of a boundary running from London to Chester. Alfred was recognized as king of all the parts of England that were not under Viking rule.

During his conflicts with the Vikings, he built up a large fleet – the first long-term English navy – to stave off coastal attacks, and reorganized the army around burhs. By the end of his reign there were about thirty of these fortified centres across England.

A scholar and devout Christian, Alfred introduced a code of laws, oversaw a revival of learning among the clergy and encouraged the reading and writing of English. Mick regards him as the first literate king of England, who recognized the importance of books, libraries and documents that recorded his decisions and beliefs.

King Alfred baptises Guthrum

Guthrum was a Viking chieftain who attacked Wessex in 875 and almost succeeded in defeating its king, Alfred the Great. Alfred finally triumphed over him at Edington in 878. The Welsh monk Asser, who wrote his *Life of Alfred* in about 893, goes into detail about the battle and describes how Alfred 'fought fiercely against the entire heathen host in a long and stubborn stand. At last by God's will, he won his victory'.

One of Alfred's great skills as a king was his ability to turn his enemies to his own advantage. Not only did he defeat Guthrum, he also converted him and thirty of his men to Christianity. The baptism took place at Aller, close to Athelney where *Time Team* carried out one of its first excavations, and was a spectacular event: Alfred wined and dined the Vikings at a feast that culminated in their being baptised, and was named as Guthrum's godfather. The baptismal procession that followed lasted for several days and wound its way through Somerset, from Aller to Wedmore and possibly on to a royal palace in Cheddar.

The Vikings' conversion may well have been a clever piece of diplomacy, and I can only imagine that Guthrum had mixed feelings about the whole series of events. He and his men occupied East Anglia in 880, and later he and Alfred agreed a treaty to maintain a common border between their territories, honour was satisfied on both sides.

The Anglo-Saxon Chronicle

The *Anglo-Saxon Chronicle* starts with a description of Julius Caesar's invasion, races at lightning speed through the history of the world to 449, and finally settles into lengthy accounts of the Anglo-Saxon period and the years after the Norman Conquest of England.

Year-by-year entries were brought together in a single compilation in the ninth century, during the reign of Alfred the Great. This ends in 891, after which versions of the *Chronicle* were continued independently in various monasteries across England. Peterborough Abbey kept its chronicle going the longest, until 1154.

Initially the monks generally based their entries on the same events, but after 915 they started to record different ones. Matching the various versions is difficult because there is no common dating system. Also, the entries can be biased by contemporary opinion – Alfred's exploits with the Vikings, for example, are the subject of many highly complimentary entries. However, despite these problems, without *The Anglo-Saxon Chronicle* we would be very much in the dark about what occurred in the early medieval period.

LLANGORSE
POWYS

SERIES 1
Broadcast
6 February 1994

Situated between the Usk and Wye rivers in the heart of the Brecon Beacons, Llangorse Lake is the biggest natural area of water in South Wales. About 40 metres (130 feet) from its northern shore is a crannog or artificial defended island. Archaeologists from Cardiff University and the National Museum of Wales had been investigating it periodically since 1987, and dated one phase of its construction to about 890 AD. The site may have been built by a king of Brycheiniog, and is reminiscent of similar royal sites in Ireland. *Time Team* went to help with the investigation of the crannog and find the location of the early settlement around the shores of the lake.

On Day One an examination of a large-scale map revealed an area of land with a curvilinear boundary, possibly indicating an early enclosure, about halfway between the lake and the church of Llangorse (an early monastic site). The geophysics team set off to survey this but when Mick and Tony went up in a helicopter for an aerial view they realized that it seemed rather too large for a Dark Age settlement. Mick spotted another area of slightly higher land, with dark patches in a ploughed field, at the west end of the lake – was this a settlement? The crannog had been built from an estimated 1,000 tons of rock, layered with bundles of branches that held it together, and the remains of a timber palisade fence were visible, sticking up out of the water. We opened Trench One on the curvilinear boundary to look for evidence of a ditch but it proved to be barren – and John and Chris announced that their survey of the area had also turned up a complete blank.

At the start of Day Two the Team was completely in the dark about what had been happening in the Dark Ages. Dr Mark Redknap of the National Museum of Wales had been sieving the silts where the edges of the crannog were eroding, but so far had found nothing more than a few pieces of charred wood, and Tony and Carenza joined them in their task. Geophysics investigated the higher land at the west end of the lake, but only located several pits where trees had been grubbed up and burnt.

Wet sieving by the side of the lake.

St Dunstan

St Dunstan revitalized the monasticism that had all but disappeared in Britain as a result of Viking attacks, and was at the forefront of the wave of monastic fervour that swept across Britain in the tenth century.

He was born near Glastonbury to an aristocratic family, some of whose members attended the court of Athelstan, the first King of England. He used his noble birth to gain royal support for his religious ideas and was chief adviser to Edmund, who succeeded Athelstan. However, Dunstan was the victim of intrigue and was about to be banished when the king narrowly escaped death while hunting a stag above Cheddar Gorge. According to legend, the stag leapt over the top of the gorge, followed by the hounds, and as Edmund was about to follow them he reproached himself for the way he had treated Dunstan. At this moment the king's horse reared up and saved him from death.

The incident had such a profound effect on Edmund that he made Dunstan abbot of Glastonbury – which, like other monastic institutions, had all but collapsed – and gave him a free rein to introduce his reforms. These were based on the rule of St Benedict, which was characterized by moderation and obedience within the framework of disciplined community life. From Glastonbury Dunstan reformed old monasteries like Peterborough, Gloucester and Ely, and created new ones. He was so successful that British monasticsm remained unchanged for at least seventy-five years, and at the time of Norman Conquest, in 1066, the majority of Britain's forty to fifty monastic houses were reformed tenth-century establishments. Dunstan was appointed Archbishop of Canterbury in 960 and crowned Edgar at Bath in 973 in a ritual which, modified, forms the basis of the modern coronation ceremony.

Robin Bush explained that the crannog had come to a fiery end. In 916, a Mercian abbot, Ecgberht, had been assassinated and Aethelflaed, the Lady of the Mercians, blamed Tewdwr Ap Elised, the King of Brycheiniog. Her army destroyed the island and captured his queen.

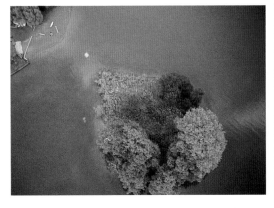

An aerial view of the crannog, with traces of a causeway linking it to the mainland.

Mick found another area suitable for settlement on the other side of the lake, at Llangasty, and it became the next target for the geophysics team who located a ditch in the field next to its church. Could it have surrounded a Dark Age settlement? While Tony and Carenza were sieving at the edge of the crannog one of the diggers found a Dark Age finger ring, made of shale and dating to the ninth or tenth century, in the silt. Other finds were less exotic: animal bones, charred grains and part of a furnace lining which implied that metal had been worked on the crannog.

On Day Three Phil opened a small trench, Trench Two, across the ditch geophysics had located at Llangasty, to try and find dating evidence. Mick thought it might have surrounded an earlier monastic enclosure and Trench Three was put in across the churchyard boundary to see if this could be dated. Phil's trench produced a neatly cut ditch but no finds, and Trench Three revealed that the church boundary also followed a ditch. The final geophysics results at Llangasty, in the field beside the church, showed what appeared to be patches of layered stones, possibly the sites of cells in an Irish-style monastery.

In three days *Time Team* showed that in 900 AD the crannog would have been full of activity, with domestic fires and the furnaces required for metalworking. There were monastic settlements on either side of the lake: one at Llangorse and the other, probably the smaller of the two, at Llangasty.

King Cnut

To most people, Cnut (or Canute) is the king who tried to hold the sea back. In fact, he was demonstrating the limits of a ruler's authority to his courtiers: even a king could not command the waves to roll back. Son of the wonderfully named Svein Forkbeard, Cnut conquered England in 1016 and later ruled Denmark and Norway. As his foreign interests frequently took him away from England, he divided the country into four earldoms – Northumbria, East Anglia, Mercia and Wessex – whose leaders ruled their territories in his absence.

Cnut left the English system of justice unchanged and married Emma, the widow of Aethelred the Unready. He promoted Christianity throughout his reign with increased links to Rome and gave gifts and land to many religious foundations.

Although he could be brutal, he brought England almost twenty years of peace and stability, and was renowned as an able and just ruler.

980   1000   1020

The Battle of Hastings

The Battle of Hastings in 1066 saw the end of Anglo-Saxon England. The Norman invasion – the last conquest experienced by the English – started a new era in British history.

The English troops, led by Harold, arrived at Hastings exhausted after defeating the king's brother Tostig and Harald Hardrada of Norway at Stamford Bridge, and by their hurried march south. Harold's sense of honour did not allow him to wait for William in London while the Norman duke destroyed English villages on his way to the city. The armies met just outside Hastings in Sussex. Although Harold had the upper hand – he was on high ground, on a hill, and his men fought with powerful axes – William's apparently endless supply of arrows threw the English ranks into chaos. The Normans faked retreats to draw their opponents off the hill, then cut through them with their cavalry.

The Bayeaux Tapestry shows the entire battle. However, it has led to some misunderstandings, including the popular belief that Harold died when an arrow pierced his eye. On closer examination, it appears that he is next to the figure with the arrow, and that the last Anglo-Saxon king was killed by a sword. Whichever way he met his death, the Normans were victorious.

William the Conqueror

William brought England into a new era of history. The illegitimate son of Duke Robert of Normandy, he was a descendant of the tenth-century Vikings who settled in Northern France and intermarried with the French – and seems to have shared some of their traits. His rule in England was characterized by the ruthlessness with which he dealt with anyone who opposed him.

After William's defeat of Harold at the battle of Hastings in 1066, he still had to deal with rebellions throughout England. There were three revolts within three years in the north and in the winter of 1069/70 he burnt and killed his way through this part of the country – an event known as the Harrying of the North. Castles were built as a reminder of his might as a king and warrior and by 1070, only three years after the Norman invasion, the conquest of England was complete. William invaded Scotland in 1072 and led his troops into Wales in 1081.

To assert his authority, William transferred land that had belonged to the English to his followers. He ruled with a firm and determined hand and, as a result, England was stable and totally under his control.

The Tower of London

The Tower of London was the ultimate monument to the Norman Conquest. There was no mistaking the permanence of its huge stone keep, the White Tower, and it was clear that the Normans were here to stay. Construction started soon after 1066 when William built three strongholds at the corners of pre-existing Roman walls – the White Tower, in the south-east, was begun in about 1078 but not completed for at least another twenty years, and was the epitome of the Norman castles that by then were seen throughout England. It was four storeys high, with the entrance on the first floor to protect it from battering rams.

The Tower remained London's principal fortress and grew along with the importance of the city. Most monarchs added their own touches, especially Edward I, another great castle builder, who built the Beauchamp Tower, but the major work was completed by the late thirteenth century when two surrounding walls were built. The Tower had become one of the largest and best defended of all Europe's fortresses – and was also regularly occupied as a royal residence until the reign of Charles I.

Not everyone shared their rulers' appreciation of the Tower. Despite the multitude of uses it has had, it is probably best known for its Traitor's Gate, which gave access to the moat from the Thames, its dungeons, and as the place where opponents of the crown were imprisoned and often executed. On a lighter note, it has also contained royal menageries and still holds the Crown Jewels.

The Domesday Book

The name suggests a morbid document predicting the end of the world, but the *Domesday Book* was actually a survey of three areas: landholding, taxation and liability for military service. It was commissioned by William the Conqueror at his Christmas Court at Gloucester in 1085/6 and in 1086 all England was surveyed. Local officials recorded landholders, the size and value of their estates, and the number of peasants, ploughs, mills, woods and churches, both in 1086 and during the reign of Edward the Confessor, the last Saxon king before Harold.

It is now thought that the book was never fully completed as originally conceived. The *Domesday Book* is really a whole collection of texts at various stages of completion including *Great Domesday* which records all England south of the Tee and Ribble rivers, with the exception of Norfolk, Suffolk and Essex which are in *Little Domesday*. This contains much more detail than its counterpart, and is perhaps a draft for a final condensed version.

The survey was already being called 'Domesday Book' by the late twelfth century and was used to settle disputes about land throughout the Middle Ages.

Despite its superb potential as a record of landscape and agriculture in eleventh-century England, its formulaic entries and complicated use of obscure units of measurement – woodland is sometimes so many pigs – make it difficult to decipher. In addition, information was often collected haphazardly so there is no continuous style or level of accuracy. Mick says looking at the *Domesday Book* is like looking at the past after three glasses of Southern Comfort. Nevertheless, it remains the first port of call for all students of medieval history.

MUCH WENLOCK
SHROPSHIRE

SERIES 1
Broadcast
30 January 1994

Tony with medieval remains, doing one of his early pieces to camera.

Much Wenlock in Shropshire is a small market town close to the Welsh Borders. It became an important religious centre in the seventh century when St Mildburga founded a convent there, and the site of her building remained a monastic precinct for more than 400 years – the remains of an eleventh-century Cluniac priory are still visible. But when did Much Wenlock become a bustling medieval town? Gerry Bowden asked *Time Team* to investigate foundations in his garden that might be linked with this development.

On Day One, while Carenza tackled old maps of the town to try and decipher how it had developed, Oliver Butler used the radar scanner to survey Mr Bowden's garden and try to locate what might have been a large masonry wall foundation not far under the surface. The line of the boundary between the properties may follow an old boundary ditch. Phil opened Trench One over it in Mr Laws' garden next door. Meanwhile Mick went to the house belonging to Mrs Gibson, Mr Bowden's other neighbour, to see if he could find clues to any earlier buildings. He decided to call in Dan Miles to dendro-date a wooden Samson post, and identified two stone arches in the living room as medieval: they would have functioned as a double doorway into the service part of the house.

Mick and Tony climbed to the top of the church tower where it was possible to see how the town had developed outside the precincts of the priory. The ends of the gardens in the area the Team was investigating formed a definite straight boundary, suggesting that the houses and gardens may have been laid out in a block. Could they be part of a planned Norman town outside the priory?

At the start of Day Two the radar results appeared to show walls under Mr Bowden's back garden and Trench Two was opened. Dr Mark Horton, a local archaeologist, explained that the Anglo-Saxon monastic precinct had been bigger than the Norman priory precinct and that a piece of its land had been divided off, probably in 1080 when the Cluniac priory was founded. This may well have coincided with the laying out of a new town. The building that the masonry wall formed part of would have fronted on to the market place opposite the gates of the priory. Documents relating to the town suggest that by 1247 it was large enough to have achieved borough status: eight freemen and thirty-nine burgesses

Durham Cathedral

The cathedral at Durham is unlike any other in Britain. Not only was it a great centre of the Northumbrian Church, but its imposing architecture and domineering position on a bend in the River Wear made it a potent symbol of English authority and power to Scottish intruders.

It replaced a tenth-century church and was built to a plan by Bishop William of Calais. Work on this Norman masterpiece began in 1093 and continued for forty years. The ultimate example of early Norman architecture, it has vaulted roofs and pillars 9 metres (30 feet) high and 2 metres (7 feet) across which are decorated with zig-zags, spirals and straight grooves.

The cathedral houses the tomb of St Cuthbert whose first resting place on Lindisfarne was so troubled by Viking invaders. However, Durham Cathedral was not impenetrable: Henry VIII took many of its treasures in the sixteenth century. Today it is a fine example of ecclesiastical power at its height.

lived there. A cobbled courtyard and small pieces of medieval pottery were uncovered in Trench Two. Some of the cobbles were removed and revealed an area of rubble infill, but there was no sign of the wall indicated by the radar scan.

Robin gets his hands on the documents.

By Day Three Mick concluded that the Team was looking for the wall in the wrong place. Measuring back from the arches in Mrs Gibson's living room suggested the walls should be closer to the house. Also, two lines on the wall of Mrs Gibson's house showing where the roof had been indicated that the main body of the medieval structure was in her garden. The position of the building and its size led Mick to suggest that it may have been an aisled hall owned by the priory and used for important visitors.

Phil uncovered the boundary ditch in Trench One and found pottery that dated it to the twelfth century – which means the town was probably laid out then. Meanwhile, in Mr Bowden's back garden, Trench Two had revealed that the cobbled courtyard was outside the medieval aisled hall and had been laid over an area of rubble that filled in an old well. The final piece of exciting evidence was the date of the Samson post – somewhere between 1254 and 1299. It is known that Henry III visited the priory and it was conjectured that some of his entourage may have stayed in the hall.

In three days, *Time Team* discovered that soon after the Cluniac priory was established in 1080 a planned development grew up outside its gates, by the market-place, and that this enabled what had been a small Saxon settlement to grow into a thriving medieval market town.

Henry II

Henry II, the first Plantagenet ruler of England, was the first monarch in over a hundred years to become the country's king without dispute from other contenders. As a result, he was able to rebuild the power of the crown after it had been weakened by the civil war between his predecessors Stephen and Matilda. He reformed English law, and created a royal bureaucracy.

Born in France, Henry inherited Anjou and Normandy from his father, Geoffrey Plantagenet, Count of Anjou, and gained Aquitaine through marriage to Eleanor. He was made heir to the English throne in 1153 and became king the following year. After his invasion of Ireland in 1171 most of its kings recognized him as their overlord. His empire spread across two-thirds of France – he spent twenty-one years there during his thirty-five-year reign – and he was renowned across Europe as one of the most powerful rulers of his day.

Despite these achievements, his four sons plotted against him throughout his life. Henry was also plagued by opposition from Thomas Becket. Although it is not known whether he intended to have Becket killed in 1170, it was his knights who assassinated the archbishop and the king did public penance for the deed in the following year.

ASTON EYRE
SHROPSHIRE

SERIES 5
Broadcast
8 February 1998

The buildings at Aston Eyre Hall Farm in Shropshire are from different periods and include a manor house and gatehouse that date from the Middle Ages. They survive around a courtyard and Dr Mark Horton invited *Time Team* to find out when they were built and what they looked like in the medieval period.

At the start of Day One, Phil opened Trench One against the side of the manor house's main medieval hall to look for the oriel – a large conservatory-style extension – traces of which could be seen where it would have joined the house. Meanwhile, Mick organized dendrochronology – tree-ring dating – on the main timbers in the hall and gatehouse to get firm dates for the manor house. The geophysics team surveyed inside the courtyard to look for lost structures, while Stewart Ainsworth went into the surrounding field to investigate the possibility of a medieval moat around the farm. Carenza found a stone culvert that took water through the hall and opened a trench along its course. Elaborate water systems are usually found in medieval monasteries, not manor houses, so Mick decided to open another trench in the courtyard to investigate further. By the end of the day, dendrochronology had dated the gatehouse to 1350 but the medieval archaeology, hidden beneath layers of cobbles and brick floors, was proving more elusive.

On Day Two attention turned to the buildings themselves. Beric Morley, *Time Team*'s buildings expert, used rectified photography to create accurate scale drawings of each wall of the hall. From these he worked out where alterations and additions had been made to the building. He was convinced that the main hall had been built in two different phases by different lords of the manor. Out in the fields,

Is it a drain, a fountain, or what? Everybody chips in with their views.

Thomas Becket

Thomas Becket is the ultimate Christian hero: a man who stood up for his religious beliefs and, as a result, was struck down in his own cathedral. His sacrifice for his faith was soon recognized and he was canonized within three years of his murder.

Becket was appointed Chancellor of England by Henry II in 1155 and remained in the king's confidence until 1162 when Henry made him Archbishop of Canterbury. The king hoped that he would support him in his many conflicts with the Church, but Becket resigned the chancellorship and became one of Henry's most outspoken opponents.

There is no proof that Henry was directly responsible for Becket's murder. It is generally thought that the king was in France and, frustrated by his archbishop's intransigency, exclaimed: 'Who will rid me of this turbulent priest?' Four knights took him at his word and crossed the channel to Canterbury where they killed Becket in the cathedral on 29 December 1170. In the year that followed Henry did penance at Becket's shrine, which became one of medieval Christianity's principal places of pilgrimage. It was destroyed in 1538, when Henry VIII declared the saint a traitor.

Stewart found earthworks from the manor fish farm, and concluded that there had been no moat, just a series of water channels and ditches.

On Day Three Phil uncovered massive foundation stones in Trench One that would have been part of the oriel as well as pottery that suggested it dated to the thirteenth or fourteenth century. In the trench in the courtyard Carenza identified the foundations of a Victorian shed and, below this, medieval drains and culverts. At the very end of the shoot, Phil found an enigmatic feature running under the hall – a small glimpse of earlier activity at Aston Eyre – but there was no time for the Team to investigate this any further.

By piecing together evidence from the hall and gatehouse, the below-ground archaeology and documentary evidence, *Time Team* was able to unravel a complicated building sequence at Aston Eyre and reconstruct what it might have looked like in the medieval period. As Mick concluded, archaeology doesn't stop at ground level: the recording and analysing techniques it uses for excavations can also be applied to standing structures.

Aerial view of the farmhouse complex. A mini digger works its way across the lawn in a desperate search for ditches.

Richard the Lionheart

The legendary Richard the Lionheart was a courageous king who left England to reclaim the Holy Land for Christianity and who, betrayed by his evil brother John, regained his kingdom only with the help of Robin Hood. The reality is that he was very detached from England. He was born in France, spoke French and wanted to be buried in the French abbey of Fontevraud.

Richard took part in the Third Crusade but, although he gained a number of impressive victories, he also showed great brutality in his slaughter of vanquished Muslims. Although he made arrangements for England to be governed in his absence and remained in touch with his officials there, the distances involved meant that it was two months before he could react to events. The main threat to his crown came from John: when Richard was captured by Leopold, Duke of Austria, John refused to pay a ransom of 150,000 silver marks. It was paid by the king's loyal English subjects – but he only spent two months in England before leaving again, to fight the French. When he died in 1199 he had spent no more than six months in England during his ten-year reign.

Robin Hood

Together with King Arthur, Robin Hood is one England's most enduring heroes. The legend has grown and developed over the centuries. A valiant, arrow-shooting figure in his Lincoln-green tights, Robin was the best and most loyal of all Richard the Lionheart's subjects, and dedicated his life to bringing down the treacherous King John and his evil henchman, the Sheriff of Nottingham.

The story of Robin Hood was first recorded in the late fourteenth century, but it is probable that it was a bard's tale, told across the land and passed by word of mouth. Early versions focus on Robin's great skill with a bow and arrow, while later ones emphasize his superior morals and how he robbed the rich to help the poor. Our medieval ancestors were clearly content with swashbuckling adventure, and had no great need for love interest – Maid Marion does not appear until the sixteenth century.

Female skull found at Launceston

1220

1250

Magna Carta

Magna Carta was a fundamental statement of English liberties, although, ironically, it was a by-product of an attempt by barons and nobles to assert their power. John I was an unpopular and discredited king, whose heavy taxes and a long-running dispute with the pope were seen as abuses of royal power. However, he was the only surviving male Plantagenet and there was no other potential leader. John's baronial opponents took the then revolutionary step of drawing up a programme of reform and the king sealed it at Runnymede in June 1215.

Magna Carta was reissued three times and it was the final, 1225, version that included the immortal phrase, 'to no one will we sell, to no one will we deny or delay right or justice', as well as the right for free men to be judged by their peers – two concepts that have gone down in history as the first laws in the English statute book. Magna Carta also criticized the system of royal government and curbed the power of the monarchy.

Although some people have dismissed the charter as a whining grumble by thirteenth-century nobility, there is no denying its importance to the British people.

Caernarfon Castle

Caernarfon Castle, the greatest of Edward I's Welsh castles, was a physical statement by the king that the Welsh had always been part of the English kingdom and that when he defeated their leader Llywelyn Ap Gruffud in 1276/77 and 1282/83 he had merely been reclaiming his property. He backed this up by constructing the castle around the ruins of an eleventh-century one built during the initial conquest of Wales.

The King's Tower is decorated with imperial eagles, implying a similarity between Edward and the Roman emperors, and the castle walls copy the banded brickwork and polygonal towers of Constantinople, the eastern Roman imperial capital. Caernarfon's importance was also reflected in the fact that the king chose it as the birthplace of his heir, Edward II.

Although Edward created his son Prince of Wales in 1301, a title that has been bestowed on the royal heir ever since, the 'medieval' ceremony for Prince Charles's investiture was invented in 1912 for the future Edward VIII.

1260   1290   1300

Robert the Bruce

Robert the Bruce's persistent battering of the English gave him his dream – an independent Scotland – when he became its king in 1306, but it was seventeen years before the Pope acknowledged his right to the throne.

Robert had taken part in William Wallace's rebellion against the English in 1297 and, spurred on by public outrage at Wallace's execution in 1305, he led an uprising against Edward I and seized the Scottish crown in 1306. Initially, not only did he face the wrath of the English king, he also had to fight for the support of his nobles. However, their doubts soon fled when he began to exercise his superb skill as a battle chief.

Robert the Bruce's crowning glory came with his victory over Edward II at Bannockburn in 1314, when the men he was leading became the only Scottish army to defeat an English king at the head of his troops. Robert's achievements culminated in the capture of Berwick in 1316, and the English called a truce. In 1328 England recognized Scotland's independence.

HIGH WORSALL
NORTH YORKSHIRE

ERIES 5
Broadcast
March 1998

Aerial photographs of fields at High Worsall in North Yorkshire show an incredible set of earthworks surrounding a ruined church, all that is left of the medieval village. Robin Daniels, field archaeologist with Tees Archaeology invited *Time Team* to investigate the earthworks and see if we could uncover evidence of the settlement's origins and find out why it disappeared.

Stewart Ainsworth started surveying the earthworks straight away on Day One, to see how the village was planned. He identified two rows of small enclosures running along the north and south of a central open area. Each of these would have contained a house, yard and paddock and it looked as if all the enclosures had been laid out at the same time. Phil opened Trench One to try and date the houses, and soon found pottery dating from the thirteenth to the fifteenth centuries. Meanwhile the geophysics team led by John Gater produced detailed evidence of the layout of the village.

On Day Two attention turned to the central area of the village. It would have been its main thoroughfare and probably the site of the village green. The small ruined church still survives at one end and Stewart thought he had identified a possible site beyond it for the manor house. We opened a trench in this area and Stewart was proved right – a silver pin and coin suggested that a high-status house once stood on this site. In Trench One, in the row of 'ordinary' houses, Phil concluded that the buildings were made of cob – a mixture of mud and straw – and not stone. This was a common building material in the medieval period.

The eastern end of the central area contained an area of irregular earthworks which Stewart and Carenza thought could be the earliest part of the settlement. This was confirmed on Day Three when Carenza opened a trench in this area and soon found pottery from the tenth to twelfth centuries. At the end of the day Robin Bush, who had been studying historical archives in Durham, returned with an explanation for the disappearance of the village. In 1354 the lord of the manor created a deer park, and it seems likely that the villagers were moved elsewhere to make room for it.

Time Team found evidence that High Worsall was a small Saxon hamlet which had been replanned in the medieval period when new rows of houses had been laid out.

Although there are many similar deserted medieval villages in England it is rare to show their development from small hamlet to planned village by excavation.

DMVs or deserted medieval villages are one of Mick's favourite areas of study. He has spent a great deal of his life looking for them, both on the ground and in the air, and then recording them by earthwork survey. The contact with the ordinary people of the Middle Ages is what he finds so fascinating. High Worsall particularly appealed to him as it was very well preserved with all the features that should be present on such sites: evidence of houses, crofts, roads and lanes, church and manor house. Mick was very cautious about digging into such well-preserved earthworks as so many of these sites have been destroyed by ploughing in the last thirty years. However, our small research excavation helped to enable English Heritage to schedule the site as an ancient monument so that it should be preserved for future generations. For some time it had been suspected that planned 'row' villages replaced the irregular hamlets of the Saxon period. *Time Team*'s work contributed to the study of medieval settlements by finding traces of the earlier irregular Saxon settlement.

A medieval stone entrance. Each of these stones will have to be painstakingly drawn by hand.

Medieval finds from Trench One: a lead belt strap end and a lead spindle whorl.

LAUNCESTON
CORNWALL

SERIES 4
Broadcast
12 January 1997

In the thirteenth century the wealthy inhabitants of the small town of Launceston, at that time the prosperous capital of Cornwall, endowed a hospital in the fields at the edge of the parish to care for lepers. Andy Reeve, a local landowner, found skeletons while digging a water pipe in the area and asked *Time Team* to find out whether they were the remains of inmates of the medieval hospital.

Leper colonies were commonly known as lazar houses after St Lazarus, the patron saint of lepers. Leprosy was once a widespread disease and was in one form highly infectious. At the height of the disease more than 200 such colonies existed in England, twenty-seven in Cornwall alone. The early houses were chapel-like buildings with half the structure set aside for worship and half for care of the sick. As they were segregated from the town, they were often self-sufficient communities, growing their own food, looking after their ill brethren and burying their own dead. The epidemic peaked in Europe in about 1300, and a century later, it had almost disappeared except in Scandinavia. It still continues to affect people but its infectiousness has been greatly reduced.

On Day One Phil started by cleaning up the water-pipe hole – which became Trench One – in order to examine the skeletal remains that had already been exposed. Margaret Cox, *Time Team*'s expert on bones, insisted that he wore a protective suit – she intended to DNA-test the skeletons for leprosy and no modern DNA from Phil could be allowed to contaminate them. Tiny amounts of DNA can be extracted, with difficulty, from ancient bones and teeth, and analysed to reveal specific details about diseases. For instance, a sample can be tested for the presence of antibodies specific to leprosy. However our worries about contamination of the graveyard bones later proved to be justified: it made it impossible to do an accurate DNA analysis and so this information was lost to us.

Meanwhile the geophysics team set off into the fields to locate the medieval hospital and Carenza, also looking for it, opened Trench Two near the road where a fragment of wall had been found by a local builder. Robin meanwhile had located a seventeenth-century document in the possession of the Town Council of Dunheved (the original name of Launceston) which describes the thirteenth-century boundaries of the leper hospital. The document contained an extract from an earlier charter granting land to the colony. A comparison of the boundaries mentioned in the charter with those on the modern Ordnance Survey map showed that some of the features mentioned had survived, whilst others had vanished. There was enough correlation, however, to show that we were looking in the right area. However, by the end of the day, there was still no sign of the hospital – geophysics had only located geological features and nothing had been found in Trench Two.

On Day Two, Phil recorded and removed a skeleton. Margaret Cox analysed it and said that it was a woman, but there was not enough information to tell whether she was a victim of leprosy. Robin Bush suggested she might have been a criminal because the grave was near the parish boundary, a common burial place for medieval wrongdoers. County boundaries were the dumping places for the unfortunates who were not entitled to receive a Christian burial and this site, near a major crossing point of the River Thames, could be just such a site.

Trench Two, Carenza's trench, produced a modern wall, so the hospital was proving elusive. However, at the end of the day, one of the local archaeologists who were helping the Team found medieval

Prior to lifting the bones, their exact positions are drawn. Note the crossed arms that hide the turned-in hands. Clench hands like these can be a sign of leprosy.

pottery in the flowerbeds of the neighbouring sewage farm. Further research showed that no 'foreign' soil had been brought in to create the beds, so we know we had our first pieces of pottery contemporary with the lepers.

On Day Three Carenza opened Trench Three in the sewage farm and soon a wall was revealed with medieval pottery *in situ*. Then, in the afternoon, a few pieces of stonework and some cobbling – perhaps part of a yard or entranceway – were found. It seemed that *Time Team* had finally found the site of the Medieval hospital and soon found pottery and stonework that was the same date as the hospital.

Phil had excavated about five skeletons by now, although not all of them were complete. Margaret Cox examined them in detail and found possible evidence of leprosy – the skull of one of them showed some bone damage around the nose which is characteristic of the disease. There was also a scourge mark across one temple, which Margaret interpreted as the result of treating a sore or infection. Lepers would have been treated with different herbal remedies in the Middle Ages. Yarrow was a well-known balm and feverfew would have been used to reduce temperature as the name suggests. Because of the numbness of the extremities, a classic symptom of the disease, sufferers were constantly injuring their hands and feet; and these injuries would lead to secondary infection, gangrene and the loss of fingers, toes and sometimes whole limbs. The disease also caused the reabsorption of calcium in the bone, including the bony structures of the nose and mouth. This led to the destruction of the nose, palate and gums, and as well as the terrible disfigurement it caused, it meant that the lepers found it impossible to eat anything but the softest food. In some cases, a surgeon would be brought in to cut the person's head, in just the same place as on our skeleton, in order to relieve the pressure of an abscess. One intriguing question was left unanswered – how long had this woman been buried here? The acidity of the soil should have had a detrimental effect on the bone, but the skeleton was in reasonably good condition. Medieval corpses were often covered in lime, however, if they were diseased to aid decomposition, but this would have neutralized the acidity in this case. To resolve the question, a bone was

The Black Death

The Black Death caused the greatest loss of life ever seen in Britain. In just two years bubonic plague killed almost half of the population. The disease came from Europe through the ports of Dorset in June 1348, and by December of the following year it had reached most parts of the country. The speed with which it spread has led some people to think that, as well as being carried by fleas, the disease was air-borne. Although this was not the only time plague had swept across Britain, the Black Death of 1348-9 was the most devasting outbreak. It resulted in economic disaster, which contributed to changes in the English landscape.

The worst death tolls came with this first epidemic, but a series of later, smaller outbreaks weakened the people of Britain still further. However, contrary to common belief, whole villages were not wiped out – rather, some rural communities became so small that the living left their settlements to regroup with survivors elsewhere.

England did not break down because of the plague – Mick has seen places in Somerset that show no signs of the disease – and the effect the Black Death had on the economy only became visible in the 1370s. Because so many peasants had died, farming changed from crop-growing to keeping animals, which needed fewer people. Workers' wages rose until only big landowners could afford to farm their land and smaller ones moved to the newly developing towns to rebuild their lives. This encouraged the growth of cities and industry that overtook England in the centuries that followed.

Fragments of bone from a female potential victim of leprosy.

extracted for radio-carbon dating. The Team gathered at Launceston churchyard at the end of the day to rebury the skeletons there. The irony was that, if our woman had been a leper, she would never have been granted this privilege at the time of her death.

By the end of *Time Team*'s three days in Launceston we had collected enough structural evidence from the trenches in the sewage farm to locate the hospital. However, there was not enough evidence to determine whether the skeletons were victims of leprosy, medieval criminals or from later burials. As with many archaeological sites, several explanations could fit the evidence that had been uncovered and we would have to wait until after the three days for more conclusive answers.

The sample of bone taken by osteoarchaeologist Margaret Cox was sent to a radio-carbon dating laboratory in Miami, Florida. According to the lab, the skeleton from which the bone was takendated from between 1040 and 1290 AD, which means that the woman we found could well have been a resident of the thirteenth-century lazar house.

SMALLHYTHE
KENT

SERIES 6
Broadcast
7 February 1999

Five hundred years ago a dockyard on the River Rother dominated life in Smallhythe in Kent. However, the village is now 13 kilometres (8 miles) inland and the mighty river has dwindled to a small stream. Christine O'Neill, the town clerk for Tenterden in Kent, invited *Time Team* to find the evidence of the medieval dockyard.

Today the village is surrounded by green fields and our first priority was to reconstruct the layout of the medieval landscape and the course of the river. Early on Day One Stewart Ainsworth and the geophysics team – John Gater, Chris Gaffney and Sue Ovenden, who was in charge of seismics – started surveying the area.

Seismic refraction is widely used in exploration geophysics to provide information about the depth of deposits. It only has limited archaeological application because most archaeology lies too close to the ground surface. At Smallhythe the method was used to trace the old course of the river. The technique involves using a sledge hammer or a small explosive charge to emit an energy wave into the ground and then measuring how long it takes for the energy to bounce back to the surface after it hits the different layers under the ground.

In addition, Jane Siddell and Keith Wilkinson, *Time Team*'s environmental experts, began removing long cores of earth that would show which soils had been part of the earlier river bed, and palaeo-archaeologist Nigel Cameron was able to take samples from the cores to carry out diatom analysis. Diatoms are microscopic algae that live in water. They have characteristic shells which are preserved in the sediments of ditches and ponds, and these can be used to identify species that were either freshwater or marine species. Meanwhile Carenza assembled aerial photographs of the area to identify where the original floodable land might have been. Phil opened Trench One in Delph Marsh a field shaped suspiciously like a dry dock, and Trenches Two and Three, both of which had negative results, were started in the field next door to it. By the end of the day five more trenches, had been opened in Delph Marsh but there was no sign of the dockyard in any of the trenches that had been dug so far. However, Stewart and the geophysics team found interesting features in nearby fields for investigation.

On the hunt for medieval dockyards. The marked finds are mainly ship nails.

The Canterbury Tales

The *Canterbury Tales* was the first written work in which English humour dictated and enriched the stories. Geoffrey Chaucer's masterpiece also played a great part in making the English of the south-east the principal language for the literature of England.

Although we may not fully appreciate some of the jokes, the *Tales* have retained their charm over the centuries. There are twenty-four in total, all but four of them complete, and all but two in rhyming verse. The characters they portray range from a battle-worn knight talking of romantic ancient Greece to a miller with comic anecdotes of English society. Chaucer's look at medieval England is mainly based in the middle and lower classes, but he cleverly shows how they see their wealthier compatriots.

The stories are a unique reminder of the importance of pilgrimage in the Middle Ages, when Christians made long journeys to shrines as acts of penance for wrong-doing, and to ensure their place in heaven.

Chaucer himself made the pilgrimage to Becket's tomb in 1388, when he was writing his *Tales*. Unfortunately, his pilgrims never made the return journey from Canterbury: he died in 1400 without completing his work.

ships' nails and roves or washers. The nail would be hammered over the washer and the tip cut off.

On Day Two, Trench Four, in Elfwick field nearer the village, revealed a layer of fine sand below the topsoil which would have been the beach at the edge of the medieval river. Further upslope, in Trench Five, Phil found medieval ships' nails and brick rubble which Mick thought could be ships' ballast or maybe an oven. Trenches Six and Seven were opened in the field behind Smallhythe Place, which had originally been the port house, and produced evidence of metalworking, while Carenza started to clear out a pond in the fields next to the house. The pond produced nothing of interest but Trench Six was opened over a geophysical anomaly next to the pond which turned out to be heaps of nails and iron slag, probably from shipbreaking or repair. The seismic survey carried out by the geophysics team identified two medieval river channels; the shallow one, near the shore, was probably used by the medieval shipbuilders.

By Day Three Phil was sure the brick rubble in Trench Five was the remains of a kiln or furnace. This, coupled with clear indications of smithing, and ships' nails and roves – the diamond-shaped washers that are placed on the ends of nails – from Trenches Six and Seven, showed we had found evidence for the dockyard. Carenza found a line of ships' nails within a boat-shaped depression which, after further digging, took on the appearance of a small boat. A final surprise came from the geophysics team, who uncovered evidence along Smallhythe's main road of the settlement where the medieval shipwrights and labourers would have lived.

In three days *Time Team* uncovered evidence of the dockyard and found slipways and associated deposits that provide, possibly for the first time, a detailed picture of a medieval shipbuilding site alongside the River Rother.

Mick found Smallhythe really interesting because the evidence that *Time Team* uncovered for medieval shipbuilding has turned out to be very important – probably the first such evidence in the country. He was especially intrigued by the change in the landscape since the Middle Ages and found it very difficult to imagine that the green fields around the site had once been a wide estuary. Nigel Cameron's work on the diatoms showed that the water channel had been tidal in an area that is now 13 kilometres (8 miles) from the sea. In his trip in the helicopter, Mick flew as far as the coast and then followed the former outline of the estuary – now flat land with many drainage ditches. The medieval town of Rye, East Sussex, and Henry VII's Camber Castle were both formerly on the coast but are now marooned inland. It is often difficult to comprehend that the landscape is not static but constantly changing, even though it is not usually apparent over just one lifetime.

Henry V

Henry V claimed the French throne through his great-grandfather Edward III and if he had not died prematurely he would have ruled both England and France. He defeated the army of Charles VI at the battle of Agincourt in 1415, and when he married the king's daughter, Catherine of Valois, in 1420 his father-in-law recognized him as his heir.

Although Henry is said to have enjoyed a misspent youth as Prince of Wales, he nevertheless suppressed a rebellion by Owain Glyn Dwr, who led the last major Welsh rebellion from 1402 to 1408. If tales of Henry's early life are true he clearly reformed when he acceded to the English throne in 1413: he was a pious and efficient ruler who believed that his victories were based on his faith in God and ruthlessly suppressed any threat to the Catholic religion. The character portrayed in Shakespeare's *Henry V* was clearly based on the accepted reality of the day and played its part in ensuring his reputation.

Henry died from dysentery at the early age of thirty-five only weeks before Charles VI, whose death would otherwise have seen him accepted as King of France.

TEMPLECOMBE
SOMERSET

SERIES 3
Broadcast
21 January 1996

Medieval walls turning up in a Somerset back garden.

The Knights Templar were among the most famous crusaders in medieval Europe, warrior-monks whose order was founded in the twelfth century to defend the Holy Sepulchre in Jerusalem and protect pilgrims to the Holy Land from bandits. Templecombe in Somerset was one of their preceptories, where they lived and owned land, and Templecombe manor house and farm are traditionally believed to contain its remains. Geoff Wilson, the owner, invited *Time Team* to investigate.

On Day One Mick, whose specialist topic is medieval monasteries, immediately set off across the fields to investigate a bank and ditch which he thought might be the preceptory's boundary wall. Meanwhile Beric Morley, *Time Team*'s buildings expert, started to examine the seventeenth-century manor house for signs of earlier structures. He was soon interested in the kitchen area. Phil opened Trench One next to the farmhouse garden in an area traditionally thought to be the location of the Templar chapel. He began finding decorated medieval floor tiles and by the end of the day had uncovered the foundations of the chapel.

Despite this promising start, Day Two was less successful. Further trenches were opened in the manor garden to locate Mick's boundary wall but failed to do so. And although the preceptory would have contained many different buildings only Trench One had so far revealed any foundations. In addition, tree-ring dating of the beams in the kitchen showed that, like the house, they dated to the seventeenth

A beautiful house which seemed to want to hang on to its secrets.

The Battle of Agincourt

The battle of Agincourt on 25 October 1415 was a historically satisfying occasion: not only did the English beat their enemy against the odds, but their victory was immortalized by Britain's greatest playwright, William Shakespeare.

A total of 30,000 French knights faced 8,400 English archers but a combination of bad weather – successive French charges became bogged down in the mud – and the English longbow decimated the French in their heavy armour. Over 7,000 of the French were killed – the flowers of French chivalry.

Leading the English was Henry V. His portrait, with his strange Norman haircut and sensuous lips, projects the image of a shrewd man whose victory was a high point of English history. For a short time he dominated England and France and was made heir to the French throne. His heroic reputation was enhanced by his premature death from dysentery in 1422, at the age of thirty-five. Had it not been for this he would have been king of both England and France.

As part of the *Time Team* shoot at Hylton Castle near Sunderland, we saw knights in hand-to-hand combat. Even on a dry summer's day they seemed to move in a restrictive, cumbersome fashion. We also heard the heavy thunp as the arrow from a longbow hit home and it seems a mystery that anyone could think the French knights at Agincourt stood a chance. Chopping down unarmed peasants, or making dents in each other's armour, is one thing – but the long-range longbow is such a lethal weapon that using it against slow-moving knights on large horses who are wading through mud seems positively unsporting.

1420   1425   1430

This templar image of a headless figure had been deliberately hidden between the walls. It came to light after a thunderstorm brought down the wall.

century – too late for the preceptory. Mick and Carenza decided to review documentary evidence for the medieval establishment overnight, in a search for fresh clues.

Their research revealed that the Team had missed a crucial piece of historical evidence: the nineteenth-century tithe map of the village showed the boundaries of the medieval preceptory – further north than most of the existing trenches. On Day Three the geophysics team led by John Gater started surveying the area and Phil opened a new trench. Carenza, Phil and even Mick were soon all digging hard and the trench began to produce medieval pottery. Finally, the boundary wall of the preceptory appeared. At the very end of the day, Carenza identified more of the wall in the farmyard, still standing but buried under a build-up of plough soil.

Time Team found remains from the Templar chapel and was able to discover the extent of the preceptory. Contrary to tradition, it was not located below the seventeenth-century manor house but was further to the north of it.

PLYMPTON
DEVON

SERIES 6
Broadcast
31 January 1999

A quiet Devon village waits to be Time Teamed.

Plympton is a small offshoot of Plymouth, its main street backed by a public park that contains a medieval castle motte. A group of local residents invited *Time Team* to investigate unusual features in their houses, and find evidence of the park's origins.

Although the frontages of the buildings on the main street look post-medieval Mick and Stewart Ainsworth realized that maps showed Plympton to have the classic layout of a medieval planned village. At the start of Day One they set off for Tan Cottage, one of the houses on the street, which has features like fireplaces that suggest it was once part of a more important building. Closer investigation revealed impressive walls and a large chimney and fireplace and Beric Morley, *Time Team*'s buildings expert, was sure these were once part of a very large medieval building. David and Sally Sheppard, Tan Cottage's owners, were renovating the house and garden and were happy to let Phil begin demolishing an outhouse to create room for a trench. We opened another trench in the next-door garden to see how far the medieval building had extended. In the park, the geophysics team and an earthwork survey by Stewart Ainsworth revealed a series of features and Trench Two was inserted to investigate.

By Day Two Carenza and Beric had produced amazing results by knocking on doors in the main street and looking at people's attics and cellars. They found an extremely rare arch-braced medieval roof in one house and organized tree-ring dating to find out how old it was. In Tan Cottage garden, Phil successfully demolished the outhouse, revealing fine medieval masonry. A further trench was opened and soon produced many medieval finds including part of a decorated glass goblet and a gold pin. Meanwhile, the Team unearthed enough evidence in the park to confirm the existence of a medieval field system of banks and lynchets – terraces formed by ploughing.

On Day Three attention turned to the cellar of the rectory, which is also on Plympton's main street. Another session of demolition – this time of walls – revealed that the cellar had once been at street level, and that the road had built up since the medieval period. Walls were emerging in the trench in Tan Cottage garden and these, together with the evidence from the other houses in the street, showed how the medieval town had been laid out.

Time Team's investigations made it clear that medieval features survive behind the frontages of later buildings. We also discovered that the park had been an open area used by the medieval inhabitants of Plympton to grow crops.

This aerial view of Plympton reveals the medieval layout of the village.

A braced medieval roof discovered on Day Two. It is amazing what some people have hidden in their attics!

William Caxton

When William Caxton established the first successful printing press in England in 1476 it was a momentous event. The transition from monks laboriously copying out texts to reproducing hundreds of copies mechanically was revolutionary. It transformed the way knowledge spread and effectively took the monopoly on communication out of the hands of the Church.

Caxton trained in the Low Countries where he produced the first printed book in English, his translation of *Le Receuil des histoires de Troye*, in 1475. He built his first press at Westminster three years later. Here he printed almost a hundred books including *The Canterbury Tales* and Sir Thomas Malory's *Morte d'Arthur*. They covered a huge range of topics from romantic or humorous stories to works on religion and art. Caxton introduced regular spelling and had an effect on writing style.

His use of pieces of wood carved into letters and numbers, woodcuts and black ink has led to criticisms that his texts are ugly and inaccurate. However, it was Caxton who made it possible to spread information throughout English society and his press remained invaluable for the next 400 years.

COVENTRY
WEST MIDLANDS

SERIES 7
To be broadcast in
early 2000

This medieval tile is
a hint of Coventry's
wonderful past.

Coventry is in the West Midlands about 24 kilometres (15 miles) east of Birmingham. At its centre stands the new cathedral which replaced one destroyed by bombing in the Second World War. But in the Middle Ages there had been yet another, monastic, cathedral under the present precinct: St Mary's, a massive building that was destroyed by Henry VIII in the sixteenth century. Its east and west ends can still be seen, but the layout of its central portion is conjectural. Coventry City Council invited *Time Team* to excavate this area in advance of development – a last chance to reconstruct the plan of the medieval cathedral.

The geophysics team set to work on the morning of Day One, but the many cables and pipes that cut across the site interfered with their survey. The Team therefore based the location of the first three trenches on a conjectural plan of the cathedral supplied by Richard Morris, *Time Team*'s buildings expert. Carenza opened Trench One across the north wall in the area of the chapter house – the most important building in a monastery after the church. It was the community's meeting place and priors and abbots were often buried there, in the belief that their spiritual presence would guide the monks. Almost immediately, the trench revealed decorated tiles and painted window glass. In Trench Two, Phil uncovered the remains of a large shaft base just under the surface.

On Day Two Carenza continued her search of the chapter house. Although an earlier excavation had shown a doorway *in situ* there was no sign of this, but other finds included a piece of glass still with part of its lead framework, and a carved rose from a ceiling boss. It was possible to see the imprints of floor tiles in the mortar floor. Excavation continued in Trench Two but there was too much rubble and masonry to locate the floor level on Day Two. A small exploratory Trench Three was opened by Phil under the position of the the the central tower. He soon revealed the first massive crossing pier which was 3 to 4 metres (10 to 13 feet) in diameter. Part of the adjoining wall survived, with plaster and some paint. Tony had earlier visited Lichfield Cathedral, Coventry's sister cathedral, to compare it with St Mary's, and revealed that the base of the pier was slightly smaller than the ones he had seen there. Phil and his diggers also found pieces of broken masonry which Mick believed to be Norman. As the

Richard III

Possibly one of the most controversial characters in British history, Richard III was branded as evil personified by Shakespeare, who depicted him as an ugly, hunched figure. Yet he has supporters, a society dedicated to clearing the name of the last Yorkist king.

Richard was the only surviving brother of Edward IV – their youngest brother, Clarence, was reputedly drowned in a butt of malmsey in the Tower – and although he had always been ambitious, it is by no means certain that he purposefully set out to gain the crown. Soon after Edward's death in 1483 there were rumours that his sons – Edward V, the rightful heir to the throne, and the Duke of York – were illegitimate and, for this reason, Richard became king in 1483.

He was a capable ruler but his nephews were never seen again and the suspicion that he was involved in their death undermined his popularity. Although his complicity can never be proved, it seems that his contemporaries were unsure of his innocence: Henry VII faced very little resistance after his victory over Richard at Bosworth in 1485.

ships' nail found
at smallhythe

1480   1485   1490

vast quantities of rubble and pipes were still frustrating John Gater – he had been unable to find any of the piers or walls the diggers had found – they decided to use ground-penetrating radar on the floor of the chapter house to see if they could locate any graves.

At the start of Day Three Phil opened Trench Four to the east of Trench Three to try to locate another pier – finding this would enable the Team to work out which corner of the crossing had already been found. Modern drains, along with an electricity cable and two manholes, caused problems. In the chapter house Carenza located the doorway from the earlier excavation but the decorative stone had been removed. Geophysics showed up two anomalies that were possibly graves and Carenza put in a sondage – a deep trial trench – to investigate one of them and soon started to find human bones. By the end of Day Three she had found a stone-lined grave. Meanwhile, Phil had found a second pier in Trench Four, again of huge dimensions, and was confident that it formed part of the crossing. This meant the nave of the cathedral was shorter than predicted – nine bays rather than ten – and that the chancel was longer, with the crossing aligned on the chapter-house wall. In Trench Two Mick Worthington had at last reached the medieval floor where one green tile remained *in situ*.

In three days *Time Team* found the exact location of the crossing and established that it was Norman with later Gothic additions to the east and west ends. The positioning of the piers indicated it would have been too small to support a stone spire and that the cathedral probably had a wooden one. Its walls were whitewashed in places and the floor was covered with green tiles.

The stone-lined grave in the chapter house had to be thoroughly excavated and, for the first time ever on a *Time Team* programme, a group of diggers stayed on to do this. The grave contained the skeleton of a prior who was shown by analysis to have been overweight and suffering from diabetes. A piece of bone was sent to be radiocarbon-dated so that the Team could establish the identity of the prior.

An urban site rich in archaeology, both Henry VIII and German bombers attempted to destroy it.

Henry VIII

Henry VIII, the second of the Tudor kings, was the first English monarch to insist on being called 'your Majesty'. Although he is generally portrayed as stout and non-athletic, in his younger years he was fit and healthy with great vitality. He waged costly wars with France in his determination to regain the regions England had lost in the fifteenth century, and a campaign in Scotland ended in 1542 at Solway Moss, where James V was killed, leaving his six-day-old daughter as Mary Queen of Scots.

Henry wanted to marry Anne Boleyn, already pregnant and possibly about to provide him with his greatly desired son and heir, and in 1534, when the Pope refused to grant him a divorce from his first wife, Catherine of Aragon, he established the Church of England with the monarch as its supreme head. Anne was beheaded, ostensibly for adultery, in 1536, and Henry went on to marry four more wives.

Between 1536 and 1539 he dissolved the English and Welsh monasteries, confiscating their lands and granting them to his supporters. It is ironic that some twenty-five years earlier the Pope had named him 'Defender of the Faith', for *The Defence of the Seven Sacraments* – a rebuttal of Martin Luther's heresy.

Tudor bricks found at Richmond

1500   1505   1510

RICHMOND
SURREY

SERIES 5
Broadcast
4 January 1998

Lying next to the River Thames in Greater London, Richmond was once the site of a royal palace, originally called Shene Palace. It was essentially a brick building – one of the first brick-built palaces in England – with only door and window frames in stone. Henry VIII added a blue decorative frieze, a reminder of the opulence of what would have been one of the greatest palaces of its day. John Cloake, a local historian, invited *Time Team* to investigate the exact location of the palace's privy lodgings – the royal private apartments. We would use his research work as well as geophysics and do a small amount of excavation in the immaculate lawns of the house now built on the site.

This wonderful 'back garden' was slightly larger than those on our usual sites and hid a famous palace.

The geophysics team were up at the crack of dawn on Day One. Their initial results did not give a very clear picture but there were signs of a wall associated with a ditch near the Thames in the area where John Cloake was expecting to find the south wall of the lodgings. We opened Trench One and excavation soon revealed a brick wall. After taking some measurements Dr Simon Thurley, an expert on palaces, pronounced it to be Tudor. Mick and Phil had a great time fitting together the medieval stonework that emerged from the trench like a Tudor Lego set. They also found pieces of window mullions, fragments of painted glass and the lead strips that held the glass in place.

Phil was called away to wade into the river to identify a piece of stonework that the local archaeology society had found some years earlier. It turned out to be part of a window and may have been dropped from a barge when the palace was being dismantled and the stonework taken away to be reused elsewhere – a common practice in the past. The geophysics team came across another possible wall on the croquet lawn, unfortunately closer to the modern house than where John Cloake had estimated the north wall should be. Phil decided to investigate it by excavation and Phil opened Trench Two. He found a wall

The Reformation

The establishment of the Church of England with Henry VIII at its head was one of the most fundamental changes in British history. The path of this religious revolution was smoothed by Thomas Cromwell, who became Henry's deputy in the Church in 1535. He systematically created a dictatorship, spread anti-Catholic rumours and sent officials to 'dig up the dirt' on the monasteries, as Mick puts it. Many sixteenth-century monks were lax in their observation of their vows and, with a little artistic licence, Cromwell had his evidence of corruption. He convinced the Church of this in 1536 and, with its backing, started to destroy Christian institutions that had been part of the English landscape for over 700 years.

Henry was half-hearted about the Reformation and it was only when his son Edward VI came to power that Protestantism was fully established. The combination of the king's needs and Cromwell's efficiency dealt almost a permanent blow to the Catholic Church in England.

but it was too narrow to be load-bearing. However, Stewart Ainsworth found a 1638 drawing of the palace that showed porches along its front. Had *Time Team* found a porch wall?

On Day Two the Team debated where the next trench should go. Geophysics showed a possible wall close to the house, but its position would make the porch too wide to be believable, so we decided to extend Trench One. Meanwhile, Phil had found another wall in Trench Two, three times thicker than the first one with signs of an interior floor. The Team were convinced that this must be the north wall of the privy lodgings. Mick and Tony went up in a crane for an aerial view of the layout of the palace. Visitors would have walked through the surviving archway into a courtyard, and through a middle gate into another courtyard with a fountain in the centre. They would then cross a footbridge over the moat to reach the privy lodgings.

Torrential rain by lunch time meant the trenches were rapidly filling with water. Spirits fell when Phil's wall turned out to be relatively modern, but revived when he pointed out there was a medieval wall underneath it. He was delighted to uncover the neck of a seventeenth-century bellarmine jug which might have been smashed by workmen dismantling the palace. We put in Trench Three over an area of high resistance, perhaps the north-west tower of the privy lodgings, and almost immediately a complex mass of stonework and brick was uncovered. It included a terracotta ornament from the front of the building dating from 1520 and a similar ornament of acanthus leaves, which was probably part of an original frieze on the front of the lodgings.

On the morning of Day Three all the Team reassessed the evidence from all the trenches. The wall in Trench One was very deep because of the cellars that had extended under the privy lodgings. The trench was becoming dangerous and was closed down. Phil finally established the width of the north wall in Trench Two and in Trench Three Mick Worthington was still searching for the turn into the west wall at the corner of the building. We opened Trench Four nearby and eventually unearthed a large medieval wall beneath modern rubble. The structure in Trench Three was indeed the north-west tower of the privy lodgings but had undergone many alterations.

By the end of three days *Time Team* had located three of the outer four walls of the privy lodgings and determined the building's exact position.

*regular find
Time Team
enches, a
llarmine jug.*

St Thomas More

Thomas More is probably one of the most famous examples of an individual trapped between personal conscience and royal power. He could not bring himself to abandon the Pope and support Henry VIII's break with the Catholic Church and, as a result, was executed on 6 July 1535.

A scholar and follower of the humanist movement, he described his philosophy in *Utopia*, a detailed description of an ideal society. He also wrote most of Henry's *The Defence of the Seven Sacraments*, the tract against Protestantism that gained the king his title 'Defender of the Faith'.

As Lord Chancellor – he was appointed to the post in 1529 – More refused to agree to Henry divorcing Catherine of Aragon. Although More resigned the chancellorship in 1532, the king could not allow a public display of disobedience and in 1534 summoned him to swear an oath recognizing Elizabeth, Anne Boleyn's daughter, as the rightful heir to the throne in place of her older sister Mary. More refused and was imprisoned in the Tower. At his trial, aware that he was doomed, he spoke out against Henry and was sentenced to death.

Thomas More, who is now seen as one of the great champions of the Catholic Church in England, was made a saint in 1935 – 400 years after his execution.

Mary Queen of Scots

Mary, who became Queen of Scotland when she was just six days old, was in line to be Queen of France at sixteen when she married the French dauphin – and the Catholic world saw her as the true ruler of England. The potential for creating a hugely powerful dynasty seemed close at hand, but she did not achieve her ambitions.

She lost the opportunity to secure the French throne when her husband died before she had produced a child, but returned to Scotland determined to gain the English one. Here she married her cousin Henry Stewart, Earl of Darnley, but the marriage was a disaster and ended when her husband was murdered in 1567. Mary was accused of being involved in his killing – and married his murderer, the Earl of Bothwell, within three months of Darnley's death. She abdicated soon afterwards and was imprisoned in Lochleven Castle.

She turned to Elizabeth for asylum from her Scottish enemies but the English queen could not allow a rival claimant to her throne go free, and kept her captive for twenty years. Mary was always the focus of plots by English Catholics and was eventually executed at Fotheringay Castle on 8 February 1587.

Elizabeth I

It is easy to picture the defiant, pale-faced queen standing on the shores of Tilbury as the Spanish Armada approached England in 1588, exclaiming: 'I know I have the body of a weak and feeble woman, but I have the heart and stomach of a king, and a king of England too…' She was showing the world that she could rule like a king and should be treated as such.

Despite her criticisms of her body, Elizabeth had her vanities. Five years after her coronation in 1558 she declared that unofficial images of her were illegal; and in 1596 she ordered the destruction of all 'unseemly' portraits. These proclamations led to the familiar, formal portrait of the queen, with pale features, red hair filled with diamonds and a large ruff around her neck. Vanity was not her only weakness and she was also capable of jealousy: when Sir Walter Raleigh secretly married Elizabeth Throckmorton, a maid of honour at the court, she imprisoned him in the Tower.

Elizabeth could be ruthlessly efficient. When Robert Devereux, the Earl of Essex, once her favourite, attempted to overthrow the government he was arrested for treason and executed.

Although she failed to marry and produce an heir, the Virgin Queen was one of England's most successful monarchs. She preserved and strengthened the concept of an independent nation, expanded its dominions throughout the world and defended it against Spain.

Sir Walter Raleigh

A courtier, writer and adventurer, Walter Raleigh was one of Elizabeth I's favourites. He was knighted in 1584 and over the following three years made several abortive attempts to colonize North America in her honour – the state of Virginia is named after the Virgin Queen. Famously, he is credited with introducing the potato to Europe and popularizing tobacco. Despite his lack of success in the New World, Raleigh's popularity with the queen continued until 1591, when his secret marriage to Elizabeth Throckmorton, one of her maids of honour, was revealed and he was imprisoned in the Tower of London. Four years later he led an expedition to South America to find the fabled El Dorado, and returned with specimens containing gold.

When Elizabeth's successor, James I, acceded to the throne in 1603 Raleigh's aggression towards Spain brought him into conflict with the king. He was found guilty of treason, on somewhat insufficient evidence, and sent to the Tower, where he lived under the constant shadow of death with his wife and son until 1616. In 1617 he was released to search for gold along the Orinoco in South America. The expedition was a failure and when Raleigh returned to London he was executed in 1618 under the original sentence of treason that had been passed fifteen years earlier.

William Shakespeare

Mick and I regard Shakespeare as a fellow Midlander. He produced thirty-eight plays, 154 sonnets and two long poems and is Britain's pre-eminent writer. He reflected the concerns and beliefs of the Tudor period which, after the constraints of the Middle Ages, was a time of individualism and exploration.

Time Team has occasionally been asked to investigate the origins of Shakespeare's family – for example, to locate a burial that might be connected with him – but the search for detailed facts about his past seems to be out of proportion to the genius in his writing.

With works like *Hamlet*, *Othello*, *Macbeth* and *King Lear*, he entered areas of human psychology hitherto unexplored in popular drama. And although his historic plays may be only loosely based on fact, the details of the Tudor view of life that they reveal – the names of flowers and medicines, the business of seamanship, the nature of country manners, make them a valuable source of material for the period.

He died on 23 April 1616, his birthday. He left the world the legacy of his plays, Stratford-upon-Avon with a rich source of tourist income and a note to archaeologists who might be contemplating an excavation at his burial site. His epitaph begins: 'Good friend for Jesus sake forbeare to dig of the dust enclosed heare.'

1560   1565   1570

HYLTON CASTLE
SUNDERLAND

SERIES 2
Broadcast
15 February 1995

The standing remains of a medieval castle in the middle of a modern housing estate.

Lying in the middle of a group of Sunderland housing estates, the gatehouse of Hylton Castle towers above the remains of its park. The local community asked *Time Team* to undertake an archaeological survey so that they could develop the castle and its park as a local amenity in keeping with the past history of the site. The castle was built by Baron William de Hylton in the second half of the fourteenth century – could we locate the buildings that would have surrounded it?

The geophysics team surveyed the area to the east of the castle at the start of Day One and found three major anomalies that might represent buildings. The Team decided to dig a series of evaluation trenches across these to see whether any structures remained and what condition they were in. Meanwhile, Stewart Ainsworth and Carenza surveyed earthworks in the park and spotted parch marks from the roof of the castle, confirming some of the geophysics results. Robin Bush found a description of the buildings that made up the castle when Baron William died. These included a hall, four chambers, a chapel, two barns, a kitchen and 'a house constructed of stone called the gatehouse'.

At the start of Day Two the first of the evaluation trenches, Trench One, wasn't producing any convincing evidence of walls, but seemed to contain a mixture of demolition rubble and natural stone which had been used as a foundation. However, we uncovered some solid stonework in Trench Two and pieces of tile started to appear. As the day wore on a clear section of wall was revealed with plaster decoration and prestigious Flemish floor tiles contemporary with Baron William. This was probably his guest hall.

In the park Stewart found a set of terraces that appeared to be aligned on a building other than the castle and could belong to an Elizabethan house built about 150 years later. We put in a trench to locate the remains of the house and found an area of badly damaged masonry. This was difficult to interpret but was associated with pottery and coins from the Elizabethan period.

Throughout Day Three the Team continued to record the stonework and other remains that had been found in the trenches and Stewart mapped many of the garden features in order to produce a survey that would form the basis of the community's redevelopment plan.

Sir Francis Drake

Elizabeth I's reign was the age of discovery and on 13 December 1577 Francis Drake, then in his early thirties, sailed west to the Pacific in search of an undiscovered continent. He had suggested the expedition to the queen, who had given it her blessing, and it was understood that if he met Spanish ships laden with gold he could relieve them of their burden.

His ship, the *Pelican* (renamed the *Golden Hind* during the voyage) passed the Strait of Magellan, the southern tip of the Americas, in 1578, and in June 1579 he arrived at what is thought to be California and annexed it to the English crown. The Spanish ships he captured included the *Acapulco* galleon, which produced 36 kilograms (80 pounds) of gold, 26 tonnes of silver and thirteen chests filled with gems.

Drake struck out across the Pacific and reached the Spice Islands where he added cloves – which were of great value in England – to his cargo. He rounded the Cape of Good Hope at the tip of Africa in June 1580 and reached England in September, thirty-three months after he had set off on his voyage. Although he had not found the undiscovered continent, he received a hero's welcome: he had become the first Englishman to sail around the world, and Elizabeth knighted him on the deck of the *Golden Hind* as a tribute to his achievement.

Bronze cannon found at Teignmouth

1580

In three days *Time Team* produced the first solid evidence of the impressive guest hall Baron William built as part of his castle 600 years ago as well as evidence for other buildings, some contemporary with Baron William, some later. English Heritage regarded the new areas of medieval buildings and gardens that we uncovered as important enough to be scheduled as an ancient monument. Later work showed that the castle had not been purely defensive. The gardens we discovered were associated with various phases of the buildings and the siting of the castle was such that it was meant to be looked at from the garden area – it must have appeared as a most prestigious and grand building.

Fragments of medieval tiles enabled some of the detail to be added to Victor's reconstruction.

The Spanish Armada

In July 1588 Philip II of Spain ordered a huge invasion fleet of 130 warships to sail to the Straits of Dover in an attempt to overthrow the Protestant Elizabeth I and seize the English throne. It was a force to be reckoned with, and if the Spaniards had reached England, Britain's history could have been very different.

Although the English had only thirty-four warships and 170 private vessels, they had bigger, better guns and Lord Effingham, commander of the fleet, made good use of these and the quicker, more agile, English ships. After a battle at Gravelines in northern France on 29 July the Spanish escaped around the north of Scotland and west coast of Ireland.

They were pursued by the English and suffered storms and shipwreck. Thirty Spanish ships were lost during the retreat and this, coupled with losses during battle, meant that only two-thirds of the mighty force that had embarked on the mission returned to Spain.

TEIGNMOUTH
DEVON

SERIES 3
Broadcast
28 January 1996

At the end of the sixteenth century Teignmouth, now a seaside town on the south Devon coast, was a small port with trading links as far afield as the Mediterranean and under threat of attack by the Spanish Armada. In 1975 a local boy, Simon Burton, found a seventeenth-century bronze cannon in the harbour while he was out fishing. Subsequently local enthusiasts found a shipwreck nearby. They invited *Time Team* to Teignmouth to help relocate, survey and identify the wreck which was now threatened by seasonal storms. It would be the Team's first underwater archaeological investigation.

Professor Aston happily at work on some 'regressive' map analysis.

On Day One our land base was established in the Royal Teignmouth Yacht Club. Out at sea the diving support vessel, the *Terschelling*, was to be the diving platform, and would also operate the pumps that would remove the sand covering the wreck. The first priority was to locate the site of the wreck and so we surveyed the seabed with sonar and a floating magnetometer that would track down any iron remains. The survey was unsuccessful and the search was continued by divers on Day Two. Meanwhile, the land-based team Mick Aston and Robin Bush attempted to identify a monograph and coat of arms on the cannon with the help of documents. Mick investigated the topography of Teignmouth and used old maps and building analysis to discover the earliest part of Teignmouth. It appeared to be the quay.

With the arrival on Day Two of Chris Preece, the underwater archaeologist in charge of the divers, the diving could begin. Underwater conditions were a new experience for Phil. The sand-suckers cut visibility to below 1 metre (3 feet) in places, and removing the sand took much longer than anticipated

– as soon as it was sucked out of an area it flowed back in from the sides of the hole. By the end of the day about 1.2 metres (4 feet) of sand had been removed, but the wreck had not been uncovered.

On land Mick and Robin were making progress with the identification of the ship. One suggestion was that it may have been a Venetian galley, possibly seized by the Spanish for use in the Armada. Against this was the fact that wrecks from the Armada are well documented because a close watch was kept along the coast when invasion threatened. It is more likely that the ship sank in the middle of the night in a storm, some time just before or after the Armada. The presence of two merchant's seals among the finds from an earlier investigation of the wreck help to confirm that it was a trading vessel.

On Day Three a piece of wooden beam, complete with 'ghost nails' – concreted impressions where the nails had been – emerged from under the sand. On shore, Mick and Beric Morley, *Time Team*'s buildings expert, explored the Jolly Sailor, a public house on the Quay, which was said to be the only building to have survived a French raid in July 1690. A 'notched lap joint' in the timber tie-beam, along with the structure of the building, suggested a pre-1690 date.

Meanwhile, a more substantial piece of timber was appearing under the waters of the bay – over 6 metres (19½ feet) of the ship's stern, complete with stern post, was uncovered. The position of the timbers together implied that the ship had broken in two as it sank, and would have scattered its contents and guns over the seabed.

Time Team's efforts were rewarded by the discovery of the wreck for the next season's work by Chris Preece, and we provided useful possibilities about the ship's identity and when it sank. Our confirmation that the Jolly Sailor is a seventeenth-century building was also important in unravelling the history of the town. Our foray into underwater archaeology was an exciting learning experience. It is said to take three times as long as its dry land equivalent and both Tony and Phil found it totally exhausting.

A fragment of Venetian wood. This was something I thought we would never see, but it turned up on the last day.

Guy Fawkes

Guy, or Guido, Fawkes was a conspirator in the Gunpowder Plot to overturn Protestant rule and reinstate Catholicism in England. Its failure led to a wave of anti-Catholic feeling that was focused on Fawkes and even today his effigy is burnt to commemorate the event.

Although Guy Fawkes is the best known of the conspirators in the Plot, he was only their agent. The main culprits were Robert Catesby and other Catholic gentry who, in retaliation for the religious persecution of Catholics in the early seventeenth century, planned to blow up James I, head of the Church of England, and the members of both Houses of Parliament. They rented a cellar underneath the House and Fawkes placed the gunpowder there on 4 November 1605. Parliament reopened the following day and Guy Fawkes was poised to light the fuse that would bring down the British government. However, the conspirators had been betrayed by fellow Catholics and he – and his fellow plotters – were captured.

Guy Fawkes faced the prospect of torture in the Tower of London equably, but confessed to the Plot when he was told of the capture of his co-conspirators. He was executed at Westminster on 31 January 1606.

TO THE MOST
HIGH AND MIGHTIE
Prince, IAMES by the grace of God
King of Great Britaine, France and Ireland,
Defender of the Faith, &c.

THE TRANSLATORS OF *THE BIBLE*,
wish Grace, Mercie, and Peace, through IESVS
CHRIST *our* LORD.

Reat and manifold were the blessings (most dread Soueraigne) which Almighty GOD, the Father of all Mercies, bestowed vpon vs the people of ENGLAND, when first he sent your Maiesties Royall person to rule and raigne ouer vs. For whereas it was the expectation of many, who wished not well vnto our SION, that vpon the setting of that bright *Occidentall Starre*, Queene ELIZABETH of most happy memory, some thicke and palpable cloudes of darkenesse would so haue ouershadowed this land, that men should haue bene in doubt which way they were to walke, and that it should hardly be knowen, who was to direct the vnsetled State: the appearance of your MAIESTIE, as of the *Sunne* in his strength,

The James I Bible

For many centuries the men and women of Britain were unable to read the Bible in their own language and depended on monks and priests to interpret its Latin texts for them. So when William Tyndale translated it into English between 1523 and 1535 this was perceived as something of a revolutionary act.

Tyndale worked closely with Martin Luther in Wittenberg and his version of the Bible was printed in Germany. Although he managed to smuggle copies into England they were seized and burnt by the Church. Tyndale himself was later caught and burnt as a heretic. However, his work was not so easily suppressed and survived to be used as one of the key texts for the James I Bible.

James commissioned this at Hampton Court in 1604, on the basis that all previous versions were corrupt. The new Bible drew on material from four earlier ones including William Tyndale's and was completed in 1611. It overshadowed contemporary translations with its rich use of language and enjoyed 250 years of exclusive use as the Authorized Version of the Bible. Its texts were also used as the basis for other religious books such as the Book of Common Prayer, a key text in Protestantism.

The Pilgrim Fathers

The Pilgrim Fathers were Puritans who had suffered at the hands of James I, whose desire for religious uniformity throughout England led to widespread persecution of non-Anglican believers. Forced to flee from their homes in Nottinghamshire, they made their way to Holland but eventually decided that they wanted to preserve their English values while practising their own form of Christianity.

They decided to emigrate to America and their cause was supported by the London Company who paid for the building of their ship, the *Mayflower*. In September 1620, one hundred pilgrims sailed from Plymouth and settled on what is now Cape Cod. They called their settlement New Plymouth – a reminder of England.

Initially, the settlers did not fare well. Although they were helped by the local inhabitants they lost forty-seven people through lack of warmth and food. When reinforcements arrived aboard the *Fortune* in November 1621 it was a cause for celebration and the settlers held a feast to give thanks for their salvation. It was the first-ever Thanksgiving meal, a tradition that is firmly entrenched in modern American society.

Charles I

Although Charles I was a good and courageous man, he lacked the values that make a good monarch. His belief that the king had a divine right to rule, inherited from his father James I, was old-fashioned and unpopular in seventeenth-century society. His autocratic views led him to dissolve Parliament three times and he ruled without it for eleven years from 1629.

He was forced to reopen Parliament in 1640, but two years later he tried – and failed – to arrest five of its dissident members. Confident that many people supported his view that the institution was becoming too radical, he withdrew from London and declared war on the Parliamentarians on 22 August 1642.

In 1645 Charles was defeated at the battle of Naseby and imprisoned in Hampton Court, where he secretly plotted a Scottish invasion. He escaped briefly, but was recaptured. At his trial his refusal to plead reaffirmed that he believed himself above the law and he was condemned as a tyrant and enemy of the nation. His execution in front of the Banqueting House in Whitehall on 30 January 1649 ended almost 800 years of continuous monarchical rule in England.

The English Civil War

Charles I's insistence on ruling England to the exclusion of Parliament reached its climax in 1642 when the king attempted to arrest five dissident members of the House of Commons in January that year. He and his family were forced to leave London and seven months later, on 22 August, he raised his standard at Nottingham. Royalists (Cavaliers) and Parliamentarians (Roundheads) met two months later at the indecisive Battle of Edghill.

Charles had no standing army and had to rely on the loyalty of his subjects. However, at the battle of Marston Moor in Yorkshire in 1644, he had only 18,000 men against a combined Parliamentarian and Scottish force of 27,000. He suffered a crushing defeat but two months later his supporters were victorious at Lostwithiel in Cornwall. This Royalist victory prompted Oliver Cromwell to form the New Model Army – which decisively defeated the king at the battle of Naseby in 1645.

The king tried to negotiate peace with Parliament as a ruse to buy time while he plotted in secret to have a Scottish army invade England. But in 1648 Cromwell purged the House of Commons of dissidents and formed the Rump Parliament to ensure that a majority of members would vote to try the king. Charles was executed in early 1649. The war continued and only ended in 1651 when Charles II was defeated at the battle of Worcester.

BASING HOUSE
HAMPSHIRE

TONY'S PIECE TO CAMERA: 'Ruins are all that remain of Basing House today, but it was once one of the biggest and grandest houses in Tudor England. Henry VIII and Elizabeth I were guests here, and most famously it was under siege for two years during the Civil War before it was finally destroyed by Cromwell in 1654. But how much of the great house is still waiting to be discovered?'

PHOTO STORY
FROM SERIES 7

Passing through modern Basingstoke it is hard to believe that hidden in its suburbs is one of the most interesting grand houses of English history. Basing House today is an impressive series of earthworks that contain fragments of what was once one of the greatest houses in England: a Tudor mansion built by Sir William Paulet, first Marquis of Winchester, on the site of a Norman castle. Mary I and Philip II of Spain spent their honeymoon there in 1554 and both Henry VIII and Elizabeth I were guests at the house. Throughout the sixteenth century members of the family played a key role in the country's government. Their downfall came in the middle of the seventeenth century: the Paulets were Catholics who supported Charles I in the Civil War, and Basing was a strategically and symbolically important fortified house. It was known to contain a large arsenal and was therefore a threat the Parliamentarians had to remove.

I was keen to do a programme at Basing House because of the role it played in what is, thankfully, a rare event in British history. One of the first things I discovered as our assistant producer Ella Galinski and researcher Pippa Gilbert went about their work was the intensity of the religious feeling on both sides. The current troubles in Northern Ireland are perhaps the closest we can get to this.

The Civil War lasted from 1642 to 1646 and was civil strife of the most horrendous kind – the first time the English had gone to war against each other since the Wars of the Roses in the fifteenth century. The root of the conflict was a constitutional issue, the king claimed to rule by divine right and Parliament believed it had rights and privileges that were independent of the Crown.

When Charles acceded to the throne in 1625 he inherited a country where anti-Catholic feeling was rife. Ever since the Armada in 1588 the public had feared invasion by Catholic Spain or France. Matters were made worse by the Gunpowder Plot of 1605 – the conspiracy to blow up the Houses of Parliament and inspire a Catholic uprising; and in 1641, a year before the outbreak of the war, news of an Irish rebellion against English and Scottish colonizers reached London, accompanied by tales of Protestants being massacred.

From the start of his reign Charles had clashed with Parliament which rejected his demands for funds to wage wars. The flashpoint came in 1642 when he entered the House of Commons and attempted to arrest five of its members. War became inevitable and the king fled north to rally his followers. The first major battle was fought on 23 October at Edgehill in Warwickshire, between over 13,000 Royalists and 12,000 Parliamentarians. Although the outcome was indecisive, Oliver Cromwell learnt valuable lessons that led to the formation of the New Model Army which eventually defeated the king at Naseby in Leicestershire in 1645.

On Day One, however, we were intent on the archaeology. Alan Turton, *Time Team*'s expert on the Civil War, was hopeful that some buildings from the time of the Parliamentary attack on the house

asingstoke's ery own Tudor arthwork and ivil War attlefield. he 'mansion' renches are to he lower left.

had survived, undamaged by the later canal. The earthworks were vast – designed to resist attack – and Alan pointed out the skill with which the ramparts had been constructed. Trench One went in where brickwork remains were visible on the surface of the earthworks and we soon began to find more of the brick structure with some plaster still attached to the walls.

A survey by the geophysics team, led by John Gater, of what we were now calling the 'mansion field' appeared to show vague traces of a building. The sixth Marquis of Winchester had built a new, but less elaborate, house towards the end of the seventeenth century and archivist Caroline Wilson showed us two recently discovered maps of this later mansion. Drawn in about 1730, they are the first documentary evidence of its existence. This Stuart house in the 'mansion field' became our second target. Trenches Two and Three were opened and soon began to reveal fragments of brick and seventeenth-century pottery.

The exact position of the Stuart mansion was unclear but the brick wall that surrounds the site, dividing the field from the road, provided Stewart Ainsworth with clues to its possible entrance. Two sets of brick piers are built into the wall and Simon Thurley, from the London Museum, showed how their complicated corners indicate a high level of skilled masonry on the site. Their construction, which involved carving the corner sections laboriously by hand, fitted the late seventeenth century/early eighteenth century date for the Stuart mansion. This was a nice example of features proving to be unexpectedly important: at first glance, the fact that they were brick suggested they were much later in date. It is easy to forget that many Tudor and Stuart palaces were made of brick, a material that is often associated with buildings of the eighteenth, nineteenth and twentieth centuries. We were also beginning to get brickwork from a much earlier period in Trench One.

We were lucky enough to find a pistol ball that had been flattened by contact with a wall – or a Royalist – and Alan described how pistols were used in the initial stages of a typical Civil War storming: after digging trenches and setting up firing positions the foot soldiers were replaced in the first attack by the dismounted cavalry who advanced with pistols. Like all musket balls, the one we found had a

Mick Worthington excavating the level of Civil War destruction.

A newly cast musket ball, you may just be able make out the sprue.

The Fairfax encampment receives visitors.

distinctive protrusion – a sprue – left after the ball was broken from the mould, which would have had four or five bullets attached in a strip.

Day Two saw members of the Roundhead Association from the English Civil War Society setting up camp as a preliminary to re-enacting the attack on Basing House – the 'cameo' for this programme. Their battalion is the Fairfax – part of the New Model Army – which historically stormed the house. Their encampment was outside the great barn at Basing, a remarkable sixteenth-century building, 36.5 metres (120 feet) long, that was an important strategic target for both sides. The Parliamentarians under General Waller captured the barn and expelled the Royalists, which gave them a protected base from which to attack the main house. The barn still bears the mark of a cannon-ball fired during the battle.

The re-enactors wore beautiful authentic clothes, researched in detail, that were a striking contrast to the gruesome reality of a soldier's role on a batttlefield. To see the steely efficiency with which the musketeers went about their work, and feel the weight of the musket balls, made one shudder at the thought of what it would have been like to be on the receiving end of a volley. A lump of lead shot from a muzzle-loader at close range would create a very large hole.

Meanwhile, Trench One had revealed brickwork arches and their strength implied to Simon that they had supported a huge tower or gatehouse. According to Civil War records it was here that Cromwell's troops broke into the main house.

Back in Trenches Two and Three we were finding traces of brick walls but they seemed too small to support a building as large as the Stuart mansion. Occasional finds, including a piece of eighteenth-century Delftware, encouraged Carenza and the diggers, but although John Howard, an architectural historian, arrived to help make sense of the site, we still had very little to go on.

I must admit I had a limited interest in the Stuart building although the archaeological crossword puzzle of the remains it eventually revealed proved to be a fascinating element of the programme.

Muskets and pikes ready for another drill.

Most of all I wanted to have some physical contact with the Civil War, and the older house, which had borne the brunt of the Parliamentarian attack, was the one that interested me most.

The inmates of Basing withstood a two-year siege until, in 1645, Cromwell himself joined the Parliamentary forces there. A Colonel Dalbier had previously bombarded the exterior of the house with cannons, and used a form of poison gas against its defenders: a combination of straw, sulphur and brimstone was burnt and the smoke blew over the trapped Royalists. Cromwell now surrounded the house with 7,000 men. He believed an overwhelming defeat of the king's supporters at Basing would be an example to other papist strongholds. A quote from *The True Informer*, a contemporary news sheet, stated that, 'the dispute was long and sharp the enemy deserved no quarter and I believe that they deserved what little was offered them. You must remember what they were. They were most of them Papists, therefore our muskets and swords did show but little compassion.'

Sources for the attack on Basing include eyewitness accounts, many of which were used as propaganda. Cromwell's own report was written immediately after the house had been stormed, on the night of 14 October; it was being sold on the streets of London the following week.

Hugh Peters, Cromwell's chaplain who was executed in Trafalgar Square when the monarchy was restored in 1660, recorded details of the defeat. He notes that seventy-four people were slain, including a woman – 'Miss Griffiths' – who died attempting to revenge the wounding of her father. Among the dead, strangely enough, was a Mr Robinson, a player or actor from Drury Lane, who was shot as he taunted the Parliamentarians from the battlements of Basing House. Eight of nine gentlewomen were 'coarsely entertained' – which probably means their valuable clothes were removed – but Peters goes on to describe their treatment as 'not uncivilly'. A soldier's account of the battle includes details of an

The great barn in the background and the 'mansion' trenches. The brick wall piers of the gateway can be seen to the next to the road.

assault with ladders, during which the Royalists threw grenades into the courtyard and killed many Parliamentarians.

Back in the re-enactors' encampment, Mick had been enrolled in the musketeers and was learning to use a matchlock musket: in battle a musketeer could fire every thirty seconds, and Mick clearly needed practice. Waiting for him to charge, load and fire his weapon we felt there must have been some heart-stopping moments for a soldier during that half-minute as the Royalist cavalry charged at him. However, the men on horseback had their own problems – they faced troops of pikemen with 5-metre (16 foot) pikes. The pikemen also had grim realities to face. Many of the Royalist horses

Excavations in th 'mansion' field.

and their beautifully dressed riders were impaled on the ends of pikes, like so many hapless kebabs.

The pikemen had agreed to train Phil and he was learning how to manoeuvre a pike into a position that would be more of a threat to the enemy than his own side. There was an enjoyable moment of confusion when all the pikemen presented their weapons towards the enemy, with one exception: Phil Harding Esq., who faced in the opposite direction – possibly, as he said later, protecting the rear!

The geophysics team returned to the mansion field early on Day Three but still found little that seemed to correspond with the likely location of the wall of the Stuart mansion. One of the 1730s maps which showed a painting of the house indicated that an earlier Tudor structure had been attached to the rear of the building and some of the older-looking wall lines we had begun to find might correspond to this. We were now looking at building remains dating from the Tudor period, a time when the Paulets had thrived.

Phil Harding Esq. pikeman, wearing a new kind of head gear.

Mick lets fly with a matchlock.

Fragments of glass and lead from the destruction during the attack on Basing House.

The family was one of many great Catholic families who were loyal supporters of the Crown, and who coexisted with a state that was often anti-Catholic. The high point of their influence came with Sir William (1485–1572). His father had served Henry VII and William was appointed a sheriff, then held a senior position at Henry VIII's court. In 1522 he became controller of the royal household, a position that brought him close to the king, who sealed their relationship by making him a lord. A consummate politician, he did not allow his religious beliefs to interfere with his duty to the king: when Henry came into conflict with the Church William was personally responsible for persecuting pro-Catholic sympathizers who attempted to delay the process of the Reformation. In contrast, in 1546, a year before the king's death, he was president of a court that prosecuted Protestant heretics.

William continued to hold high office throughout the reigns of Edward VI and Mary I and, like many of Mary's counsellors, was retained by Elizabeth I when she came to throne in 1558. Sir Robert Nawton, an Elizabethan historian, is quoted as noting that the Marquis of Winchester 'had served four princes in these various and changeable times and seasons, that I may well say in time nor age has yielded the like precedent'. When asked the reason for his success William is quoted as saying: '*Ovtus sum salice non exquercus* – I am made of pliable willows not the stubborn oak'. He lived to the ripe old age of ninety with, as Alan Turton puts it, 'all his offices intact'.

With the exception of the third Marquis of Winchester, who was one of the commissioners at the trial of Mary Queen of Scots, and lord steward of her funeral, the Paulet family had little impact on public life in the years following William's death. It was the fifth marquis, John Paulet (1598–1675), who defended Basing during the Civil War. His brother Edward betrayed him by attempting to do a deal with the attackers and was forced to hang his fellow-conspirators in the grounds of the house. After the attack John was imprisoned and his property was confiscated.

By Day Three we were beginning to excavate building remains that might belong to this period in Trench One – a tower with wings on either side linked the two courtyards of the main house. The outer one was where visitors like Elizabeth I would have alighted from their carriages before entering the central building. The queen visited Basing and admired both the house and William Paulet's qualities. She is quoted as saying that if he had been younger she would have considered him as a husband.

Below the towers we had begun to uncover two rooms used for storage, and evidence that one of them had been set on fire during the Parliamentarian attack. Victor's drawing beautifully captured the dramatic moment – the Paulets' darkest hour.

By the end of three days *Time Team* had found evidence of the attack that had breached the gatehouse of Basing House. This, the pistol ball and Victor's drawing are perhaps my most vivid memories of the shoot – a programme that delved into what is, thankfully, a rare event in British history. We never made sense of the remains of the Stuart mansion – there are structures but, as Mick said, it would take a large-scale excavation of the entire area to sort them out. The remains that we did find show that the Paulets managed to survive and prosper as a family after the Civil War.

Modern Britain

The Great Fire of London

The diarist Samuel Pepys shrugged his shoulders and went back to bed, but most Londoners were not so blasé about the Great Fire. Though fire was a fairly common occurence the Great Fire was on the largest scale ever seen. It started in the early hours of Sunday 2 September 1666, in Thomas Farrier's bakehouse in Pudding Lane near London Bridge, and in five days it ravaged 187 hectares (463 acres) of the city – more damage than the Blitz inflicted during the Second World War.

Urged on by a strong east wind, the fire swept across firebreaks, destroying timber-built houses and shops with ease. Although fewer than twenty people died, it engulfed the old St Paul's Cathedral, the guildhall, royal exchange, eighty-seven parish churches, fifty-two company halls, markets and gaols, and 13,200 houses – losses valued at the then mind-blowing sum of over £10 million.

However, some good came out of the disaster. Although a number of the rebuilding schemes were rushed, most were well thought out with improved sanitation and access and the new buildings were brick rather than wood. The Monument, which still stands close to the site of the bakehouse, was erected in 1677 to commemorate London's Great Fire.

St Paul's Cathedral

There have been a number of St Paul's Cathedrals in London. The first was built in 604 on the site of a Roman temple and endowed by King Aethelbert. It burnt down and was rebuilt in stone between 675 and 685, but was laid waste by the Vikings in the ninth century. Once again it was rebuilt, and once again it was destroyed by fire – in 1087. 'Old St. Paul's', the fourth cathedral, was completed in 1220 and was a magnificent building whose Gothic splendour reflected its status as England's largest church and the third largest in Europe. It too underwent a trial by flames in the Great Fire of 1666 – and lost. What followed is the famous landmark that stands out on the London skyline.

In 1675 Sir Christopher Wren started work on the new cathedral, the only one built under the same architect from start to finish. The building is famous for its distinctive dome, which is reminiscent of Eastern churches, and whose shape inside creates a whispering gallery that allows words whispered against the wall on one side to be heard near the opposite wall. St Paul's is a resting-place for the good and the great of Britain, and of Wren himself.

Castle Howard

Castle Howard is one of Britain's grandest private houses, comparable to Chatsworth, the Derbyshire home of the dukes of Devonshire. Designed by John Vanburgh, it was commissioned by Charles Howard, Earl of Carlisle, as part of a plan to transform the local village and Henderskelfe Castle, the previous house which had burnt down in 1693, into a great family estate. It was to be a grander residence than its predecessor, and Vanburgh created a masterpiece in the strict classical style, with architectural features that had never before been seen on such a scale: the magnificent south front, the central dome and entrance hall – Castle Howard was the first private house to have a dome – and the temple of the four winds.

Work started in 1699, but all this grandeur did not come cheap and Howard spent £78,000 on his house before he died in 1738. Even then, Castle Howard was not finished for another twenty-two years.

Captain James Cook

In 1768 the Royal Society selected James Cook to command the *Endeavour* on a voyage to make astrological observations from Tahiti. Travelling south-west, he discovered and charted New Zealand before arriving at the coast of Australia, where he landed at what soon became known as Botany Bay: the scientists who had accompanied him were astounded at the range of new and unusual plants. Cook systematically charted the coastline of this land and raised the English flag on a tiny island – later Possession Island – to claim the 3,200-kilometre (2,000 mile) coast for George III.

From 1772 to 1775 he commanded two ships, the *Resolution* and the *Adventure*, on an expedition during which he successfully disproved the existence of a great continent in the southern hemisphere – a region, unconquered by any nation, that was known as *terra australis incognita*, the 'unknown southern land'- and charted some of Antarctica.

Captain Cook's third great expedition, from 1776 to 1779, took him to the South Pacific and then to North America, where he tried to find the North-West Passage. He was killed on the return voyage during a skirmish with Hawaiians.

1710

1720

John Wesley

John Wesley was the founding father of Methodism, a movement that organized Christians into societies whose members lived according to the teachings of the Church. His followers owed much to Calvin, and their direct approach to the people, particularly the poor, was seen as a threat by the traditional clergy and the upper-class society of Georgian England.

As a young man at Oxford Wesley had been rigidly High Church, but in 1735 he went to Georgia in America on a mission and was struck by the practices of the Moravian brethren. On his return to London in 1738 he experienced a 'sudden conversion' and became an ardent evangelical. He spent the next fifty years travelling the country, preaching the word of God. His teachings made the Church suspicious and when its doors were closed to him he spoke in the open air, to huge gatherings that had been organized by his local followers.

Wesley had not broken with the Church of England – on the contrary, he wanted to be integrated into it – but the Anglicans refused to ordain his preachers. This refusal and the spread of the movement made an organization separate from the established Church necessary and in 1784 Wesley established a permanent Methodist Conference.

Handel's Messiah

Handel said that as he wrote the *Messiah*, 'I did think I did see all heaven before me, and the great God himself'. He wrote it in 1742, some thirty years after he settled in England rather than his homeland Germany.

As a young man George Frederick Handel had travelled in Europe where his posts had included that of *kapell-meister* to the Elector of Hanover, the future George I of England. After his arrival in Engand he wrote thirty-five operas. These were initially very popular, but his audiences declined and in about 1730 he turned his hand to the dramatic style of the English oratorio. It took him only twenty-three days to write the *Messiah* – the pinnacle of these pieces – yet it has remained a classic of the music world for 250 years.

Handel's music is for ever intertwined with the English Crown. At the first performance of the *Messiah* in London, George II was so roused by the 'Hallelujah Chorus' that he stood – a rare and extraordinary tribute for any composer – and thereby established a longstanding tradition. 'Zadok the Priest' the anthem Handel composed when George II was crowned in 1727, has been performed at every coronation since then.

His death was a fitting one: he attended a performance of the *Messiah* in Covent Garden on 6 April 1759, and collapsed just as it ended. He died eight days later.

The Battle of Culloden

The Battle of Culloden, near Inverness, was the last land battle fought in Britain, and the last stand of Prince Charles Edward Stuart, the 'Young Pretender' to the British crown. Bonnie Prince Charlie's army had defeated government forces at Prestonpans towards the end of 1745 and marched into England, but had been turned back at Derby by the Duke of Cumberland's forces.

After a failed attack on the advancing English army on 15 April 1746 the Jacobites chose Drumossie Moor above Culloden House as the site of the main battle the following day. It was a strange choice as the ground was flat and boggy, an unfamiliar surface for Charles's Highlanders. The Jacobites had 4,000 fewer men than Cumberland's army and, as Bonnie Prince Charlie fatally hesitated before ordering them to charge, the English guns ripped through their ranks. When the armies came to blows, the superior reach of the enemy's bayonets dominated over the Scottish broadswords.

The MacDonald clan on the Jacobite right flank started the retreat and the English forces pursued the thwarted Highlanders on horseback. The Duke of Cumberland's order to kill even the wounded earned him the title 'the butcher', and made Culloden one of the most horrific episodes in Anglo–Scottish history. The Young Pretender spent five months as a fugitive in the Highlands before escaping to France.

Bonnie Prince Charlie

Bonnie Prince Charlie is a Scottish hero, the champion of the Jacobites who wanted to put the descendants of James II back on the British throne. The grandson of James II and son of James, the Old Pretender, Charles – the Young Pretender – was born in exile in Rome, and came to Scotland in July 1745 to claim the crown. The Highlanders rallied to his call, and it was a combination of their total self-confidence and the military skill of their general, Lord George Murray – rather than Charles's slightly limited grasp on reality – that got them as far as Derby. Bonnie Prince Charlie was hailed as a hero, but his glory was short-lived, snuffed out by the shadow of the Duke of Cumberland.

The massacre of the Jacobites at Culloden forced Charles into hiding and, with a price of £30,000 on his head, he spent the ten weeks after the battle in the Hebrides. On his return to the mainland he spent five months wandering the Highlands to avoid capture, reputedly dressing as a woman to throw off his pursuers. It seems he was in high spirits during his time as a fugitive, whistling and singing Gaelic ditties as he crossed the Scottish moors.

Charles finally escaped to France, never to return to his beloved Scotland. He lived for another forty-two years, drifting through failed relationships and finally turning to drink: a sad ending for someone who was once a glamorous figure.

1740

1750

BURSLEM
STOKE-ON-TRENT

SERIES 6
broadcast
January 1999

Josiah Wedgwood is one of the most famous names in the history of pottery-making, and the factories he established still sell ceramics all over the world. A huge exhibition centre celebrating Burslem's ceramic history was planned and, perhaps fittingly, it was to be located where Wedgwood's first factory, the Ivy House Works, once stood. Bill Klemperer, Stoke-on-Trent's city archaeologist, invited *Time Team* to investigate the site before the centre was built.

The area we would be excavating was not promising – it consisted of a 1960s paved area, complete with benches, flowerbeds and bandstand, and a car park. Undeterred, John Gater and Chris Gaffney began to survey it with ground-penetrating radar (GPR) to build up information about the depth and form of deposits. Stewart Ainsworth consulted old maps in order to estimate the parts of the site that were least likely to have been destroyed by nineteenth-century building, and might contain remains of the Ivy House Works. Trench One, in the first area he suggested, was not hopeful: it revealed the floor of a Victorian market building. However, a brick structure was uncovered in Trench Two and the day ended amidst rampant speculation: was it a pottery kiln?

The pottery kilns in Burslem were known as bottle ovens, and until the 1950s their continual firing produced a very unhealthy environment full of smoke. The ovens were shaped like a bottle (hence the name) and consisted of two distinct parts: the outer shell or 'hovel' which acted as a chimney and protected the kiln from the weather; and inside, the kiln or oven which was stoked with coals through holes around its base. It would have taken about forty-eight hours for the maximum temperature (between 1000°C and 1250°C) to be reached, and this had to be maintained for two to three hours before the fires were allowed to go out. Would there be any evidence of a kiln in our trench?

Throughout Day Two, the Team gradually worked backwards through the history of the site. The brick structure in Trench Two turned out to be a nineteenth-century kiln, so it was recorded and excavation continued. The market floor in Trench One was removed and eighteenth-century pottery, as well as another possible kiln, was found beneath it. At this point the excavations were suddenly taken over by

The distinctive
curve of a pottery
kiln, can clearly be
seen, but would it
turn out to have
been in use in
Wedgwood's time?

Josiah Wedgwood

In the eighteenth century Josiah Wedgwood made pottery a fashionable commodity in wealthy and aristocratic households, rather than a poor second to silver. Aware of the need for fashion labels, he gained the permission of Charlotte, wife of George III, to call his improved creamware 'Queen's Ware' and sales across Europe rocketed. He had clearly found his niche in the market and gained the title 'Potter to the Queen'.

Born into a family of potters in 1730, Wedgwood set up his own business in 1758, in Burslem, and opened his great Etruria factory nearby eleven years later. He was always keen to try new types of ceramics and glazes, and kept meticulous records of his experiments. Commissions flowed in from all over Europe and in 1774 Catherine the Great, Empress of Russia, requested a 952-piece dinner service. It was one of the great peaks in his career and he responded with dishes, plates and bowls that were exquisitely decorated with scenes of the countryside and depictions of eighteenth-century houses.

Despite his illustrious clients, Wedgwood was greatly concerned with the plight of the poor. He went to great lengths to improve the living conditions of his workers, building schools for their children and paying them wages that were higher than normal. He publicly supported the American War of Independence and the French Revolution and was a member of the Society for the Abolition of the Slave Trade.

Wedgwood's achievements are summed up in his epitaph, which tells us that he 'converted a rude and inconsiderable manufactory into an elegant art and an important part of national commerce.'

Wedgewood creamware pottery found at Burslem

1755

incredible discoveries in Trench Three. Our mechanical digger uncovered a huge deposit of pottery, dating to the 1830s and numbering thousands of pieces. It had all been manufactured by Enoch Wood, an important local potter, who was famous for tipping waste pottery into any available hole! This had supplied material to keep researchers busy for some time.

By the end of the day the site had produced pottery dating to before Wedgwood's time and a kiln dating to after it, but nothing from the period when his factory occupied the site.

Overnight, Mick Worthington decided to take matters into his own hands and on Day Three he dug a new trench in the car park. Meanwhile, the first pieces of early Wedgwood creamware were discovered below the nineteenth-century kiln in Trench Two – much to everyone's relief. Soon results were coming in thick and fast as Phil revealed workshops that dated to Wedgwood's time below the Enoch Wood pottery in Trench Three. However, Mick's trench, in the far corner of the car park, stole the show at the end of the day. He discovered pottery and waste dating from the fourteenth to the sixteenth centuries.

Bill Klemperer, the city archaeologist, confirmed that this was a great find. Whilst they had previously found the odd fragment of medieval ceramics around Burslem, they had never uncovered anything as wonderful as this collection and he had never seen such a large cache in Staffordshire. It would change the way archaeologists viewed the history of pottery production in Burslem. Before Josiah's first factory was established in Burslem, the pottery had been produced in small kilns in the back gardens of the cottagers who made these relatively crude ceramics that we had found next to the back wall of the Ivy Hall Works.

In three short days, on one small site, *Time Team* managed to uncover a long history of pottery-making – from the Middle Ages through Josiah Wedgwood's time and up until the nineteenth century. The new exhibition centre would now be built in a way that would conserve the surviving archaeology and the plans would be altered to incorporate the bottle oven and Wedgwood's floor (in Trench Two) into the permanent exhibition!

George III

It is unlikely that George III would have been pleased to know that he is best remembered for going mad – a reputation for drifting in and out of insanity and producing strangely coloured waste-products is not the most desirable memorial for a monarch. Nor is talking to trees – although many people today would agree that this encourages them to grow. His insanity has been retrospectively diagnosed as being a sympton of porphyria, a rare kidney disorder that caused toxins to be released into his blood and affected his brain.

Quite apart from his madness, George III was not suited to being a king. 'Farmer George' – his nickname because of his manners and interests – was nervous in public and, although he was hard-working, he was not gifted in the affairs of government and has been criticized by later politicans and scholars who have said that he 'inflicted more profound and enduring injuries upon his own country than any other modern British king'. This is perhaps unjust. It was not entirely his fault that Britain lost her American colonies during his reign – Parliament was largely in control during the War of Independence, and it was later propaganda that blackened George's name by blaming him for the loss.

George III reigned for sixty years from 1760 to 1820. After two bouts of illness and subsequent recoveries, he descended permanently into insanity in 1811 and lived on, totally incapacitated, for another nine years.

Edward Dod clay pipe found at Basing

1760

Earlier pottery than Wedgwood began to appear on the final day – the result of a digger's initiative.

Lord Horatio Nelson

Horatio Nelson was a popular hero, who had lost an arm and the sight of one eye in conflicts with Britain's enemies, but he also stood out as an officer who treated his men humanely at a time when flogging was a regular event in the Royal Navy.

His flagship, the *Victory*, is now moored in Portsmouth and it was on this ship that he paraded on the morning of the Battle of Trafalgar, his medals glittering on his uniform in defiance of French snipers.

Napoleon had been victorious on land in Europe and victory at sea would pave the way for his invasion of Britain. On 21 October 1805 Nelson faced a large fleet of French and Spanish ships under the command of the French admiral Villeneuve. He issued his famous signal – 'England expects that every man will do his duty' – and attacked the lines of enemy ships at right angles, cutting across them. The *Victory*'s seamen had been well trained and were capable of firing a 100-gun broadside every eighty seconds. The enemy were decimated and Nelson was within sight of victory when he was shot by a sniper. Comforted by his great friend Thomas Hardy, he died in his cabin.

Time Team made a connection with Nelson on the island of Nevis in the West Indies, where he had stopped to water his ships and met Fanny Nisbet who later became his wife. However, it was to his mistress Lady Emma Hamilton that his last thoughts were directed.

1770

The American War of Independence

It is said that when George III heard the British had been defeated in America in 1781 he wept and proclaimed that his country had 'lost a kind of Eden'. Whether this is fact or fiction, it seems to express a great feeling of loss. Certainly, America was seen as the land of opportunity, where the common man could become a big landowner.

Dissent in America had been building for some time before the outbreak of war, but fear of attack by the French in Canada made the colonists stick close to Britain. However, when the British defeated France in the Seven Years War of 1756-63 and gained control of Canada the Americans felt they could make their bid for freedom.

The war started with the battle of Lexington in 1775, and lasted for six years. The end came when Major General Charles Cornwallis failed to unite with southern allies of Britain and was forced to surrender at Yorktown in October 1781. The defeat hit the British hard. They were accustomed to glorious victories, and there were close family ties between Britain and America. In Mick's words, 'It was a fight amongst relatives'.

1775

ST MARY'S CITY
MARYLAND

One of Britain's earliest colonies, Maryland was developed by the second Baron Baltimore, primarily as a haven for Catholics who were being persecuted in their homeland. Lord Baltimore was English secretary of state until 1625 when he resigned after becoming a Catholic. His conversion was extraordinary given the tide of feeling against Catholics at the time which was fuelled by the Spanish Armada of 1588 and the Gunpowder Plot of 1605. The first settlers (Protestant as well as Catholic) arrived there in 1634 and St Mary's City – its first capital and now a small village – was established in the same year. Lord Baltimore never got to the New World as he had died two years earlier, and Leonard Calvert, the baron's son, became the colony's first governor.

Time Team were invited to Maryland by Dr Henry Miller. He and his team had built a living museum recreating the lifestyle of colonial Maryland. Dr Henry Miller had established a clear set of targets for the three days, each related to elements of the colony's early history. Six years' research and excavation had located the site of the brick chapel and a number of burials and *Time Team* would try to find the extent of this early cemetery. In addition, we were to explore the site of the governor's mansion, one of the first to be built in colonial America. It was blown up in 1694 in mysterious circumstances, and despite a small excavation in the 1930s, its exact location was now lost. Stewart Ainsworth was keen to find the site of Fort St George which would have been built somewhere in the area to protect the colony. The first settlers encountered the local Yaocomico tribe of Native Americans who were friendly and showed them how to make bread from maize and where the best supplies of game and other foods could be found. The Susquehannock tribe to the north, however, were much more aggressive, making the wooden fort an important place of refuge for the colony.

Day One opened with the geophysics team, John Gater and Chris Gaffney, searching for Leonard Calvert's mansion. This had been partially excavated in the 1930s but its location had been lost because the excavation had not been properly recorded. Geophysics soon revealed a square anomaly that could be the building and Phil opened Trench One there. It soon became apparent that American excavating techniques are very different to British ones – every shovelful of earth was sieved to look for artefacts, so digging was a slow process. Geophysics set off to locate the seventeenth-century settlers' graveyard and Stewart Ainsworth focused his attention on the site of the fort, using aerial photographs. Phil was happy at the end of the day because he had found an American Indian spearhead made from white quartz.

On Day Two the discovery of brickwork in Trench One confirmed the location of the governor's mansion. English pottery and building materials were also found as well as ammunition, probably from the armoury in the cellars of the house. Carenza joined Stewart in his examination of the aerial photographs of the area, and they proposed at least three possible locations for the fort. In the graveyard near the settlement's chapel, we had begun to excavate a body. Progress was still slow, however, and by now Phil was suffering from the heat.

Day Three and the excavation of the skeleton was complete. Mick was delighted by its 'pipe facets'– worn areas on the teeth that showed where a clay pipe had been clamped. *Time Team* were joined at this point by Doug Owsley from the Smithsonian Institute in Washington DC. His research included

SERIES 4
Broadcast
5 January 1997

scene that isn't changed much in the last ∞ years: an rial view of St ary's.

experimental work on the proportions of carbon 12 and carbon 13 in skeletons. As we eat, carbon is incorporated into our bones and he had found that people brought up on a diet of wheat, barley and rye had a larger amount of carbon 12 than those whose diet was predominantly maize - their bones contain carbon 13. Doug hoped to use this information to distinguish between the skeletons of early European settlers, and those who had been born in St Mary's and raised on the maize diet. Enough excavation had been done at the governor's mansion to reveal how the bricks had been laid and allow us to make a reconstruction of the house. Debate raged until the last moment of the shoot about the location of the fort.

John and Chris were unable to find any clear geophysics targets indicating a fort wall, but they did find an area of high resistance in the middle of their survey area. With only a few hours remaining Phil opened a final trench and almost immediately located brickwork. As it was uncovered it became clear that we had found the chimney stack of an unknown colonial house and there were pieces of English pottery associated with it. Whilst the fort still eluded us, Dr Miller and his team were delighted with the new discovery. A final trench revealed a previously undiscovered house, but no fort.

Extreme heat and humidity, as well as the risks posed by ticks and other burrowing insects, made conditions on this dig more gruelling than normal. However, St Mary's City was an important site for *Time Team* to visit because it allowed us to explore what life was like for the pioneering settlers, and also to experience American archaeology. Because the remains below the ground are so different to those in Britain, the approach to excavating them also has to be completely different. Unlike Britain, where archaeologists often uncover sites with deep layers of occupation over many centuries, in America, the archaeology is often very shallow and ephemeral, and consists of finds in the topsoil. Thus in America, it is common to sieve all the soil dug up to recover as many artefacts as possible. Nevertheless, the normal *Time Team* approach yielded valuable results, and gave the American team new avenues to explore in the future.

An early settler i America, complei with dental face caused by pipe smoking.

Ironbridge

The cast-iron bridge that spans the River Severn in Coalbrookdale, Shropshire, was a wonder of its age and has given its name to the industrial valley of Ironbridge. Part of an early eighteenth-century iron-manufacturing centre, run by the Darby family, it was the first iron bridge in the world and an advertisement for the region's booming ironworks. Many local factories contributed to its manufacture.

The bridge, originally a toll bridge, was built by Abraham Darby the Third between 1776 and 1779 and used so much iron – more than 378 tonnes in all – that a charcoal furnace last used in 1706 had to be rebuilt in 1777 to cope with the demand.

Although an iron bridge conjures up images of an ugly, chunky structure, the details are delicate, with fine, intricate patterns and tracery. This is because it was built using carpentry techniques as at this time new methods of construction suitable to iron had not yet evolved. It is little wonder that it caused such a stir when it opened, with sightseers and industrialists from all over Europe visiting it. Today, Ironbridge is a heritage centre and a superb example of the Industrial Age.

James Watt & Matthew Boulton

By the 1780s 'Britain had gone steam-mill mad', thanks to the efforts of Matthew Boulton and James Watt. The combination of Boulton's business sense and Watt's brilliance with steam power launched a new technological age. They first met in 1774 when Watt was struggling to find the money to develop his new steam engine and Boulton needed more power for his factories. Each could provide what the other needed and their partnership was sealed.

Their success was assured as Watt created better engines and Boulton ensured they were sold across the country. The high point of their joint career came in 1781 when Watt's rotative engine, which was more efficient than its predecessors and able to cope with the heavy machinery of the Industrial Age, was patented. The partners developed a production line to produce the engines and they were shipped in large numbers throughout the world. In one sense they were the first portable power units and represented a revolutionary transition from a period when the only power source was human or animal muscle.

The partnership ended in 1800 when Watt retired. Boulton, however, continued their work and applied steam power to minting at Soho in Birmingham and in the Tower of London.

MALTON
NORTH YORKSHIRE

SERIES 4
Broadcast
2 February 1997

Malton in North Yorkshire has been an important strategic point on the River Derwent since prehistoric times. The Romans built a fort there to control the crossing. Roman Malton was called Derventio and was an important strategic site. The fort has been excavated and can still be seen as a series of grassed-over humps and bumps. To its east, the Normans built a castle – added to during the following centuries – for the same reason. Today, only one wall of the castle survives, in the garden of a Jacobean lodge that was built after the castle had been demolished. Local plans to turn the castle area into a public park meant archaeological assessment was needed,

so the local council invited *Time Team* along. It was our first excavation on a scheduled site – one protected by English Heritage – and we worked closely with John Ette, their local inspector. Because of the scheduling a number of strict criteria had to be agreed before *Time Team* were allowed access to the site. Our investigations were restricted to five trenches of a set size, and John Ette would have to give his approval for each of them.

The original stone castle at Malton, which may have been preceded by a motte and bailey, had two advantages that would secure it into the Middle Ages and beyond. Firstly, the position was a strategic one, commanding a crucial route north at the crossing point of the River Derwent. Secondly, there was a plentiful supply of building material, both from the remains of the Roman fort and from a local outcrop of limestone. The castle had been visited by Richard

Floored by his fall down a holy well, Mick finds alternative transport.

Captain Bligh

Bligh sailed on Captain Cook's last voyage from 1776 to 1779, and in 1787 he commanded the *Bounty* on a voyage to transport breadfruit from Tahiti to the plantations of the Caribbean islands. His second-in-command was his friend Christian Fletcher. On 28 April 1789 Fletcher led the crew in a mutiny against Bligh and set the captain and eighteen men adrift in an open boat. He and his fellow mutineers took the *Bounty* to Pitcairn Island where they settled. Their descendants still live there today.

Bligh and his men reached Timor after forty-one days at the sea. They had travelled over 5,600 kilometres (3,500 miles) and only lost one man. It was an amazing journey and it was Bligh's stubborn character that enabled them to survive. He returned to England and in 1805 he was appointed Governor of New South Wales, where he once again provoked a mutiny. Bligh returned to Britain and was made an admiral in 1811.

1790

I in about 1194 and Edward II in about 1307. It was later occupied by Robert the Bruce, who used it as a military base in 1322. During the reign of King John (1199–1216), the castle was 'slighted' – that is, made militarily useless by having its walls pulled down, and any wooden structures within them burnt – but it was later rebuilt.

Day One began with a huge nettle-clearing programme in the lodge garden so that John and Chris could begin the geophysics survey. Straight away, the clearance revealed a large earthwork bank and platform, so Phil immediately opened Trench One there. Meanwhile Carenza and Beric Morley, *Time Team*'s buildings expert, set off through neighbouring back gardens to look for remains of the castle walls. Beric soon identified some eleventh- to twelfth-century buttresses and even a medieval garderobe (toilet) – more than anyone thought had survived of the castle. As Trench One was above this area, it seemed possible that we might find features associated with this period and even with the castle itself.

Endless sieving produced a superb collection of finds.

The day ended on an optimistic note as Phil had uncovered a stone structure in his trench. Mick was handicapped by his plastered leg which he had broken a month before. This called for a new archaeological method of investigation: one of his research students, Nick Corcos, was called in to rove across the site with a camera connected to a close-circuit television, whilst Mick directed him from the comfort of *Time Team*'s four-wheel drive vehicle, thus enabling him to take part in advising the Team.

With John Ette's permission it was decided to extend Trench One at the beginning of Day Two. We began to locate large stones that might just be the edge of a freestanding building. Beric was convinced that the structure was the corner of a medieval building, and probably part of the castle and on Day Two two new trenches were opened near Trench One to investigate. The Jacobean lodge had originally belonged to a much bigger house, but this had been demolished and its location lost. With the search for the castle going well, Stewart Ainsworth concentrated on looking for the mansion. Stewart had looked at a number of possible models for this mansion, and Howley Hall in Yorkshire seemed the closest bet. It had a very similar gatehouse, with the same arrangement of columns at the entrance. According to Beric such estates were arranged in nine symmetrical squares, and this resembled the existing layout of the surviving lodge and garden. He set off with John and Chris into the orchard to tackle more nettles and the results at the end of Day Two revealed they had located a possible site for the house. Trench Two, in the woods near the town, had revealed a mortared base that could be the return of a wall, and Trench Three was producing lots of late medieval finds including a water jug. Beric was particularly excited by the discovery of part of an aquamanile – a decorated water jug that would have graced a 'posh' medieval table. The finds suggested that we were in the demolition layer of a medieval building – perhaps part of the castle destroyed in the fifteenth or sixteenth century.

At the start of Day Three, with some trepidation, Stewart opened Trench Four on the site geophysics had identified. Would it be an inside wall of the mansion or just the edge of the courtyard. Relief was visible when a plaster floor was soon revealed and pieces of window-lead and stone window-fragments

William Wordsworth

One of Britain's poetic masters, William Wordsworth's early work was fundamental to the romantic movement in Britain. As a young man he was in Paris in 1791, during the time of the French Revolution, and returned to England imbued with republican principles. However, he became disillusioned when the Revolution became the Terror.

A fortunate inheritance in 1795 allowed him to concentrate on his poetry and he formed a close friendship with Samuel Taylor Coleridge, with whom he created *Lyrical Ballads*, which starts with Coleridge's 'Ancient Mariner' and ends with Wordsworth's 'Tintern Abbey'. In 1799 he moved to the Lake District with his sister Dorothy and married Mary Hutchinson in 1802.

As Wordsworth's literary fame grew he became more conservative and his early radical poems are generally more admired than his later ones. He worked on his poetic autobiography, *The Prelude*, throughout his life and it was published posthumously in 1850.

Coin blanks manufactured using steam found at Soho

dating to the Jacobean period confirmed that it belonged to the lost house. The building appeared exactly where Beric and Stewart had predicted and we were delighted to have relocated it. Back in the castle trenches, Phil had identified mortared walls and concluded that he had found the demolition layer from the time when the castle was pulled down.

John and Chris, carrying out a geophysical survey of the area where the gardens of the mansion should have been located, had come up with what looked like a definite structure. Here, we were close to the Roman fort's gateway and also not far from the castle, so great care had to be taken. However, John Ette and the team finally decided to place a small trench, Trench Five, over the mysterious feature. From the evidence of small pieces of pottery, apparently flowerpots, it seemed that we had begun to uncover evidence for the formal gardens of the mansion. Given the scheduling restrictions, it was not permissable to destroy the evidence for the gardens in order to see what lay underneath so this trench had to be closed. This was a very frustrating, but archaeologically correct, decision for us to have to take. It raised interesting questions for the Team about the relative importance of different archaeological features. We might have had a Roman structure underneath a medieval building on top of which were the Jacobean gardens. Far fewer gardens have been excavated than Roman buildings, so it would not be acceptable to destroy the gardens in order to reach the Roman levels. As John Ette reminded us, the bias of scheduling is in favour of preservation, not investigation.

By working closely with English Heritage, *Time Team* managed to locate part of the medieval castle and the lost Jacobean mansion in three days. We were able to show where the remains are, and also how well-preserved they are, and future work in the area will be able to take these findings into account.

Mick was still very immobile at Malton and this gave him some insight into the difficulties that physically disabled people have in getting around ancient monuments. He felt that Malton, in particular, showed the problem of trying to investigate one period alone. It is not uncommon to have Romano-British, medieval and post-medieval sites all mixed up together. Nevertheless, much was learned about the castle, and details of the Jacobean mansion turned out to be of great interest.

The Discovery of Electricity

Electricity, the basis for most of modern technology, was discovered, produced and mastered through the combined efforts of many scientists. The first discoveries were made by two Italian physicists: Galvani created an electric current in 1786 by observing its effects on frogs' legs; and Volta devised a battery in 1800. Also in 1800, two English scientists, William Nicholson and Anthony Carlisle, used electricity to discover electrolysis. Each invention and experiment built on previous results.

Two of the main movers in this force of electrical scientists were Humphrey Davy and Michael Faraday. Davy undertook a number of chemical experiments with electricity, which enabled him to isolate volatile elements like sodium and potassium. As a result he realized that firedamp posed a danger in mines, and invented the safety lamp.

Faraday, who became Davy's personal assistant in 1812, concentrated on electromagnetism. On Christmas Day 1821 he made his first electric motor. He recognized that development was spurred on by scientists co-operating with each other and started the Friday lectures at the Royal Institute.

1800

NEVIS
WEST INDIES

SERIES 6
Broadcast
21 March 1999;
28 March 1999

In the eighteenth century Nevis, a small island in the West Indies between Monserrat and St Kitts, was an important centre of the sugar trade, which produced great wealth for the British empire. Slaves from Africa were shipped to the Caribbean and worked on large plantations making sugar and rum for transportation to Europe. *Time Team* went to Nevis to investigate several different sites. Initially we were working with David Small, a historian from Bristol who had been researching the history of a wealthy merchant family from the city – the Pinneys. We were going to investigate the remains of their plantation on the island. After this, we intended to look for the first town on Nevis, and then the first inhabitants – American Indians. Everyone knew it would be busy, but we were looking forward to a six-day shoot rather than the usual three!

The surviving parts of Mountravers, the Pinney plantation house, are high on the side of Mount Nevis and deep in the jungle, so on Day One our first task was to clear vegetation from the ruined buildings with the help of local machete experts. Carenza and Phil were soon excavating a midden full of nineteenth-century pottery, while Mick Worthington scrabbled in the cellars of the eighteenth-century house. Out in the jungle, Stewart Ainsworth located the foundations of an animal mill – driven by oxen – for crushing sugar.

Coastal excavation of the prehistoric Indian site.

By the end of Day Two Phil had uncovered evidence of the eighteenth-century Pinneys who built the house, and had also found seventeenth-century pottery that suggested the site was inhabited before the family arrived there.

On Day Three our attention turned to the coast. Charlestown is the capital of Nevis but the first settlement on the island was Jamestown, which was reputedly destroyed in 1690 by a tidal wave. Its exact location was lost but the geophysics team had been surveying fields at its traditional location and Carenza opened three trenches there. She was soon finding wall foundations and pottery dating from the seventeenth to the nineteenth centuries. It seems certain that the settlement had not been completely

Our old friend the bellarmine jug turned up yet again in the Caribbean.

First Locomotives

Adapting steam power, which had previously been used for static machines, to create moving vehicles revolutionized transport technology. It is generally believed that the first effective steam locomotive was George Stephenson's *Locomotion*, which served the Stockton-Darlington line, Britain's first railway, which opened in 1825.

The Rainhill competition, organized by the directors of the London and Manchester Railway in 1829 to decide whether their new line should use a steam engine or one drawn by horses, is the start of railways as we know them. Stephenson's *Rocket* steamed into first place at a stunning 35 mph, a speed unheard of at the time, and George and his son Robert won first prize.

George Stephenson's earlier engine, the *Locomotion*, ran on the first line in the world to use locomotives and carry both passengers and freight, but the engine was expensive and tended to break down. The *Rocket* spelled the end to this kind of frustration. However, the technology was developing at such a rate that even this great locomotive became redundant. However, although the *Locomotion* has been given this place in the history books, the first efficient locomotive was in fact built by Cornishman Richard Trevithick in the early nineteenth century. Trevithick was ahead of his time though and gave up his work because the engines were too heavy for the brittle cast-iron rails. Hence, Stephenson has taken the credit.

Bottle made in Bristol found on Nevis

1810

A pottery fragment from an Indian jar reveals the face of a rather unhappy shark.

destroyed by the tidal wave: although the capital moved to Charlestown, Jamestown did not die out until the nineteenth century.

On Day Three Stewart returned to the Pinney plantation to try and find the village where its slaves would have lived. Following just one old map, he spent several days clearing a path through the jungle until he came to what he thought was the right location. A search yielded a handful of beads and pottery, and he discovered some ruined foundations and the terraces on which the houses had been built. It was the first slave village ever found on Nevis.

From 5,000 BC until the fourteenth century the Caribbean was home to tribes of American Indians and Phil spent three days at Coconut Walk, on the windy side of Nevis, investigating them. He was astonished to find their prehistoric flint, stone axes, pottery and carved shells littering the beach. In addition, geophysics found a series of anomalies nearby. A large trench revealed post holes from an American Indian house, which would have been a round thatched structure with an outside cooking area.

Looking out to sea on another sweltering day under the Caribbean sun.

Time Team's six days on Nevis was hard work, but extremely interesting. We pieced together several elements of the Pinney plantation – the family house, the animal mill and the slave village. We found the earliest European settlement on the island and even uncovered something of its early American Indian inhabitants. Most importantly, we all felt that the archaeology on Nevis had taught us a lot about British history and the ramifications of the sugar trade in the eighteenth century.

The Battle of Waterloo

At Waterloo on 18 June 1815 British, Prussian and Dutch troops, led by the Duke of Wellington, saved Europe from the domination of Napoleon Bonaparte. However, on the duke's own admission, 'it was a damn near thing – the nearest run thing you ever saw in your life'.

Napoleon was the first to attack and separated the Prussians from the British, who took up a position on a ridge near Waterloo and waited for the French to do their worst. At 11.30 am Napoleon struck, bombarding their centre, and following through with a great charge. Courageously the British rifles held their fire until the French were nearly upon them, then let loose a volley that rained confusion on the enemy.

The Prussians joined the British at 1.30 pm and after several more hours of fighting, Napoleon hesitated – fatally. The allies took full advantage of this and the French were forced to retreat as the Prussians swept down the ridge. The battle was won, but the bloodshed was sickening with nearly 30,000 French soldiers dead on the battlefield.

Wellington had seen enough war. He cared a great deal for his men and felt that a victory was almost as bad as a defeat because of the bloodshed involved. After Waterloo he said, 'I hope to God that I have fought my last battle'. His wish was granted.

Queen Victoria

To many people today Victoria's reign is dominated by the personality she presented after the death of her consort Albert. This image of a small dour woman, clad in black, who insisted that even piano legs should be covered, is mixed with the hazy notion of a vast empire. Victoria ruled over 400 million subjects and her reign saw great advances, however there was a sense that, beneath the surface glitter and achievement, there was a hypocrisy that had a darker side. However, she presided over changes that came to fruition in the modern world and took Britain into the twentieth century. During her reign there was a renaissance in science, while revolutionary developments in industrialization were led by men like Isambard Kingdom Brunel and Matthew Boulton.

Victoria was nineteen years old when she was crowned in 1838, a popular heroine with much of the world at her feet. After Albert's death in 1861, after twenty-one years of marriage, she reigned without the support of the man she loved. The Albert Memorial in London, recently restored, is a remarkable monument to her dead husband, and symbolizes the 'state of mourning' that dominated most of her reign.

1830   1835   1840

The Houses of Parliament

The Clock Tower which houses 'Big Ben' is one of the best-loved symbols of Britain, along with red telephone boxes and double-decker buses. However, it is just one part of the Houses of Parliament. Its medieval appearance, like that of the Victoria Tower, is nineteenth-century mock Gothic – a tribute to the past.

The Palace of Westminster, where Parliament originally met, burnt down in 1834, leaving only Westminster Hall, the crypt of St Stephen's Chapel, some of the cloisters and the Jewel Tower. A new building was needed, and in 1836 a design by Charles Barry, which incorporated the late eleventh-century Westminster Hall, was selected from ninety-seven entries in an open competition. With the help of Augustus Pugin, Barry built one of the finest examples of Gothic architecture in Britain. Work started in 1840 and it took twenty-seven years to construct the complex.

The House of Commons was destroyed on 10 May 1941 during the Blitz, but a new chamber in the same Gothic style as the old one was designed by Sir Giles Gilbert Scott and built in 1948-50.

Florence Nightingale

The 'lady with the lamp' is the ultimate image of care and comfort. Florence Nightingale's work in the Crimea breathed new life into nursing. Wounded soldiers regarded her as an angel, and it is said that she never left a dying man's side. She gained her nickname from her nightly rounds, checking on her sleeping patients, when she lightened the darkness with the oil lamp she carried. The British public warmed to her, and she was hailed as a national heroine.

The Crimean War was Britain's attempt to stop the Russians expanding into Europe. The battles were fierce, but in the hospitals themselves conditions were so horrific that more than 250,000 men died. Florence's real talent lay in administration. She systematically reorganized the military hospital at Scutari, cleaned, repaired and brought in new medical equipment.

Her reforming work continued after the war and, although she was desperately ill with brucellosis, she established the first nursing school at St Thomas's Hospital in London in 1860. Her aim was to improve the standard of nursing and she succeeded in changing what had been a disreputable profession into an honourable vocation.

Charles Darwin

Charles Darwin's theories about the 'survival of the fittest', or natural selection, and man's evolution, rocked the foundations of the scientific world and shocked Victorian society. He was bombarded with criticisms from all over the world, particularly by those who believed in a literal interpretation of the book of Genesis.

Darwin was the naturalist on the *Beagle*'s expedition to South America and the Galapagos Islands from 1831 to 1836 and identified many new plant and animal species. *The Origin of Species by Means of Natural Selection* was published in 1859 after he had spent twenty years collecting evidence to support his ideas about evolution. When he followed this controversial book with the *The Descent of Man* twelve years later, he added further insult to civilized man. However, despite cries of denial from his colleagues, Darwin was convinced he was right. He retreated to Kent, where he studied the less controversial subject of barnacles.

By the end of his life, natural selection was accepted throughout the scientific world. Darwin's theories on evolutionary development obviously link well with the kind of evidence archaeologists search for and make the unique fragments of early human bone from sites like Boxgrove in West Sussex even more important.

Charles Dickens

Charles Dickens was probably Britain's most famous nineteenth-century novelist, and could certainly lay claim to being the most successful: his writing was consistently popular during his life, and in the twelve years after his death almost 4¼ million copies of his books were sold in England. He still commands a huge following today.

Dickens used his work as a forum to speak out for reforms and against injustices, and his fiction is often intermingled with political statements against aging institutions like the Poor Law, the prison system and the civil service.

Although books like *The Pickwick Papers* and *Great Expectations* are set in a fictional version of Chatham where his father once worked, most of his writings focus on London and Dickens successfully reveals the many facets of Victorian society. However, his characters are often caricatures of contemporary people and, although he paints a vivid picture of London life, his delight in mirth and drama removes them a little from the reality of nineteenth-century society. The city is dark and mysterious in novels like *Bleak House* – an image that is commonly associated with the Victorian period. It would be as well to remember that the London of Dickens is a London of fiction and not necessarily of fact.

1865   1870

SOHO
BIRMINGHAM

SERIES 4
Broadcast
19 January 1997

Soho marked an important departure for *Time Team* – it was our first industrial site, and our first urban excavation. Birmingham was one of the leading cities of the Industrial Revolution because it was where Matthew Boulton, together with James Watt, set up the Soho Manufactory: a huge, steam-powered factory and mint. Established in 1761, it revolutionized mass production. Today, the site is covered by a residential area. We were called in by Dylan Close, a local resident, to examine a brick structure he had found while digging in his garden.

Industrial archaeology presents some unusual challenges for archaeologists. It is usually associated with sites in existence since the seventeenth century or later. Many sites that have been excavated are those connected with the start of the Industrial Revolution and this period marks a massive increase in artefacts and the beginning of machine

shafts from the steam engines passed along brick tunnels to drive other machines. They still exist under Soho back gardens today.

production which makes it harder to say where particular objects come from. Mass production was on its way and new industrial centres developed next to large coalfields: the Soho Manufactory was one such. The site had been important enough to have had a good number of plans, drawings and engravings associated with it, but there were still many gaps in the records. Could we relocate the mint that Boulton had set up in 1788?

Trench One was the re-excavation of the hole in the garden and showed the base of a brick-lined tunnel which was important as we could see that parts of the factory had survived intact. Many plans and drawings of the factory exist so our first strategy was to use these to identify the different factory parts on the ground and work out its entire location. George Demidowicz, the local industrial archaeology expert, identified the brick structure as one of the shafts that linked the engine to the presses that made coin blanks. At Boulton's mint in 1826, one steam engine drove four coin presses, and the engine was also linked by shafts running through brick tunnels to six presses that cut out coin blanks in another building. By locating one of these tunnels, we hoped to follow it to the 'cutting-out' room and then trace it back to the main steam engine. Armed with this information, Phil planned to open Trench Two to find the room where the coins would have been cut. After a lot of clambering over hedges and measuring over fences, his calculations led him to a site under a patio that was hastily removed.

Our second target was to find the front wall of the factory, which would also fix its location. After calculations by Stewart Ainsworth, a mechanical digger was brought in to dig Trench Three, through the concrete forecourt of a modern factory.

By Day Two, an overwhelming smell of petrol pervaded Trench Three and work stopped while the fire brigade arrived to make it safe – it turned out that the fumes were leaking from a large underground tank. Meanwhile, Phil continued digging in several back gardens to try and locate more of the factory. He found shafts of machinery and junctions in the tunnels that made it possible to map the position of the engine room, using the old plans. The steam engine would have been supplied with water by a deep well shaft, and the radar team were brought in to try and locate its position. Radar is reckoned to be the best method for finding voids underground. By using the data from the scan along with the information from the plans, we got an approximate fix for the well.

To get an idea of the kind of machine we were looking for, Mick took a trip to the Birmingham Museum of Science and Industry to view one of the few surviving examples of Boulton's steam engine in action. Boulton and Watt had sold construction plans for these machines and their key parts to factories all over the country and later throughout the world. Many are over 9 metres (27 foot) in height and the main beam can weigh several tons. Each needed to be supplied with thousands of gallons of water to produce the steam, and all this required masses of piping. It was a far cry from the water mill that had existed on the site when Boulton first came to Soho in 1761. He continued to use the mill until but employed the help of a steam-powered pump to recycle the water to the channel that supplied the mill. It was in 1774, when Boulton met James Watt, that the real revolution began. Watt's improvements to the steam engine increased its power and efficiency.

Towards the end of Day Two Phil uncovered some bone button-blanks that would have been manufactured by Boulton. Phil continued to navigate his way around the factory on Day Three, putting in small trenches to find out where different rooms and workshops were located. In the 'latchet room' he found copper coin-blanks, confirming that this was the area where coins were minted. This room was so called because before it was used for minting coins, latchets, or buckles, had been made here. Boulton was a great enthusiast for minting coins. He employed skilled engravers to create magnificent

Sir Edward Elgar

Britain's most popular composer since Handel, Elgar was one of a long line of artists who effectively gave voice to a national feeling. His music carries the ring of a nation that still has an empire and, at the same time, the memory of its historic past: traditional folk music combined with stirringly triumphant melodies captured the mood of late Victorian England, and the *Pomp and Circumstance* marches epitomize the wealth and patriotism that were present in Britain at the turn of the last century. His contribution to the nation was recognized by his knighthood in 1902.

Elgar made his name with the *Enigma Variations* in 1899. A tribute to his friends at his home in the Malvern Hills, its serene theme is intertwined with a touch of the loneliness that he believed all artists suffered. *The Coronation Ode*, written for Edward VII's coronation in 1901, is perhaps his most famous work. It was an adaptation of a *Pomp and Circumstance* march, but is more commonly known as *Land of Hope and Glory*. With lyrics by the poet A. C. Benson, which Elgar disapproved of, thinking them jingoistic and detrimental to his composition, it is like a second national anthem and now ends the Proms every year.

portraits to adorn them, and he also introduced the 'cartwheel' coin, which was worth its weight in metal. This coin had a secure value at a time when counterfeiting and devaluation were severe problems. Prior to the eighteenth century, coins were generally made by hand-powered presses, which could turn out fifty to sixty coins an hour. With the invention of the steam-driven mint, that rate increased to tens of thousands, and the objects produced had a regularity and consistency that had not been seen before. Boulton's Manufactory made other goods which were sent throughout the world: not only humble buttons and buckles, but also, as the factory flourished, sophisticated lamps and gilded clocks, one of which found its way to the royal court of Catherine the Great in Russia.

Finally, Trench Three in the forecourt, now deep, unstable and hampered by mains gas supplies as well as the petrol tank, uncovered a set of massive whitewashed foundations – the front wall of the factory or 'Principal Building'. This had been designed with a grand classical front by the architect James Wyatt in order to make it look like a great country mansion! The building was demolished in 1863.

Birmingham demonstrated the amazing potential of industrial archaeology. Although there were maps and plans of the factory, archaeological skills were still necessary to locate it on the site and show how well-preserved it was. By finding the main mint building, parts of the latchet works, the front wall of the Principal Building and the steam-engine well, we had been able to locate the information contained in the drawings and plans of Boulton's factory. This should protect the Manufactory's remains should any redevelopment of the area be contemplated.

Time Team also learnt a lot about the problems of digging on urban sites – problems like petrol tanks and dangerously deep trenches. Birmingham is Mick's home town and it was difficult for him to believe that *Time Team* were making a programme near where he came from in such apparently inhospitable archaeological circumstances. He found the end results stupendous, however: Boulton's Manufactory for its time and of its type is one of the most important archaeological sites in the world. It was the beginning of the end of a world in which objects were made on request. Mick's favourite moment of the shoot was the visit to see the 1779 working steam engine in the museum. At each stroke it lifted a ton of water and the smoke, steam, noise and smells all brought the Industrial Revolution to life!

Coin blanks from the Soho digs.

Scott of the Antarctic

Captain Robert Scott led a famous and fateful expedition to the South Pole in 1912. During the first decade of the twentieth century there was intense competition between explorers of all nationalities to see who could be the first to reach the centre of the southern hemisphere. Scott, who had commanded a previous expedition that had discovered King Edward VII land, was chosen to lead the official British team.

He and his four companions reached the South Pole on 18 January 1912, only to find that the Norwegian Roald Amundsen had arrived a month earlier. There was nothing left to do but start the crippling journey back to base camp. In his diary Scott wrote: 'We shall stick it out to the end… It seems a pity but I do not think I can write any more.' That was his last entry. He and all the members of his party died just 18 kilometres (11 miles) from a vital food station.

News of their tragic death left the entire nation in mourning. Scott was awarded a posthumous knighthood, and his diaries, which were found eight months later, were published in 1913.

The First World War

The abiding image of the First World War is of thousands of young men, filled with patriotic fervour, advancing out of trenches only to be slaughtered. It was the first time Britain had sent an army to Europe since Wellington's victory at Waterloo and tactics had, unfortunately, changed very little since then. The belief was that an artillery bombardment would reduce the enemy to a defenceless rabble, and that an advance in neat strategic lines would encounter very little resistance. The reality was that the Germans hid in their shelters, waited for the bombardment – which was often inaccurate and ineffective – then set up their machine guns and waited.

On 1 July 1916, as the noise of the big guns died away, British and French divisions started their long walk towards German lines. It was the start of the battle of the Somme and on that day there were almost 60,000 Allied casualties, to little effect. Battles like this were a tragic mix of raw young recruits, out-of-date tactics and the new industrial dealer of death – the machine gun – and produced losses that, in scale and speed, were totally new in the history of war. Britain was confident in its manufacturing capacity, and surprised that it could be outgunned by a nation determined to turn its industrial skills more effectively to the cause of warfare and imperial expansion.

The British and their allies, including French, Australian, Irish and Canadian troops, returned to the Somme two years later and, thanks to the use of tanks and a less suicidal regard for enemy machine guns, were victorious: 21,000 Germans were killed or declared missing. Sir Douglas Haig, the commander-in-chief on the Western Front, presided over both battles of the Somme. The war ended with victory for the Allies and the abdication of the Kaiser.

The First World War saw the industrialization of death and introduced the horrors of poison gas, which was used by both sides. For many, it was the end of innocence. However, despite Germany's defeat, it would be only twenty years before it was on the march again.

The Invention of Television

The invention of television was a momentous event because it allowed information to spread rapidly across countries and the world and made instantaneously shared experiences, and concepts like Marshal McCluhan's global village, possible. Large numbers of people watching a programme like *Time Team* and talking about it the following day is a new kind of human communication – the next stage of which is being developed on the Internet.

In the 1870s Thomas Edison was the first man to dabble with the idea of a 'telephonescope'. About thirty years later a company called Campbell-Swinton worked out the basic ideas behind modern television, building on inventions from the end of the nineteenth century: the scanning disc and cathode ray tube. Their work was put on hold during the First World War, but in 1925 John Logie Baird produced a machine that showed a primitive 30-line picture and could even send images to America. After negotiations with the BBC he put out experimental transmissions in 1930. The first-ever outside broadcast – of the Derby horse race – was in the following year.

Baird's 'seeing-by-wireless' was not ultimately successful, and was replaced by a basic electronic model made by Marconi-EMI.

Edward VIII

Edward's father, George V, was not overly confident in his son's ability. He is quoted as saying, 'After I am dead, the boy will ruin himself in twelve months.' How right he was: Edward VIII's reign lasted just under a year, from January to December 1936.

In his youth Edward was a popular figure, with his easy charm and concern for the unemployed. However, he did not take well to his official duties and it was often obvious that he found them boring. He preferred London society, and Fort Belvedere, his home in Windsor Great Park, was regularly the scene of private parties and soirées. In 1930 he met Wallis Simpson, an American divorcée, then married for the second time, and two years later she visited Fort Belvedere. After his accession she filed for divorce from her second husband. Legally there was nothing to prevent Edward marrying her, but the establishment considered that it would be unacceptable for the head of the Church of England to marry a divorced person.

The king's suggestion of a morganatic marriage – Wallis Simpson would not be accorded royal status and their children would not have the right to succeed to the throne – was also unacceptable, and by the end of the year few options were open to him. Edward abdicated on 11 December in favour of his brother, who became George VI, and left England for France where he married Wallis Simpson in June 1937. He was created Duke of Windsor, and was governor of the Bahamas from 1940 to 1945, but spent the remaining thirty-six years of his life in exile.

Jet Engines

In the late 1930s the development of the jet engine and subsequent changes in aircraft design were swept along in the race for better warfare technology. The jet engine was a modification of the gas-turbine system that used jet propulsion to achieve higher speeds, and allowed planes to be bigger and fly higher than before. With the outbreak of the Second World War, it was a critical invention. The jet engine has a better power-to-weight ratio, and is capable of taking heavier loads for longer distances. It helped to establish the mass transport of large numbers of people throughout the world, in a relatively short time and at low cost. In terms of cultural exchange, it opened up the world.

In Britain, the first theories behind jet propulsion were being propounded in 1928 by Frank Whittle. However, the Germans were also developing a new jet engine and they achieved the first-ever jet-powered flight on 27 August 1939. It was another eighteen months before Britain achieved this, with a Whittle engine (W-1) in a Gloster plane at Cranwell. The English technology moved to America where General Electric continued research and production which culminated in the Lockheed XP-80 prototype, flown in 1944.

By 1945, the Germans' jet engine was in full production for the Messerschmitt Me 262 fighters. On the Allied side, the Gloster Meteor twin-jet fighter was in limited production, but very few served in the war.

The Second World War

Until the rise of the Third Reich, epitomized by the unpleasant shape of Adolf Hitler, Britain had not been threatened with invasion since the Spanish Armada and Napoleonic Wars. *Time Team*'s work on the Spitfire programme brought home to us how close Germany had come to invading Britain: but for Hitler's mistaken strategic decisions, the determination of a small number of RAF pilots and the faith of the British people, the Germans might have succeeded in their objective.

The early phase of the war was Britain's darkest period, with a string of German successes in Europe. In 1940 Allied troops were evacuated from the beaches of Dunkirk and France surrendered. It was probably the RAF's defeat of the *Luftwaffe* and Churchill's inspired leadership that won the day – even though, in the years that followed, victories like Montgomery's at the battle of El Alamein were followed by setbacks. More than a quarter of a million service personnel and 60,000 civilians died between 1939 and 1945.

The armed forces had developed an egalitarian structure and troops returning from the war were determined to create a different Britain, less dominated by class. In July 1945 the Labour Party won a landslide victory and Clement Attlee became prime minister of a government that nationalized many key institutions and established the National Health Service in 1948.

The archaeology of the Second World War is increasingly valued and English Heritage's 'Defence of the Realm' project has helped to preserve evidence of a time not so long ago, when Britain's existence was threatened.

REEDHAM MARSHES
NORFOLK

SERIES 6
Broadcast
21 February 1999

In February 1944, two American B–17 'Flying Fortress' aircraft returning from a bombing mission in Germany collided in mid-air over Reedham in Norfolk, just minutes from their base. The bodies of the airmen who were killed were salvaged and parts of one plane were removed in the 1960s. Ian McLachlan, an aviation archaeologist, suggested the site to *Time Team* and our aim was to excavate the B–17 that had remained buried in the peat marshes for over fifty years, and try to add to the information about the causes of the crash.

Day One began with a talk from an RAF bomb-disposal team about safety procedures during the dig. There had been no large bombs on the plane when it crashed, but there would still be hundreds of bullets in the ground. There was also the possibility that we might encounter inflammable aviation fuel and dangerous metalwork.

On Day One John Gater and Sue Ovenden, the geophysics team, identified two anomalies that could relate to the plane and mechanical diggers were brought in to start removing layers of soil and peat. Trench One quickly filled with water and mud from the waterlogged peat and underlying clay layers, making excavation difficult. But by lunchtime Trench Two had begun to yield pieces of plane, as well as machine-gun rounds that were immediately made safe by the bomb-disposal team.

Local aircraft enthusiasts were on hand to help with the dig and, as bits of metal were uncovered by the mechanical diggers, it became apparent that they work very differently to archaeologists. Phil carefully excavated and recorded the metal like any other archaeological find, while the enthusiasts wanted to pull everything out as quickly as possible.

By Day Two a compromise had been reached between the archaeologists and aircraft enthusiasts and Trench Two was extended to find more of the wreckage. Recognizable parts of the plane came up, including the pilot's seat and perspex from the cockpit window. Finding personal items like a boot and glove brought home the tragedy of a crash that killed twenty-one airmen. Stewart Ainsworth and Bernie Ford, the air-crash investigator, were trying to piece together the exact order of events from official records and eyewitness accounts – and even telephoned America to get the opinions of men who had flown in the B–17's squadron.

A B–17 machine-gun round, still live and potentially lethal.

Sir Winston Churchill

Winston Churchill is probably one of Britain's most famous prime ministers: the man who saved the nation from a Nazi invasion. His stubbornness in the face of imminent German victory, and his inspirational command as a war leader, turned the tide of the war to Britain's advantage. Churchill's desire to destroy the Nazis began to be fulfilled in June 1944 when Allied troops stormed the French coast in the D-Day landings. It has been said that George VI himself had to prevent his prime minister going with them to watch the historic event.

Churchill entered politics for the first time in 1900 when he was elected Conservative member of Parliament for Oldham. His career developed quickly and by 1908 he was the youngest cabinet minister for forty-two years. However, he was clearly at his best, and sometimes his worst, during times of war and, although he held government office during the 1920s, he did not stand out as a superb leader until the outbreak of the Second World War.

Churchill was the rock on which the British public could rely. While the world was in chaos and families were torn apart, he became a beacon for raising the country's morale. His insistence that Britain would be victorious and his characteristic 'V' sign inspired and encouraged the nation. However, his brilliance as a war leader was counterbalanced by his lesser abilities at home affairs and in 1945, in the first general election after the war, he lost to the Labour Party.

Pilot's boot found at Reedham

Plunging deeper into the black stuff, our search for the B-17 involves civil engineering on a grand scale.

The combined efforts of the Team produced a lot of information about the crash by Day Three and, by combining eyewitness accounts with photographs of the area after the crash and comparing what this revealed with the excavated evidence, Bernie Ford was able to build up a picture of what had happened: two planes had collided in heavy cloud and plummeted to the ground. The trenches were therefore extended to include the proposed new crash site and the mechanical digger removed two machine guns from Trench Two.

By the end of the three days there was still no sign of the B-17's enormous engines or any large pieces of fuselage, despite the huge and unstable trenches - up to 5 metres (15 feet) deep - that we had dug. Either the force of the crash had propelled these remains further down into the watery peat than we could reach, or the salvage teams in 1944 had removed more than we thought. Either way, *Time Team* had to some extent unravelled the circumstances of the crash, and used archaeological methods on a very modern mystery.

Elizabeth II

Elizabeth II became Queen of England in 1952, on the death of her father George VI. Although some people believe the monarchy is perhaps outdated in today's society, a medieval institution that has no place in the twenty-first century, something deep in the British psyche seems to need a royal presence as a balance to the politicians about whom we are healthily sceptical.

Although the power of the monarch was greatly limited by the time Elizabeth acceded to the throne, she carried out her duties with an energy that would have impressed the previous incumbents of the role. In particular she was concerned to develop the Commonwealth as an effective world body. Over the considerable period of her reign, she has become an invaluable source of experience for successive prime ministers and it is perhaps in embodying the permanence of one our great British institutions, that she plays her most valuable role.

WIERRE-EFFROY
NORTHERN FRANCE

TONY'S PIECE TO CAMERA: 'Nearly sixty years ago, on 23 May 1940, a twenty-four-year-old Englishman called Paul Klipsch climbed into his Spitfire and flew across the English Channel. It was the first day any Spitfire based in England met a German aircraft in combat. It was Klipsch's first day of real war. And it was also his last. The combat report simply says 'Killed in Action'. We know where his plane came down in northern France, but why — and how — did it crash? Time Team will be uncovering the wreck of one of the war's earliest Spitfires, and telling the story of its pilot.'

Paul Klipsch entered French air space and was shot down by a Messerschmitt 110 at about 6 pm on 23 May 1940. He was one of the first Spitfire pilots to be killed over French territory, and his Spitfire almost the first to be lost in France.

His death came at the moment when only the courage of the pilots of the Royal Air Force, and the technical excellence of the planes they flew, stood between Britain and what might have turned into the first phase of a German invasion. The men of the British Expeditionary Force were being evacuated from Dunkirk and German Panzer tanks were speeding through the small villages around Boulogne in an attempt to encircle them.

Two brothers, Auguste and René Mierlot, saw the Spitfire come down in the fields outside the small French village of Wierre-Effroy. Their memory of the events of that day are particularly vivid because less than half an hour after the plane crashed, the German army entered the village. The local coffin-maker risked the anger of the Germans in order to remove the pilot's remains and they were interred in the village cemetery.

The remains of our Spitfire. This hole may have been created by a 20-mm bullet.

Professor Aston and the fieldwalk team, searching for clues on the morning of Day One.

Nearly 1,500 pilots gave their lives in the early years of the Second World War, a war that was to include countries on a worldwide scale. It was the closest Britain has come since the Napoleonic Wars to experiencing the threat of invasion. Somewhere on the horizon an alien culture lurked, intent on the country's destruction or subjugation.

When I jumped at the chance to excavate a Spitfire everyone wanted to know why. The answer was complicated. The fact that the programme would be part of a series broadcast in the millennium year was one reason. I imagined two ends of a historic continuum that expressed our past in terms of weapons: at one end a palaeolithic hand-axe, which I was hoping to find at Elveden, and at the other a Spitfire – an icon of a lost age. To me the pilot and the plane are the modern equivalent of a knight on his charger, standing against the forces of darkness.

I also felt that we should continue to excavate sites people don't normally associate with archaeology. Watching archaeologists at work on the unexpected provides new insights into what they do. I also knew that I wanted to see a Spitfire fly and listen to the people who had flown the plane. These airmen are the last remnants of a group of fighters who enabled Britain to win the war against fascism and they represent a kind of warfare that could be regarded as lost for ever. My father was an RAF engineer during the Second World War and both Mick and I had memories of attempting to build Airfix models of planes as children, so on one level the Spitfire aspect of the site could be viewed through somewhat rose-tinted spectacles. Other realities were harsher, including the fact that someone had died in the crash.

Both Mick and I had found excavating the B–17 in Reedham Marshes in Norfolk, in 1998, a bit depressing. We had not found much evidence of the plane and Mick kept muttering that it was like digging a car crash. It had also taken us some time to adjust to what might be called the cultural differences between archaeologists and aviation enthusiasts. It had felt like a difficult dig and after it was broadcast we received quite a bit of e-mail along the lines of 'it's the wrong subject for *Time Team*'. Set against this was the excellence of the programme and the enthusiastic response from the majority of viewers.

To return to the Wierre-Effroy shoot, members of the pilot's family were willing to give their permission for the excavation to go ahead and also to join us at the site. This and the prospect of including a Spitfire that was still in flying condition in the programme made me certain we should go ahead.

With the enthusiastic support of researcher Alex Finch, Justin Pollard, the assistant producer, and the vital translation skills of Katy Segrove, we ventured into France and began negotiating with French farmers. There were a number of obstacles to overcome. Would we be allowed to dig up French fields? Would a representative of the British Embassy stand by to help us through the red tape? Would anything be left of the Spitfire?

On the evening before the shoot started, an ancient French farmer in the local bar assured us, after complimenting us on the beauty of our lady excavators, that the plane had been taken away and the engine was lost. With the clouds tipping down buckets and mud sticking to everything, this was one of the low points of a shoot that was an emotional roller-coaster and left everyone exhausted for days afterwards.

We worked closely with Steve Vizard and his group of aeroplane enthusiasts. His research had led us to the site and he guided us to the exact location of the crash. As soon as we began walking in the field fragments of aluminium and the odd bullet showed we were in the right place.

We were on the land of Jacques Charlet, which is now farmed by Jean-Michel Louvet. Steve had been alerted to the site by Alan Brown, an ex-docker and aviation enthusiast, and had established a good relationship with the farmer with the invaluable help of Jean Michel Goyet, our French contact. This helped us to gain access to the location of the crash, but the production team had to do a lot of negotiating with M. Louvet to finalize an agreement, and also with official bodies to secure the necessary permission to excavate. Digging in a crash site which resulted in a fatality requires an agreement with the Commonwealth War Graves Commission. RAF Assistant Air Attaché Steve Gunner of the British Embassy in Paris liaised at an official level. He was present for most of the shoot and did an excellent job ensuring we were not tied up by too much red tape and that our relationship with our hosts was as friendly as possible.

We were keen to handle the excavation in the same way as a dig on any archaeological site and on Day One our first priority was a fieldwalk over a grid laid out by the geophysics team. Mick organized everyone into teams who walked over a large area of the field and systematically picked up anything they found on the surface. Locating finds in this way and plotting them on a map often reveals hot spots of activity that may indicate the presence of archaeological remains under the ground. One of the first conclusions we drew from the fieldwalking was that there had been quite a lot of Roman activity on

Mick on his spoil heap contemplates the fuselage wreckage.

the site. Guy de la Bédoyère, who often helps the Team on Roman sites, had come in his other role – as an aeroplane archaeologist – but became quite excited at the amount of Roman pottery that appeared. We decided to leave it in place as a record for future archaeologists and concentrate on later finds.

Bernard Thomason located each piece of the Spitfire accurately in three dimensions with a Global Positioning System (GPS). We combined the fieldwalk results with the geophysical survey and the two corresponded. John found a massive anomaly and Steve Vizard's team also surveyed the site with metal detectors, pegging the location of each find. All the different methods of surveying pointed to the same area. There was an air of quiet satisfaction, not to say smugness, amongst the fieldwalkers, who had come to the same conclusion with their very low-tech method.

Caroline Barker, a key person in our digging team working on the fuselage.

We were certain we had located the main area of the Spitfire remains – but what would we find there? We knew from research that villagers had gone to the field and that some of them had, at great risk to themselves, helped to remove the pilot's body. At this time the village was the full of advancing Germans. Some aircraft parts had recently been found in the hedgerows and it was uncertain just how much of the plane was left on the site as farmers, inevitably, tend to move bits of metal that get in the way of the plough.

All surface finds were removed from the topsoil and we used trowels to start scraping back the soil in a 30 x 30 centimetre (1 x 1 foot) area – Trench One – that showed the greatest concentration of finds.

We hoped to recover as much of the plane as possible. We knew that early Spitfires had certain distinctive elements, and that the one Paul Klipsch flew had been a Mark I. One of the goals of the excavation was to see if we could locate any of the identifying features of this model.

One of the great advantages of working with Steve and his team was that they had excellent background knowledge about the plane and its component parts. Archaeologists rarely have the opportunity to talk to people who know how an artefact was constructed. Steve's firm on the Isle of Wight maintains and rebuilds Spitfires so he knows every nut and bolt intimately. As small pieces of squashed metal emerged from the clay he matched them to parts of the plane.

The Spitfire was designed by a team led by Reginald Mitchell and was based on the Supermarine Schneider trophy aircraft, one of the fastest seaplanes of the time. The first prototype was flying within a year. In early Spitfires – more than twenty-four model types and over 22,000 planes were eventually produced – the Supermarine logo was embossed on the rudder pedals. The Supermarine's V–12 Rolls-Royce engine was renamed the Merlin and proved to be so effective that it was used by the Americans to power their Mustang fighter planes. The Spitfire engine was fed petrol and air via a carburettor whereas the German Messerschmitt used fuel injection, giving it a slight advantage when manoeuvring at altitude. Spitfires were just as fast as the Messerschmitts and more manoeuvrable. Pilots said the plane was a joy to fly.

It had always been assumed that the crash was the result of enemy action, but nobody was certain about this. Steve Moss, an air-crash investigator, was on hand to see if any of the evidence we found would clarify the situation. He would need to see every piece of wreckage if he was to stand a chance of establishing what had happened.

By the end of the morning of Day One we were using a mechanical digger to remove topsoil from a wider area and gradually opening a 5 x 5 metre (15 x 15 foot) trench – Trench Two. A combination of Katy's French and Mick Worthington's hand signals had established a good level of communication with the French driver of the digger.

By now we had been joined by members of Paul Klipsch's family. They had given their blessing to the excavation and it was important to all of us that we had their support during the three days of the shoot. Paul's half-brother, Eric Wynn-Owen, who had been in the infantry in Normandy during the war, took a keen interest. He told us about Paul's early days in the RAF, and how his half-brother kept an illegal motorcycle on the base and buzzed his mother's house in his Spitfire. Paul was made sergeant pilot on 27 January 1940 and joined 92 Squadron on 10 February. He was twenty-four when he died in May of the same year.

By mid-afternoon Trench One – our initial trench – began to reveal large numbers of bullets. Mark Kirby, a member of Steve Vizard's team, believed we had located the ammunition box for one of the

RAF Assistant Air Attaché Steve Gunner and members of Paul Klispch's family.

Spitfire's eight guns. As each find emerged it was bagged and tagged, then sent to a washing area to be cleaned.

line of spitfire machine gun bullets.

Time Team had established a good working relationship with the aviation enthusiasts by now. They understood that we would excavate carefully around objects and not just pluck finds out of the ground, and we began to use their background knowledge to identify parts and look for identification numbers. As the diggers pointed out, it is a rarity to excavate an object that has a number that not only describes what it is, but also shows where it came from. A label on the first machine gun we discovered identified it as being from the starboard of the plane and a Number One – the gun nearest the fuselage.

We already knew that the Spitfire was number P9373 and that it was first flown by chief test pilot George Pickering on 22 February 1940. It was armed with eight machine guns each of which fired 303 rounds of bullets which were the same size as those used in the army's rifles. The Messerschmitt 110, the type of plane the RAF was probably up against on the day of the crash, had four machine guns of 7.92 mm and two 20-mm cannons. The cannon shells were much larger than the Spitfire's bullets. This kind of knowledge about armaments could be critical if we discovered any holes in the fuselage. As Steve Moss pointed out, crashes like the one we were excavating often cause pieces of the plane to fracture and puncture the skin and the holes they make can look as if they were caused by bullets.

This was the first time many of our excavators had dug in circumstances like these. The B–17 dig in Norfolk had revealed so little of the main aircraft that we felt that much of the excavation had

A change of
strategy discussion
around the trench.
We needed to
expand the area
quickly to see if the
'crushed can' theory
was correct. There
was no general
agreement.

taken place in an area already disturbed by United States Air Force recovery teams. Here, we were the first people to dig on the site, and the family of the man who had died was with us.

At the end of Day One the mechanical digger started stripping Trench Two. It was difficult to know what we were looking for – would we recognize the marks in the soil caused by the plane's impact, as well as finding metal fragments of the Spitfire itself? Finally, small patches of metal and solid features started to appear in the clay.

Day Two became a battle against the elements. Heavy clay stuck to everything and we had to dig drains under the air shelter to allow the water to run away. What soon became apparent was that we had begun to excavate a column of metal – the rear of the Spitfire fuselage. Gradually, recognizable pieces of plane, including the tail wheel tyre with the word 'Dunlop' clearly visible, emerged from the tangled mass of clay-covered metal. The tyre appeared to be partially inflated. There were also puncture marks in other pieces of the fuselage. These were bent inwards, which implies an exterior entry point, but it was too early to describe them as bullet holes.

At this stage I talked to a number of the aviation enthusiasts about the exact nature of a vertical plane crash. Spitfires could reach 640 kph (400 mph) in a dive, so a speed in excess of this was likely at impact. Would the forces this produced be enough to bury the entire 4-metre (12 foot) fuselage deep into hard clay? It was difficult to accept this, and a crash that had in some way spread debris over the surface of the field seemed more likely. If this was the case, the more conventional, archaeological, layer-by-layer approach would be necessary, to establish a relationship between the various fragments of plane. However, Steve Vizard and members of his team who had dug at a similar site referred to the 'crushed can' analogy – a column of metal that has almost driven itself into the ground. What if we were dealing with this? Mick, Phil and Carenza, supported by some of the diggers, were reluctant to abandon the traditional archaeological approach, but it was clear that if we went down inch by inch in a 5 x 5 metre (15 x 15 foot) area we would not get to the base of the crash within three days.

After much discussion and a bit of argument we decided to use a small digger bucket to dig some test trenches immediately adjacent to the plane's entry hole. I was relieved and encouraged when the first bucketloads were full of clay and topsoil with no spread of debris. As Eric Wynn-Owen poignantly remarked, his half-brother had made a 'right good job of it'.

As more bits of soil were cut out of the main trench by the mechanical digger, more metalwork was revealed, but all within a column of fuselage 1.2 metre (4 foot) in diameter. The crushed-can theory was proving to be right. We began to see recognizable bits of plane including sections of fuselage and the armour-plating from the rear of the cockpit. We also started to hit patches of oil which began to combine with the mud to form an unpleasant soup at the base of the excavation. We were now below 2 metres (6½ feet) and had to widen and step the trench to ensure everyone's safety.

Wiring from the instrument panel and a piece of what might have been a control column appeared. We continued to dig down. Although there was evidence from the War Office that the body had been removed from the plane, or had possibly been thrown clear on impact, the knowledge did not make it any less moving when we began to discover small personal artefacts – a glove, a piece of uniform, a pen and what might have been a wallet – from the cockpit area. All these objects would be carefully cleaned and preserved and, after the Commonwealth War Graves Commission had been notified, they would be returned to the family.

Extra help shovelling around the edges of the fuselage.

harlie Brown – pitfire pilot.

the thrills of Day
Three - a spitfire
flies overhead.
Assistant producer
Justin Pollard
captures people's
reactions.

By the end of Day Two we had started to work at the base of the column of wreckage and uncovered what seemed to be two halves of the main engine, each with the famous Rolls-Royce lettering engraved on its covers. Huge pistons and crank rods, and the tip of a propeller blade, appeared.

On the evening of Day Two we were joined by Charlie Brown, who flies a Mark V – one of only a handful of Spitfires that are still airworthy. He had flown it across the Channel to Calais airport near Boulogne, and would overfly the site on Day Three as a tribute to Paul Klipsch's memory. Alan Wright, who had flown in Paul's squadron, had his first opportunity in forty years to sit in the cockpit of a Spitfire.

Alan exemplified the quiet toughness that enabled young pilots to keep flying when their friends were being killed. He described how Spitfires had handled, how they were flown in combat – and how pilots constantly looked over their shoulders because Messerschmitts attacked from behind. *Time Team*'s researchers had found Alan's combat report of 23 May 1940, the day Paul had been shot down.

'While patrolling the French coast the squadron became involved with about 20 ME 110s which were escorting a number of bombers. I joined in the lower part of the dog fight, and fired a number of deflection shots with little result. The pilot's cockpit of one, however, burst apart and the E/A [enemy aircraft] went down in a spiral. I followed another which was diving with white smoke coming from its engine.'

On that day the RAF flew over 250 sorties and 92 Squadron lost three Spitfires. Three German bombers were shot down and five fighters. Five more were unconfirmed, as although the pilots believed they had hit the plane, they had not seen it crash or blow up.

On Day Three Charlie performed aerobatics to show what the Spitfire is capable of doing. Then as Tony stood in the middle of the field, carefully timing the introduction to his piece to camera to allow for the plane's approach, Charlie made a low-level pass over the camera. No one was prepared for the force and excitement that was generated as the plane passed overhead. The blast of sound, the blur of the fuselage, the glimpse of Charlie in the cockpit combined to create an unforgettable moment.

A typical repair job for the RAF ground control was replacing a damaged flap, something Alan Wright remembers from his flying days. For the cameo Steve Vizard suggested that we try to reproduce this aspect of the work that the RAF ground crew would have done to keep the planes flying. Phil's practical skills were put to the test but by the middle of Day Three we had a newly repaired flap. This had been created from aluminium and beaten into shape using Phil's shovel. The hardest part had been drilling out the rivets and this had given us some idea of the pressure that must have been on the ground crew to get the planes back in the air in time for another attack.

Later, with the weather worsening, Charlie flew over the trenches and the cemetery where Paul Klipsch is buried. The tension was palpable in the moments before the fly-past. We heard the noise of the plane's engines first – a low hum that grew louder and louder – then the Spitfire appeared out of the

Alan Wright,
ecstatic to be back
in the spitfire
cockpit again.

Paul Klipsch's gra
in the Wierre Eff
cemetery.

clouds and did a series of low swoops over the site. It was an exciting experience, but also a moving one: the contrast between the two aeroplanes, one working and one buried, vividly brought home the tragedy of the crash we were investigating.

By the end of the day we had uncovered a 2-metre (6½ foot) column, from the tail wheel to the base of the propeller hub. The tangled wreckage looked like a bizarre modern sculpture. There were rivulets of black oil around the base of the column and fuselage sections, with large holes puncturing the metal, at the top.

The main pieces were carefully peeled away from the wreckage and as each one came off a member of Steve Vizard's team took it to be washed, then put it on the relevant part of a full-sized layout of a Spitfire. We could clearly see how the force of impact had buckled and crushed the structure. Some bits, including the rear of the pilot's seat and the pedals from the cockpit, were recognizable. Engine remains were the last to come out. Steve Vizard estimated that we had recovered fifty to sixty per cent of the fuselage.

In the last few minutes Paul Klipsch's family asked to be left in quiet to contemplate the excavated remains of his plane.

Time Team's diggers had done an incredible job under exhausting – and eventually draining – conditions and it was appropriate that they should carry out the final task of the shoot: handing over the small number of personal items to a representative of the Commonwealth War Graves Commission.

Steve Vizard continued working on the dig after the shoot and identified most of the plane's key parts, including the rudder pedals with Supermarine embossed on them, instruments and the firing button for the Spitfire's machine guns. The button was set to fire which suggests that Paul Klipsch had taken part in an aerial battle and fired his guns before his untimely death. Steve also found the map box, which contained a number of papers including some signed by Squadron Leader Roger Bushell, the flight officer who commanded Paul Klipsch's squadron. He was later captured and led the break-out from Stalag Luft IV, as featured in *The Great Escape*, but was eventually shot by the Gestapo.

Once the metal fragments had been cleaned a hole the size of a small calibre bullet matching a contemporary German machine gun was found on the left-hand side of the cockpit. The angle that it had penetrated the metal suggested that it had been fired from above. As there was no evidence of the plane breaking up in the air, and the weather reports on the day of the accident showed that visibility was good at low altitudes it is probable that Paul Klipsch had been incapacitated in the air, possibly from this bullet.

*...fire foot pedal
...m a Mark One.*

The shoot at Wierre-Effroy was traumatic for everyone involved. The sadness of the pilot's death, the presence of members of his family and the fact that we found some personal items amongst the wreckage, all created an atmosphere that was more emotionally charged than the usual three-day *Time Team* dig. There was also elation because we actually found the plane and we were all thrilled by the sight of a Spitfire in flight. It made us all realize that it wasn't so long ago that people of an earlier generation than ourselves were fighting a war in defence of our country and that the remains of the Second World War are equally the stuff of archaeological investigation.

THE FUTURE

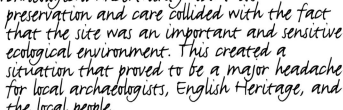

Two programmes in 1999, the documentary on the timber circle at Holme-next-the-sea in Norfolk and 'the live' at York, illustrate the way Time Team is developing and where it will be going in the future.

The site at Holme, dubbed 'sea henge' by the press, came to light when coastal erosion and storms revealed the remnants of a circle of timber posts, with the upturned stump of a tree in the centre, dating from the Bronze Age. Massive press interest, combined with archaeological uncertainty about its preservation and care collided with the fact that the site was an important and sensitive ecological environment. This created a situation that proved to be a major headache for local archaeologists, English Heritage, and the local people.

One of the earliest pictures of the exposed timber circle.

We had known about Holme for some time, thanks to our contacts with Francis Pryor and Maisie Taylor at Flag Fen, with whom we had worked earlier in the year, but it was clearly a site that required more than the usual three days. I had been keen for some time to widen *Time Team*'s remit to allow us to tackle sites like this. The unique nature of the archaeology and the popular interest in Holme – English Heritage had received more enquiries about it than any other site in the recent past – meant Channel 4 were keen to support a *Time Team* documentary on the subject. After months of tortuous negotiation with local wildlife groups, English Heritage and landowners, we were finally given the go-ahead.

The Holme site raised considerable passions on all sides. Local interest groups, keen to exploit the discovery as a tourist attraction, battled against residents worried about the expected flood of visitors – some had already conducted a naked dance of celebration around the timbers! Local wildlife wardens and ornithologists cared less about the archaeology than protecting the habitat of rare birds and English Heritage and the archaeologists were in the middle.

The facts were clear enough. Continued coastal erosion and deterioration of the exposed timbers would eventually destroy the site and this unique part of our heritage would be strewn along the Norfolk coast like so much rotting flotsam. A physical structure to protect Holme would be a vast civil engineering project that would cost millions and be ecologically damaging. The only real archaeological solution was to remove and conserve the timbers, and it was agreed at a meeting with representatives of English Heritage and the concerned groups that a reconstruction of the site could be built somewhere that was local, but in a less sensitive area.

It was at this stage that the Druids arrived! They held the sincere but historically inaccurate view that the Bronze Age site was part of their inheritance and wanted to defend it. They visited it regularly and believed the archaeologists would destroy this sacred area, rather than save it. As a result Graham

One of the most enigmatic and mysterious
monuments to appear in recent times.

The upturned tree stump that may have been a platform for the dead.

Johnston, the director, was able to capture a variety of strange scenes including one of an archaeologist patiently laying sandbags around the timbers in preparation for the excavation while, in the background, a Druid was removing them.

Graham had worked on sensitive sites before, in particular those with threatened habitats, and could talk the same language as the ornithologists. He operated as a cameraman as well as director, a vital factor in getting access to the key moments that might occur at any time on this remote site.

Holme is unique in having an upturned tree stump at its centre – timber circles usually survive only as post holes. The most likely theory is that the original tree was an excarnation platform on which bodies of the dead were laid while their flesh decayed. After a period of time the main bones would have been removed and buried elsewhere, possibly in a barrow. Certainly the timber circle – despite its size which occupied a space hardly larger than the average sitting room – had a strange effect on people, partly because of the beauty of its setting but also because, even in its deteriorating state, it fascinated anyone who saw it. Its structure spoke of ancient practices from the mysterious past and the inverted tree stump communicated the strange atmosphere of a world turned upside down.

Graham and his crew recorded some of the more sociological events surrounding the circle – look out for some fine sequences of local Norfolk policemen versus Druids, and clandestine night-time archaeological activities – but the excitement finally died down and they were able to concentrate on recording the vital processes of lifting, preserving and examining the remains.

Francis and Maisie were responsible for the conservation work and the timbers were eventually removed to Flag Fen and examined there. The fascinating details that began to emerge would have been lost for ever if the sand, tides and 'piddocks' – local molluscs, large numbers of which had already bored into parts of the timbers – had been allowed to do their work.

The amazing moment when for the first time in 4,000 years the tree trunk is lifted.

A female skeleton found in the Roman cemetery in the gardens of the Royal York Hotel.

On the first day of filming at Flag Fen we began to appreciate the amount of information that could be revealed by a detailed examination of the timbers. Bronze Age tool marks, 4,000 years old, had been cut into the tree stump and there were indications that a rope, posssibly made from honeysuckle vines, had been used to drag the tree into position.

Damian Goodburn would use these details, and the survey of the original site that had been carried out by the Norfolk Archaeological Unit, to build the reconstruction – the first time this has been attempted in Britain. With a month to go before he started work he, Maisie and *Time Team* were involved in intensive discussions about how to interpret the information. The result, the first of our documentary specials, will be broadcast around Christmas 1999, and will show how we handle longer excavations and projects that cannot be completed in three days.

The live programme is a regular event in *Time Team*'s year and in 1999 was based in York. Because of the pressures and tight time scale, it is ultimate television of a particular kind – the polar opposite in some ways of the documentary. It involves a huge technical and logistical support system – more than a hundred staff, camera crews, edit suites, satellite vans, a web site team and three teams of archaeologists alongside our presenters: Tony, Sandy Toksvig our live 'stalwart' and, in York, Paul Thompson.

The financial investment is huge, as is the pressure for the archaeology to deliver. Although *Time Team* accept that we will not always find what we hope for, and that this is the reality of archaeology and part of the ethos of the programme, the atmosphere of a 'live' makes it difficult if there are too many archaeological dead ends. There were three sites in York and this, and the knowledge that wherever you dig there you are likely to find archaeology, gave us a certain amount of security.

Each transmission for live television has to be a specific length, and must be timed and scripted so that Tony can read the linking pieces to camera that introduce each new section on autocue. From the start, the script assumes a certain progress in the archaeology. The researchers and I try to be as realistic as possible, but there is something slightly unreal about a script, prepared a month before a shoot, that reads: '11 o'clock day one, locate remains of Roman burials on the cemetery site.' Somehow reality, technology and expectation have to be matched up.

The director, Jeremy Cross, has to attempt to keep a grip on the production, transmission and developing story lines while the researchers, assistant producers and Philip Clarke, the executive producer, adjust the storyline, scripts and autocue pieces to camera so that they show what is actually happening. I keep them aware of where the archaeology is going and push or drag the excavations and discoveries in the direction that is best for the programme. I also have to make sure the archaeology is not misrepresented, which involves negotiating both the speed and the strategy of the excavations with the local archaeologists – in York they were John Oxley from the City Council, Keith Emerick from English Heritage

Over the three days of the live, thousands of people turned up to watch our excavation. Here Phil is working on the excavation of a child's grave in the Roman cemetery.

and the site supervisors Nick Pearson, Patrick Ottaway and Barney Sloane. I also receive vital information from our *Time Team* diggers. We need to achieve the programme's archaeological goals without pushing the archaeology further than is appropriate.

On Day Two of the York dig we faced a situation that is typical of the issues that arise on *Time Team* excavations. A third burial had emerged at the Royal York site and there was also additional evidence from geophysics – who had, with their usual accuracy, located the first burial site for us. They had found a 'curved shaped' anomaly which might indicate a building. The local archaeologists were concerned that there was not enough time left to excavate both targets. At the end of the day, the key parties – John, Keith, Nick, Mick and I – tucked ourselves into a cosy corner at the Royal York Hotel to go over the options. The script team and directors were meeting upstairs to develop the next day's story lines and needed to know, as soon as possible, the direction the archaeology would take. Despite a certain amount of pressure from them, Mick and I were determined to listen to what the archaeologists had to say.

After an hour we arrived at an agreement that allowed the excavation to expand into the new sites but ensured that the excavators would have as much time as they needed to do their job properly and record the results. With *Time Team*'s diggers, York's experienced excavators, and Margaret Cox and her team of osteoarchaeologists on hand, we made a good case that the work would be carried out to the highest standards.

This kind of discussion – balancing programme requirements with archaeological need – is a regular and vital event on *Time Team* shoots, and the fact that we achieved this within the pressure of a live programme is a measure of its importance.

We were delighted to receive many letters of thanks and encouragement from archaeologists with whom we worked this year. I feel this is additional confirmation that our system is working. One in particular from Paul Austen, Senior Archaeologist at one of the most important monuments, Hadrian's Wall, was typical and particularly heartening: 'I thought the standards of excavation and recording were most professional and indeed exemplary. For an investigation within a strict time limit, and even without making allowances for the appalling weather conditions on the first two days, the excavations were always tidy with no damage caused by trample etc. and I am extremely pleased with the way they were carried out.'

A final memory of York illustrates another crucial element to the balancing act that is *Time Team* was at the end of Day Three. Everyone was exhausted as we approached our last segment of the transmission. I had walked through all Tony's next sequences with Phil, Margaret and the other archaeologists, checking responses and giving them a sense of how long they might have for spontaneous chat. When Tony arrived, surrounded by cameramen and sound crews trailing cables and accompanied by his autocue operator, he talked to Margaret about the first two burials and then turned to Phil who would be taking him on to the next trench.

Tony's opening question didn't get the usual obvious answer. Live sequences are usually high on adrenaline and scattered with words like 'amazing' and 'incredible', but Phil had been given space to respond. The crowds of local people who had looked on patiently for three days were attentive. Phil had been watching the excavation of the skeleton of a four-year-old child, who had died in Roman York over 1,700 years ago. He commented on the smallness of the ribs and Tony told him that the results of DNA tests showed the skeleton was that of a girl. Phil, clearly moved, talked for a few moments about his feelings about the child's death.

Watching Phil and Tony create that moment – the cameras and microphones capturing it for transmission to an audience of millions – was for me a defining event. We hadn't glossed over that small tragedy and rushed on to the next item. In a way, the balance *Time Team* achieves between television and archaeology was encapsulated in that moment – which happened because of the teamwork of the people who had taken part in the programme, and was made possible by the relationships that had been forged over three days with the local archaeologists and diggers, and the people of York who came in their thousands to see the sites.

It made me feel that *Time Team* is heading in the right direction in a way that augurs well for the future as we face more challenges and adventures.

The whole family at Cirencester in front of our much-prized mosaic.

Index

PICTURE CREDITS

22: The Natural History Museum, London. 25: CORBIS/Archivo Iconografico, S.A.. 27: CORBIS/Carol Havens. 29: CORBIS/Adam Woolfitt. 30: CORBIS/Archivo Iconografico, S.A.. 31: e.t. archive/Meyrick and Smith. 50: CORBIS/(c) Werner Forman. 54: e.t. archive/Jan Vinchon Numismatist Paris. 56: (t) Portrait bust of Emperor Claudius I (10 BC-54 AD), 1st century AD (marble), Museo Archeologico Nazionale, Naples, Italy/Bridgeman Art Library. 56: (b) 'Our Own Country'/Mary Evans Picture Library. 57: (t) e.t. archive/Meyrick and Smith. 57: (b) e.t. archive. 60: CORBIS/Robert Estall. 61: e.t. archive. 78: St Constantine and St Helena, 17th century icon Russian School, Kremlin Museums, Moscow, Russia/Bridgeman Art Library. 95: British Library/e.t. archive. 98: Jarrold/e.t. archive. 100: St Augustine in his cell, fresco by Sandra Botticelli (1444/5-1510), Ognissanti, Florence, Italy/Bridgeman Art Library. 102: (t) CORBIS. 102: (b) British Museum/e.t. archive. 103: (t) Whitby Abbey, Yorkshire, Private Collection/Bridgeman Art Library. 103: (b) British Library/e.t. archive. 104: A scribe (probably Bede) writing, by Bede, Latin (Durham) Life and Miracles of St Cuthbert, (12th century), British Library/Bridgeman Art Library. 105: e.t. archive. 108: Louvre Paris/e.t. archive. 109: British Library/e.t. archive. 110: CORBIS/Patrick Ward. 111: Harry Payne/Mary Evans Picture Library. 112: (t) York Archaeological Trust. 112: (b) CORBIS/Geoffrey Taunton; Cordaiy Photos. 113: (t) James Doyle, Chronicle of England (1864)/Mary Evans Picture Library. 113: (b) Folio text from the Anglo-Saxon Chronicles, COTT.TIB.BI. f128v, British Library. 114: Thomas Dean & Co after H H Watts/Mary Evans Picture Library. 115: CORBIS/Bettmann. 116: (t) Many fall in battle and King Harold is killed, detail from the Bayeux Tapestry, before 1082 (wool embroidery on linen), Musee de la Tapisserie, Bayeux/Bridgeman Art Library. 116: (b) By courtesy of the National Portrait Gallery, London. 117: (t) e.t. archive. 117: (b) Public Record Office Image Library. 118: Whitworth Art Gallery/e.t. archive. 119: By courtesy of the National Portrait Gallery, London. 120: Mary Evans Picture Library. 122: (t) Richard I 'Couer de Lion' (1157-99) King of England from 1189, from his effigy on his monument in Fontevrault, engraved by the artist (engraving) by George Vertue (1684-1756), Private Collection/The Stapleton Collection/Bridgeman Art Library. 122: (b) CORBIS/Bettmann. 123: (t) Public Record Office Image Library. 123: (b) Caernarvon Castle by Thomas Girtin (1775-1802), Victoria & Albert Museum/Bridgeman Art Library. 124: Robert the Bruce, and his second wife, the daughter of the Earl Ulster, Seton's Armorial Crests, National Library of Scotland/Bridgeman Art Library. 128: The Black Death, 1348 (engraving) (b&w photo) by English School (14th century), Private Collection/Bridgeman Art Library. 130: Victoria & Albert Museum/e.t. archive. 133: By courtesy of the National Portrait Gallery, London. 134: British Library/e.t. archive. 137: Two pages of a printed book by William Caxton, (c.1422-91), Private Collection/Bridgeman Art Library. 138: By courtesy of the National Portrait Gallery, London. 139: By courtesy of the National Portrait Gallery, London. 140: CORBIS/Nathan Benn. 141: By courtesy of the National Portrait Gallery, London. 142: (t) By courtesy of the National Portrait Gallery, London. 142: (b) By courtesy of the National Portrait Gallery, London. 143: (t) By courtesy of the National Portrait Gallery, London. 143: (b) By courtesy of the National Portrait Gallery, London. 144: Sir Francis Drake, 1581 by Nicholas Hilliard (1547-1619), Kunsthistorisches Museum, Vienna, Austria/Bridgeman Art Library. 145: National Maritime Museum/e.t. archive. 147: By courtesy of the National Portrait Gallery, London. 148: (t) Dedication page in 'The Holy Bible', pub. by Robert Burke, 1611 (b&w photo), Private

Collection/Bridgeman Art Library. 148: (b) The Landing of the Pilgrims at Plymouth, Mass. Dec. 22nd, 1620, pub. 1876 (engraving) (b/w photo) by N. Currier (1813-88) and Ives, J.M. (1824-95), Library of Congress, Washington D.C./Bridgeman Art Library. 149: (t) By courtesy of the National Portrait Gallery, London. 149: (b) Emile Bayard/Mary Evans Picture Library. 162: (t) London Museum/e.t. archive. 162: (b) Jarrold/e.t. archive. 163: (t) Castle Howard by Francis Nicholson (1753-1844), Christopher Wood Gallery, London, UK/Bridgeman Art Library. 163: (b) By courtesy of the National Portrait Gallery, London. 164: (t) By courtesy of the National Portrait Gallery, London. 164: (b) By courtesy of the National Portrait Gallery, London. 165: (t) e.t. archive. 165: (b) By courtesy of the National Portrait Gallery, London. 167: 'Absolom's Pillar' blue and white transfer-print dessert dish, Wedgewood, c.1822 (earthenware), Private Collection/Bridgeman Art Library. 168: By courtesy of the National Portrait Gallery, London. 169: By courtesy of the National Portrait Gallery, London. 170: Signing the Declaration of Independence, July 4th, 1776 by John Trumbull (1756-1843) Yale University Art Gallery, New Haven, CT, USA/Bridgeman Art Gallery. 172: e.t. archive. 173: Boulton and Watt's rotative engine, known as the "lap" engine (used for lapping or polishing steel ornaments), erected at Soho Manufactory, near Birmingham, 1788, Science Museum/Bridgeman Art Library. 174: By courtesy of the National Portrait Gallery, London. 176: By courtesy of the National Portrait Gallery, London. 177: Le Petit Journal/Mary Evans Picture Library. 179: Public Record Office. 180: British Museum/e.t. archive. 181: By courtesy of the National Portrait Gallery, London. 182: (t) The New Houses of Parliament, engraved by Thomas Picken (fl.1838-d.1870) pub. 1852 by Lloyd Bros. & Co. (lithograph) by Edmund Walker (fl.1836-d.1882) (after) Guildhall Library, Corporation of London/Bridgeman Art Library. 182: (b) By courtesy of the National Portrait Gallery, London. 183: (t) By courtesy of the National Portrait Gallery, London. 183: (b) By courtesy of the National Portrait Gallery, London. 185: By courtesy of the National Portrait Gallery, London. 187: (t) By courtesy of the National Portrait Gallery, London. 187: (b) e.t. archive. 188: (t) Mary Evans Picture Library. 188: (b) CORBIS/Hulton-Deutsch Collection. 189: (t) CORBIS/Museum of Flight. 189: (b) Bill Brandt/e.t. archive. 190: CORBIS. 191: By courtesy of the National Portrait Gallery, London.

Chris Bennett's photographs appear on pages: 24, 25, 76, 77(t), 88(b), 131, 132, 166, 169, 178, 179(t), 180, 181, 190(t) and 191.

Professor Mick Aston's photographs appear on pages: 22, 23, 26, 27, 28, 29, 30, 31, 33, 34, 35, 50, 51, 52, 53, 54, 55, 58, 59, 60, 61, 63, 66, 67, 68, 69, 70, 71 (Victor Ambrus), 72, 73, 74, 75, 78, 79, 99, 100, 104, 105, 108, 109, 110, 111, 114, 115, 118, 119, 120, 121, 124, 125, 134, 136, 137, 139, 140, 141, 144, 145, 146, 147, 150, 155, 158, 167, 168, 170, 173, 174, 175, 176, 179(b), 184, 186 and 190(b).

Tim Taylor's own photographs appear on pages: 32, 62, 64, 89(t), 94, 95, 101, 106, 107, 127, 129, 138, 195, 202, 206, 208, 209 and 211.

Karla Goodman's photographs appear on pages: 152(t), 153 and 156(b).

Carenza Lewis's photographs appear on pages: 96 and 97.

Francis Pryor's photograph appears on page: 204

Chris Chapman's photograph appears on page: 135.

Alun Bull's photographs, © English Heritage, appear on pages: 205 and 207.

Paul Lewis Isemonger has photographed widely in the UK, Europe and America, covering subjects as diverse as the Centre Court at Wimbledon, conferences in Rome, and wildlife in Alaska. He specializes in atmospheric action, event and 'people' photography. His photo-led books include *The English Civil War – A Living History, Wellington's War – A Living History* **and** *The Fighting Man.* **Paul's photographs appear on pages:** 6, 7, 8, 9, 10, 11, 12, 13, 14, 15, 16, 17, 18, 19, 36, 37, 38, 40, 41, 42, 43, 45, 45, 46, 47, 77(b), 80, 82, 83, 84, 85, 86, 87, 88(t), 89(b), 90, 91, 152(b), 154, 156(t), 157, 192, 194, 196, 197, 198, 199, 200, 201, 203 and 216.

AUTHOR'S ACKNOWLEDGEMENTS

I am indebted to a number of individuals whose help has been invaluable in the compilation of material, in discussion and help with illustrations.

Many people worked on the five main photo stories and I hope I have acknowledged them in the text, but I would particularly like to mention the directors: Graham Dixon, Jeremy Cross, Mel Morpeth, Amanda Fidler, Michael Douglas, Gary Hunter and Simon Everson; the assistant producers: Ella Galinski and Justin Pollard; the researchers: Pippa Gilbert and Alex Finch; the production team: Zarina Dick, Malaine Kegg, Karla Goodman and Katy Segrove; the diggers: Barney Sloane, Mick Worthington, Jenni Butterworth, Ian Powlesland, Katie Hirst and Caroline Barker; and the geophysics/ground Radar team: John Gater, Chris Gaffney and Sue Ovenden.

Thanks must go Graham Johnston and Simon Raikes, director and producer on the 'sea henge' programme, Nick Corcos for his work on the hundred key events, Mick Aston, Teresa Hall, Alun Bull, Francis Pryor and Victor Ambrus for sourcing and supplying additional photos and illustrations.

With special thanks to Liz Warner, *Time Team's* current Commissioning Editor and her deputy Ben Frow for their continued encouragement during these programmes.

And finally once again to Karla Goodman for her contributions, photography and collation of all material, and without whose support and commitment this would have been an impossible task.